OFFICE MACHINES

OFFICE MACHINES

With Excel Applications

Sixth Edition

Jimmy C. McKenzie
Tarrant County College District

Robert J. Hughes
Dallas County Community College District

Prentice Hall
Upper Saddle River, New Jersey   Columbus, Ohio

Library of Congress Cataloging-in-Publication Data

McKenzie, Jimmy C.
    Office machines: with Excel applications / Jimmy C. McKenzie, Robert J. Hughes.–6th ed.
        p. cm
    ISBN 0-13-048688-4
    1. Business mathematics. 2. Calculators. I. Hughes, Robert James II. Title.

HF5695 .M38 2003
651'26–dc21   2002072101

Publisher: Stephen Helba
Executive Editor: Frank J. Mortimer
Editorial Assistant: Barbara Rosenberg
Managing Editor: Mary Carnis
Production Management: Linda Zuk, WordCrafters Editorial Services, Inc.
Production Liaison: Brian Hyland
Director of Manufacturing and Production: Bruce Johnson
Manufacturing Manager: Cathleen Petersen
Creative Director: Cheryl Asherman
Senior Design Coordinator: Miguel Ortiz
Formatting: Clarinda Co.
Marketing Manager: Tim Peyton
Composition: Clarinda Co.
Printer/Binder: Banta Menasha
Copyeditor: Judy Coughlin
Proofreader: Shirley Ratliff
Cover Printer: Phoenix Color Corp.

Pearson Education Ltd.
Pearson Education Australia Pty. Limited
Pearson Education Singapore Pte. Ltd.
Pearson Education North Asia Ltd.
Pearson Education Canada Ltd.
Pearson Educación de Mexico, S.A. de C.V.
Pearson Education—Japan
Pearson Education Malaysia, Pte. Ltd.
Pearson Education, *Upper Saddle River, New Jersey*

V036 20 19 18 17 16 15 14 13 12
ISBN 0-13-048688-4

This book is dedicated to our wives,
Janie McKenzie and Peggy Hughes,
in recognition of their encouragement and support
during the preparation of the manuscript.

CONTENTS

Chapter 5   Multiplication on the Electronic Calculator   86

Chapter 6   Division on the Electronic Calculator   115

Chapter 7   Multiple Operations on the Electronic Calculator   146

PREFACE

Today employers demand a higher degree of competence from their employees than ever before. In fact, the ability to work business applications problems that require addition, subtraction, multiplication, and division with the help of a ten-key office machine is a prerequisite for many positions in the accounting and clerical fields. With this fact in mind, we have revised *Office Machines* in order to provide both students and instructors with the *best* textbook possible: one that is relevant, accurate, up to date, and interesting.

SPECIAL FEATURES OF THE SIXTH EDITION

As authors, we're especially proud of the sixth edition of *Office Machines,* but we also realize that it is impossible to rest on past performance. Although *Office Machines* has now been revised and improved five times since it was first introduced in 1978, we have tried to incorporate not only the latest changes that affect the world of business, but also the suggestions from both instructors and students who have used previous editions of the book. Among the special features contained in the sixth edition of *Office Machines* are the following:

- A review of the basic mathematics needed for successful completion of an office machines course
- Generic operating instructions for the electronic calculator and the calculator functions on the computer
- The use of objectives, practice problems, narrative problems, self-checks, and self-evaluations in each chapter
- An abundance of business applications problems that are identical to the type of work performed by employees in the real world
- A self-contained, cumulative simulation (Woodside Apartments) that lets students gain practical, on-the-job experience before leaving the classroom
- An option that allows students to use Microsoft Excel Software to complete the Woodside Apartments simulation

INCREASED COVERAGE OF BUSINESS MATHEMATICAL APPLICATIONS

Research indicates that students learn best when they can apply what they are learning to real-life situations. As a result, special effort has been made to choose business mathematical applications problems that are like the ones a typical employee would encounter in the real world. Specific business mathematical applications problems presented in this edition of *Office Machines* include the following:

Chapter 4
- Check Registers
- Bank Statement Reconciliation

- Consumer Payment Cards
- Accounting Forms
- Payroll Records

Chapter 5

- Markdowns
- Cash Discounts
- Compound Interest
- Commissions
- Cost Markup

Chapter 6

- Retail Markup
- Percent of Increase/Decrease
- Statements of Financial Position
- Income Statements
- Straight Line Depreciation

Chapter 7

- Declining Balance Depreciation
- Series (Chains) Discounts
- Invoices
- Simple Interest
- Distribution of Expense

Each of these topics is introduced with a real-life business situation and then thoroughly explained. Finally, examples are used to show students how each type of problem should be worked correctly on an electronic calculator.

TWO CHAPTERS PROVIDE ADDITIONAL INSTRUCTIONAL MATERIAL

For students who want to gain more practical on-the-job experience, two chapters provide additional instructional material in the sixth edition of *Office Machines*. In Chapter 8, a quick review of basic calculator operations is provided. Then detailed explanations and practice problems for seven advanced business applications are provided, including the following:

- Statistical Averages
- Dividend Yield and Stock Earnings
- Inventory Valuation
- Financial Ratios
- Corporate Taxation
- Insurance Premiums
- Installment Loans

A self-contained, cumulative simulation (Woodside Apartments) is included in Chapter 9. Woodside Apartments is an 80-unit apartment complex in the North Dallas area. Students are asked to maintain the day-to-day accounting and clerical records required to manage this small business. Specific activities include working with checks and bank deposits, bank reconciliations, invoices, accounting statements, and other jobs that must be completed on a day-to-day basis. The skills required to complete the typical office machines course are reinforced when the simulation is used as a conclusion or capstone activity for the course.

ORGANIZATION OF THE TEXTBOOK

The material in the textbook has been divided into three major parts. Part One, "The Ten-Key Office Machine and Basic Mathematics," reviews the mathematical skills that are necessary for the successful study of business applications, introduces the ten-key touch method of operating a ten-key keypad, and develops speed and accuracy while using the ten-key touch method. There are three chapters in Part One. Part Two, "The Electronic Calculator," provides instructions for basic operations and business applications problems that may be completed on an electronic calculator or computer. There are four chapters in Part Two. Part Three, "Advanced Business Applications," provides a quick review of basic calculator operations, seven advanced business mathematical applications, and a cumulative, self-contained simulation. There are two chapters in Part Three.

Each major part has been divided into flexible chapters that may be used either in a self-paced, individualized instructional approach or in the traditional method of lecture/demonstration. Each chapter contains student objectives, thorough instructions, practice problems, narrative problems, self-checks, and self-evaluation posttests. All of these components are designed to enable the student to successfully complete the material contained in each chapter.

TEACHING MATERIALS

The Annotated Teacher's Edition that accompanies the sixth edition of *Office Machines* contains Parts One through Three of the student text, with answers provided for all of the problems. It also contains the following resource materials to make teaching as efficient as possible.

1. Informational material for professors teaching the course
2. A complete set of test masters that are ready for duplication
   a. Pretest and Posttest for Chapter 1
   b. Form A tests for formal evaluation of both skill and business applications problems
   c. Form B tests for formal evaluation of both skill and business applications problems
   d. Solutions to Pretest, Posttest, Form A Tests, and Form B Tests
3. Transparency masters that can be used for business applications instruction

A SPECIAL NOTE TO STUDENTS

It's important to begin your office machines course with a basic idea: *Office machines don't have to be difficult.* In fact, we have done everything possible to eliminate the typical problems that students encounter in an office machines course. Let's begin with an overview of how this text is organized.

Organization of the Text

Take a moment and look at the table of contents. Notice that the first chapter provides review material on basic mathematics. Even if you have never been successful in math, the material in this chapter will help you build a foundation for the skill material and business applications that follow in Chapters 2 through 9.

Chapter Format

All of the features in each chapter have been evaluated and recommended by instructors with years of teaching experience. In addition, office machines students were asked to critique each chapter component. Based on this feedback, the following features are included in each chapter.

Objectives   If you have a purpose for studying the material in each chapter, you will learn more than if you simply wander aimlessly through the text. Therefore, each chapter in *Office Machines* contains clearly stated learning objectives that signal important concepts.

Introduction   Every chapter in *Office Machines* begins with an introductory section that provides generic instructions on how to use specific keys on your electronic calculator or computer.

Clearly Written Explanations and Examples   We have paid special attention to word choice and sentence structure to help you understand the procedures required to work individual problems. We have also provided examples that illustrate the correct methods to use when working both skill problems and applications problems.

Realistic Practice Problems and Business Applications   As soon as a concept is presented, problems are used to reinforce that concept. Special effort has been made to choose problems that allow you to apply concepts to real-life applications and situations. Answers for selected problems are located in Appendix B.

Self-Checks and Self-Evaluations   Each chapter contains self-checks and self-evaluations, which are provided so that you may verify skills and the attainment of the knowledge required to work business applications problems.

ACKNOWLEDGMENTS

We would like to acknowledge the contributors for *Office Machines*: Lawrence J. Folwell, CPA, Stengraph Institute of Texas; Carol Hanggee, Lee College; Becky Jones, Richland College; and Susan Calhoun, Richland College.

A FINAL WORD

A text should always be evaluated by the students and instructors who use it. We welcome and sincerely appreciate your comments and suggestions.

Jimmy McKenzie
Northeast Campus of the Tarrant
  County College District
828 Harwood Road
Hurst, TX 76054
jmckenzi@mindspring.com

Bob Hughes
Dallas County Community
  Colleges District
12800 Abrams Road
Dallas, TX 75243
rjh8410@dcccd.edu

OFFICE MACHINES

PART ONE

The Ten-Key Office Machine and Basic Mathematics

There are two things fundamental to the successful operation of a ten-key office machine: operating the machine with the touch method and understanding the basic mathematic concepts that affect machine calculations. In Part One, Chapter 1 will help you to review the arithmetic concepts that are essential for successful machine operation. Chapters 2 and 3 will give you an opportunity to learn and develop accuracy and speed in the touch method for the ten-key office machine.

PART ONE

GENERIC ID FOR THE TEN-KEY OFFICE MACHINE

The following are descriptive illustrations of the ten-key machines you will be working with in Part One. Read the description for each of the machines and proceed to Chapter 1.

1. **Electronic calculator**   Electronic machine that operates in milliseconds and displays solution to a problem on a printed tape or display; is capable of performing varied mathematical calculations with the depression of a key. Most efficient operation is with a ten-key touch system.

2. **Computer calculator**   Most computer software packages contain a computer function that uses the numeric keypad located on the right side of the keyboard for input purposes. This software application performs varied mathematical calculations with the depression of a key, a click of the mouse, or the depression of a command sequence. The solution to a problem will be shown on the screen display. Most efficient operation is with a ten-key touch system.

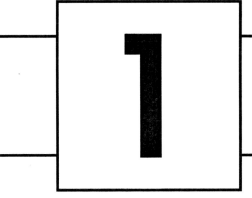

Business Mathematics Review

OBJECTIVES

When you have successfully completed this chapter, you will be able to

1. Identify the parts in addition, subtraction, multiplication, and division problems.
2. Correctly place the decimal point in addition, subtraction, multiplication, and division problems.
3. With the aid of a conversion chart, convert fractions to decimals and decimals to fractions.
4. Round answers from three or more digits after the decimal point to two digits after the decimal point.
5. Proofread your machine tape against a column of numbers to check accuracy.
6. Identify portion, rate, and base.
7. Analyze and identify necessary information contained in narrative problems.
8. Perform addition, subtraction, multiplication, and division calculations.
9. Calculate the base, rate, or portion when given the other two factors.
10. Using the information provided, solve narrative problems.
11. Estimate answers for verification of answers.

INTRODUCTION

The four basic arithmetic functions are performed on various office machines almost the same as they would be when using paper and pencil. Since there is such a close relationship between machine calculations and manual (paper and pencil) calculations, it is essential that you understand the basic functions of mathematics. Before you begin the various sections containing practice in machine calculation, you may want to review this section thoroughly, making sure you understand the material. The material is directed toward paper and pencil calculations.

Note: Before beginning the work in this segment, take Pretest I, which will be provided by your instructor. After taking the pretest, discuss the results with your instructor and proceed with the material that is recommended.

ADDITION

In adding, you combine two or more numbers to produce an answer. The parts in addition are

$$\underbrace{\text{addends}}_{} \qquad \text{sum}$$
$$23 + 4 + 56 + 7 + 8 + 90 = 188$$

When decimal points appear in addends, they should always be aligned (one decimal point under the other). The decimal point in the sum is also aligned with the other decimal points.

■ **EXAMPLE**

```
$  742.15
     14.88
    163.10
     47.98
      5.03
    207.99
 $1,181.13
```
■

If there are numbers with varying digits after the decimal point, the decimal points are still aligned in a straight line. Some find it helpful to add zeros to help in aligning decimals.

■ **EXAMPLE**

Incorrect	*Correct*	
3.92	3.92	3.920
42.1	42.1	42.100
6.032	6.032	6.032
0.08	0.08	0.080
	52.132	52.132

■

Practice Problems	Complete the following problems by placing the decimal point at the correct location.

Note: Appendix B is provided to give you an opportunity to verify selected answers. As you complete each section of Practice Problems, check your answers against those in Appendix B.

Practice Problems

1. _72.82_

2. _155.78_

3. _9.29_

4. _34.882_

5. _201.733_

6. _197.398_

7. _80.386_

8. _72.716_

9. _3430.6048_

10. _88.47_

11. _19.762_

12. _98.883_

13. _12.160_

14. _70.775_

15. _799.00_

1.	16.98	2.	9.42	3.	4.92	4.	7.68	5.	44.01
	4.29		19.22		0.03		0.032		0.003
	44.77		0.34		0.34		9.17		7.62
	6.78		126.80		4.00		18.00		150.1
	72 82		155 78		9 29		34 882		201 733

6.	3.2	7.	72.1	8.	44	9.	3.2968
	191.124		7.126		1.79		0.01
	3.07		0.940		0.006		3426
	0.004		0.22		26.92		1.2980
	197398		80386		72716		34306048

Complete the following problems by adding the columns and placing the decimal point at the correct location.

Hint: You may find it helpful to rewrite some of the problems before adding.

10.	5.06	11.	6.855	12.	8.233
	17.66		0.161		5.110
	2.82		4.926		3.040
	62.93		7.82		82.500
	88.47		19.762		98.883

13.	1.867	14.	56.76	15.	0.0158
	3.03		8.043		9.05
	7.214		4.99		755.8
	0.049		0.882		34.14
	12.160		70.775		799.00

Recommendation: If you missed any answer, determine why and make the correction; then proceed to the next section.

SUBTRACTION

In subtracting, you find the difference between two numbers. The parts in subtraction are

    minuend   subtrahend   difference
     76   –   52   =   24

    When decimal points appear in subtraction problems, they should be aligned (one decimal point under the other), as in addition. The decimal point in the difference is also aligned with the other decimal points.

■ **EXAMPLE**

     $986.88
   – 702.35
     $284.53   ■

Practice Problems

1. $\underline{32.77}$

2. $\underline{3.89}$

3. $\underline{236.26}$

4. $\underline{11.941}$

5. $\underline{35.48}$

6. $\underline{636.0012}$

7. $\underline{37.520}$

8. $\underline{107.621}$

9. $\underline{4005.41}$

10. $\underline{3.42}$

11. $\underline{2.815}$

12. $\underline{3.650}$

13. $\underline{0.9395}$

14. $\underline{8.2604}$

15. $\underline{26.4472}$

If there are numbers with varying digits after the decimal point, the decimal points are still aligned in a straight line. Some find it helpful to add zeros in aligning decimals.

■ **EXAMPLE**

Incorrect	Correct	
4.039	4.039	4.039
− 3.6	−3.6	−3.600
0.439	0.439	0.439

■

Practice Problems	Put the decimal point at the correct place in the following subtraction problems.

1.   129.05
   − 96.28
     32 77

2.   44.95
   −41.06
     3 89

3.   982.55
   −746.29
     236 26

4.   49.201
   −37.26
     11 941

5.   490.6
   −455.12
     35 48

6.   678.2962
   − 42.295
     6360012

7.   47
   −9.480
     37520

8.   268.9521
   − 258.19
     107621

9.   9426.541
   −   5421
     4005541

Complete the following problems by subtracting and placing the decimal point at the correct location.

Hint: You may find it helpful to rewrite some of the problems before subtracting.

10.   6.75
   −3.51

11.   8.707
   −5.892

12.   4.728
   −1.078

13.   1.154
   −0.2145

14.   9.027
   −0.7666

15.   28.47
   −2.0228

Recommendation: If you missed any answer, determine why and make the correction; then proceed to the next section.

Practice Problems

1. _21.252_

2. _0.004767_

3. _308.18247_

4. _869.04_

5. _0.00027125_

6. _1688.192_

7. _.47544_

8. _38.98644_

9. _2.64825_

10. _.117872_

MULTIPLICATION

In multiplying, you are adding by a shortcut. The parts in multiplication are

multiplicand multiplier product
23 × 11 = 253

When decimal points appear in the multiplicand, the multiplier, or both, use the following rule when placing the decimal point in the product: Place as many digits after the decimal point in the *product* as there are digits following the decimal points in the *multiplicand and the multiplier.*

■ EXAMPLE

14.23 × 7.2 = 102.456

| 2 + 1 | | 3 |

∠ digits after   ∠ digits after the
the decimal   decimal point in
points in the   the product
multiplicand
and the
multiplier

■

| **Practice Problems** | Put the decimal point at the correct place in the following multiplication problems. |

1. 0.92 × 23.1 = 2 1 2 5 2

2. 0.681 × 0.007 = 0 0 0 4 7 6 7

3. 96.007 × 3.21 = 3 0 8 1 8 2 4 7

4. 142 × 6.12 = 8 6 9 0 4

5. 0.125 × 0.00217 = 0 0 0 0 2 7 1 2 5

6. 479.6 × 3.52 = 1 6 8 8 1 9 2

7. 169.8 × 0.0028 = 4 7 5 4 4

8. 57.333 × 0.68 = 3 8 9 8 6 4 4

9. 9.63 × 0.275 = 2 6 4 8 2 5

10. 8.48 × 0.0139 = 1 1 7 8 7 2

11. ___3.2805___

12. ___18.063___

13. ___9.23019___

14. ___91.45290___

> **Recommendation:** If you missed any answer, determine why and make the correction; then proceed to the next material.

In completing a multiplication problem, subtotals are obtained first, then the final answer is obtained, and finally the decimal is placed correctly. The following examples illustrate the multiplication process.

■ **EXAMPLES**

```
      354
   ×  35
     1770   (354 × 5) partial product, or subtotal
     1062   (354 × 3) partial product, or subtotal
   12,390            final product
```

Reminder: You are to combine the number of digits after the decimal in the multiplicand and the number of digits after the decimal in the multiplier in order to know how many digits to mark off in the product.

```
     5.16   (2 digits after the decimal)
   × 2.7    (1 digit after the decimal)
     3612
     1032
   13.932   (3 digits after the decimal)           ■
```

Practice Problems	Complete the following problems by multiplying and placing the decimal at the correct location.

11. 7.29
    ×0.45

12. 0.27
    ×66.9

13. 3.457
    × 2.67

14. 7.062
    ×12.95

> **Recommendation:** If you missed any answer, determine why and make the correction; then proceed to the next section.

DIVISION

In dividing, you are subtracting by an arithmetic shortcut. The parts in division are

```
   dividend   divisor   quotient
     735   ÷   125   =   5.88
```

The division process is illustrated in the following example.

Practice Problems

1. 226.875

2. 6.4

3. 81.5

4. 78.5

■ **EXAMPLE**

```
        236
  51)12,036
    10 2
     1 83
     1 53
       306
       306
```
■

Decimal placement for division presents somewhat more of a problem in that there must be adjustments made to both the divisor and the dividend when there are digits after the decimal in the divisor. The procedure for decimal placement for division follows.

Step 1 Change the divisor to a whole number by adjusting the decimal to the right.

Step 2 Adjust the decimal in the dividend the same number of places to the right as the divisor.

Step 3 Locate the decimal in the quotient immediately over the adjusted decimal in the dividend.

■ **EXAMPLE**

```
                        3.68
  5.7)20.976     5.7 )20.9 76
                     17 1
                      3 87
                      3 42
                        456
                        456
```
■

Practice Problems

Complete the following problems by dividing.

Hint: Make any decimal adjustments necessary to correctly place the decimal in the quotient.

1. 32)7,264   **2.** 10.4)66.56

3. 4.86)396.09   **4.** 0.373)29.28050

Recommendation: If you missed any answer, determine why and make the correction; then proceed to the next section.

1. *46.35*
2. *9.29*
3. *76.67*
4. *72.47*
5. *406.01*
6. *476.45*
7. *129.6675*
8. *1.2902*
9. *4.0076*
10. *0.0001*
11. *77.2001*
12. *1067.1235*

ROUNDING NUMBERS WITH DECIMALS

In rounding numbers, use the following steps. (Assume you have already obtained the correct answer and inserted the decimal point in the correct position.) For problems in this book, an answer correct to two digits after the decimal point (hundredths), unless otherwise indicated, will be sufficient.

1. When rounding to two digits after the decimal point, the third digit is the determining factor.
2. If the third digit after the decimal point is five or larger, increase the second digit by one. The number 5.846 would be rounded to 5.85 because the third digit after the decimal point is five or larger.
3. If the third digit after the decimal point is four or less, leave the second digit as it is and drop the remainder of the number. The number 3.752 becomes 3.75 because the third digit after the decimal point is four or less.

The procedure for rounding decimal numbers is the same whether you are rounding to one, two, three, or more digits after the decimal point. You must obtain one more digit after the decimal point than is needed. In the examples in the list above, the numbers were to be rounded to two digits after the decimal point; therefore, the problems were worked to at least three digits after the decimal point. If the numbers were to be rounded to the fourth digit after the decimal point, the fifth digit after the decimal point would have to be obtained in order to determine how you would round the fourth digit (5.84636 = 5.8464).

Practice Problems	Round the following numbers to two digits after the decimal point.

1. 46.345 =   2. 9.294 =   3. 76.667 =

4. 72.4745 =   5. 406.007 =   6. 476.449 =

Round the following numbers to four digits after the decimal point.

7. 129.66754 =   8. 1.29017 =   9. 4.007649 =

10. 0.000076 =   11. 77.200055 =   12. 1,067.12345 =

Recommendation: If you missed any answer, determine why and make the correction; then take the following Self-Check test.

Self-Check

1. 58.63
2. 42.03
3. 9.29
4. 13.78
5. .94
6. .33
7. 78.8
8. 38.45

Self-Check

Work the following problems, placing the decimal correctly and rounding your answer to two digits after the decimal.

1. 46.023
    9.6
    2.031
    0.98

2. 7.628
   19.5
    3.2
   11.7

3.   16.291
  −7.0036

4.   96.5473
  − 82.771

5.   26.71
  ×3.524

6.   99.576
  ×0.0032

7. 252.16 ÷ 3.2 =

8. 682.5 ÷ 17.75 =

> **Recommendation:** If you missed any answer, determine why and make the correction. You may want to review the appropriate sections before proceeding to the next section.

CONVERTING DECIMALS AND FRACTIONS

Fractional portions, or fractions, will be encountered when working with various problems. The ten-key electronic calculator is not capable of working all problems containing fractions; therefore, in some instances the fractions will have to be converted to their decimal equivalents.

In the fraction 3/8, the 3 is called the *numerator,* and the 8 is called the *denominator.* The process for converting a fraction to its decimal equivalent is to divide the numerator by the denominator.

■ **EXAMPLE**

$$
\begin{array}{r}
0.375 \\
8\overline{)3.000} \\
\underline{2\,4} \\
60 \\
\underline{56} \\
40 \\
\underline{40}
\end{array}
$$

■

The decimal equivalent of the fraction 3/8 is 0.375.

Any fraction can be converted to its decimal equivalent by this process. The conversion of fractions to decimals becomes a simple matter once the division process on the various machines has been mastered.

The following table will aid you in converting fractions to decimals and decimals to fractions. The fractions given in the table are the ones most frequently used. Your goal should be to convert these fractions soon without using the chart or without going through the division process.

Common Fractions	Decimal Equivalent
1/4	0.25
1/2	0.5
3/4	0.75
1/3	0.333
2/3	0.667
1/6	0.167
5/6	0.833
1/5	0.2
2/5	0.4
3/5	0.6
4/5	0.8
1/8	0.125
3/8	0.375
5/8	0.625
7/8	0.875
1/10	0.1
3/10	0.3
7/10	0.7
9/10	0.9

Practice Problems

Convert the following fractions to their respective decimal equivalents.

1. 5/8 =   **2.** 9/10 =   **3.** 4/5 =   **4.** 1/8 =

5. 1/6 =   **6.** 2/3 =   **7.** 1/10 =   **8.** 5/6 =

9. 3/4 =   **10.** 1/5 =

Convert the following decimals to fractions.

11. 0.2 =   **12.** 0.167 =   **13.** 0.625 =   **14.** 0.3 =

15. 0.75 =   **16.** 0.333 =   **17.** 0.50 =   **18.** 0.833 =

19. 0.875 =   **20.** 0.7 =

Practice Problems

1. .625
2. .9
3. .8
4. .125
5. .167
6. .667
7. .1
8. .833
9. .75
10. .2
11. 1/5
12. 1/6
13. 5/8
14. 3/10
15. 3/4
16. 1/3
17. 1/2
18. 5/6
19. 7/8
20. 7/10

Self-Check

1. ___.4___

2. ___.333___

3. ___.9___

4. ___3/8___

5. ___2/5___

6. ___1/4___

Recommendation: If you missed any answer, determine why and make the correction; then proceed to the following Self-Check test.

Self-Check

Work the following problems by converting the number given to a decimal or a fraction.

1. 2/5 =   **2.** 1/3 =   **3.** 9/10 =

4. 0.375 =   **5.** 0.4 =   **6.** 0.25 =

Recommendation: If you missed any answer, determine why and make the correction. You may want to review the appropriate sections before proceeding to the next section.

PROOFREADING NUMBERS

After numbers have been entered into the machine, the accuracy of these numbers must be verified. To verify the numbers, compare the numbers printed on the machine tape with the numbers that were entered into the machine (the problem). To make this comparison, it is important that you develop or maintain a superior proofreading ability. The following exercises are designed to stress the importance of accurate proofreading and to aid in developing proofreading abilities.

Practice Problems

In the following two columns, the numbers and symbols in the first column are accurate, while the numbers and symbols in the second column are supposed to be accurate reproductions of the first column. If there is any variation between the second column and the first column, write the correct numbers and symbols in the answer blank column. If there is complete accuracy between the first column and the second column, place an X in the answer blank column.

Column I	Column II
1. .7211	.7211
2. 9811.88	9811.81
3. .11	.11¢
4. 22,561	22.561
5. 8.9%	8.9%
6. 10	.10
7. 15.91	15.19
8. 6,583	6,835
9. 14¢	.14
10. $9.72	9.72
11. 9%	9%
12. $140.00	$14.00
13. 78,963	78,936
14. 48.5%	485%
15. $17.10	$171.00

1. ☓
2. 9811.88
3. ☓
4. 22,561
5. ☓
6. 10.
7. 15.91
8. 6,583
9. ☓
10. ☓
11. ☓
12. 140.00
13. 78963
14. 48.5%
15. 17.10

When proofreading numbers entered into the machine, place the statement of the problem and the machine tape as near each other as is physically possible. It then becomes a matter of accurate proofreading to check your work. A suggestion that could aid in proofreading when complete accuracy is required is to place a check mark beside each number on the tape when its accuracy has been verified. Normally, when proofreading problems, it is better to simply verify the numbers through eye contact rather than to take the time to place individual check marks. Another help in proofreading is to read a large number in groups, that is, 721.567923 could be read as 721. 567 923.

Self-Check

Verify the following by comparing the "tape" to the problem. Circle any errors found on the tape.

Note: Some calculators automatically print decimal points on the tape. If the problem you are working does not have decimals, ignore the decimal points printed on the tape.

1.		2.	
1.87	1.87	8.75	8.75
4.06	4.06	1.23	1.23
9.36	(9.63)	5.17	5.17
1.57	1.57	8.37	8.37
5.49	(4.59)	3.25	3.25
2.59	2.59	3.45	3.45
4.69	(4.68)	9.85	9.85
8.34	(8.43)	6.48	6.48
5.17	5.17	9.07	(9.70)
2.74	2.74	4.50	4.50
	45.33 T		60.75 T

1. 9.36
   5.49
   4.69
   8.34
2. 9.07

Self-Check

3. 6.54
    4.06
    3.25
    _____

4. 3.53
    4.99
    4.96
    6.64

3.			4.		
	987	9.87		487	4.87
	654	6.45		353	5.35
	321	3.21		652	6.52
	750	7.50		499	4.90
	406	4.60		324	3.24
	111	1.11		676	6.76
	467	4.67		496	4.69
	325	3.53		328	3.28
	994	9.94		79	.79
	591	5.91		664	4.66
		56.79 T			45.06 T

Recommendation: If you missed any answer, determine why and make the correction; then proceed to the next section.

BASE, RATE, AND PORTION

One of the most fundamental processes used in solving business problems is the calculation of an equation known as the *percentage formula*. There are actually three variations to the formula:

$$\text{base} \times \text{rate} = \text{portion}$$

$$\text{portion} \div \text{rate} = \text{base}$$

$$\text{portion} \div \text{base} = \text{rate}$$

These variations are used in calculating commissions, discounts, sales pricing, interest, invoices, or any other business applications that involve percents.

The three components of the formula are base *(B)*, rate *(R)*, and portion *(P):*

—The *base* is the main amount or total units referred to.
—The *portion* is a part of the base and will be measured in the same units as the base. (If the base is stated as dollars, the portion will also be stated as dollars.)
—The *rate* is a factor that indicates the relation between the base and the portion. The rate will always be stated as a percent, fraction, or decimal.

One of the first problems you will encounter in working with these formulas is identifying which factors you know and which factor you need to determine. If you use the following sentence to help you identify what you know, determining the unknown will become much easier:

This part is what % of this total?
    P   *R*   *B*

In this sentence, the word *is* indicates an = sign and the word *of* indicates a multiplication process, so we can read this sentence as

This part = what % × this total?
    P   =   *R* ×   *B*

As stated, this sentence results in the portion formula $P = R \times B$, although the formula is traditionally stated in the following form:

$B \times R = P$

By transferring the problem statements in the following examples to the suggested sentence, you can identify the missing factors.

■ **EXAMPLE 1**   14% of 385 is _____ .

This part is what % of this total?

?	is	14%	of	385
P	is	R	of	B

The missing factor is the portion. The formula for determining the portion is $B \times R = P$. ■

What is the unknown factor in the following example?

■ **EXAMPLE 2**   39 is 50% of what number?

This part is what % of this total?

39	is	50%	of	?
P	is	R	of	B

The unknown factor is the base, and the formula for determining the base is $P \div R = B$. ■

Determine the unknown factor for the following example.

■ **EXAMPLE 3**   20 is what percent of 100?

This part is what % of this total?

20	is	?	of	100
P	is	R	of	B

The unknown factor is the rate, and the formula for determining the rate is $P \div B = R$. ■

The three percentage formulas are

$B \times R = P$

$P \div R = B$

$P \div B = R$

For Example 1 (14% of 385 is _____), if you use the first formula ($B \times R = P$) for working the problem, you will obtain the following answer.

$B \quad \times \quad R \quad = \quad P$

$385 \times 14\% = \quad P$

$385 \times 0.14 = 53.9$

Note: Observe that it was necessary to convert 14 percent into its equivalent decimal number, 0.14.

Practice Problems

1. *70.80*

2. *146.40*

3. *187.50*

4. *635.35*

5. *145*

6. *357.5*

7. *20*

8. *780.882*

9. *10 %*

10. *20 %*

Practice Problems	Using the correct percentage formula, complete the following problems.

1. 20% of 354 is _____ .   **2.** 30% of 488 is _____ .

3. 50% of 375 is _____ .   **4.** 75% of 849 is _____ .

To obtain the answer for Example 2 (39 is 50 percent of what number?), you use $P \div R = B$ as your formula.

$$P \div R = B$$
$$39 \div 50\% = B$$
$$39 \div 0.50 = 78$$

Note: Observe that in this example, as in Example 1, the rate or percent must always be converted into its equivalent decimal number before solution begins.

Practice Problems	Using the correct base formula, complete the following problems.

5. 58 is 40% of what number?   **6.** 143 is 40% of what number?

7. 16 is 80% of what number?   **8.** 531 is 68% of what number?

The answer to Example 3 (20 is what percent of 100?) is obtained by using the formula $P \div B = R$.

$$P \div B = R$$
$$20 \div 100 = R$$
$$20 \div 100 = 0.20$$
$$0.20 = 20\%$$

Note: The answer obtained was in its decimal form. Before recording the answer, it would be necessary to convert the decimal into its equivalent percent.

Practice Problems	Using the correct rate formula, complete the following problems.

9. 36.5 is what percent of 365?   **10.** 149.8 is what percent of 749?

11. 840 is what percent of 2,100? **12.** 562 is what percent of 917?

11. _40 %_

12. _61%_

Self- Check	Using the correct portion, base, and rate formulas, complete the following problems.

Hint: Notice the wording of each problem for an indication of which formula to use.

1. 15% of 539 is _____ .

2. 43 is what percent of 128?

3. 35 is 62% of what number?

4. 38% of 280 is _____ .

5. 113 is 40% of what number?

6. 27% of 398 is _____ .

7. 63 is what percent of 564?

8. 42 is 35% of what number?

9. 217 is what percent of 277?

10. 16% of 844 is _____ .

11. 42% of 539 is _____ .

12. 136 is 41% of what number?

13. 600 is what percent of 1,238?

1. _____

2. _____

3. _____

4. _____

5. _____

6. _____

7. _____

8. _____

9. _____

10. _____

11. _____

12. _____

13. _____

> **Recommendation:** If you missed any answer, determine why and make the correction. You may want to review the appropriate sections before proceeding to the next section.

SOLVING NARRATIVE PROBLEMS

After reviewing the basic mathematical operations for whole numbers, decimals, and fractions, a review of the process for solving narrative problems is recommended. The following procedure will help you in solving this type of problem.

Step 1 Analyze the problem by asking yourself the following questions: What must I find in solving the problem? How shall I proceed to solve for what I need? Can I check my results?

Step 2 Work the problem by estimating the results in advance and then solving the problem using the procedure selected in Step 1.

Step 3 Check your work by comparing your worked solution with your estimated solution, by working the problem again to verify calculations, and by checking your answer using the opposite math action (check + by −, − by +, × by ÷, ÷ by ×).

Practice Problems

1. _____

2. _____

3. _____

Step 4 Use a businesslike work attitude: Arrange your workstation before starting work. Concentrate on what you are doing. Work accurately and with speed.

■ **EXAMPLE** On your way home, you stop at a store and buy one item that costs $9.15. If the sales tax rate is 7 percent, how much change do you receive from a $10 bill?

According to Step 1—analyzing the problem—you need to answer three questions to solve this narrative problem.

What must I find in solving the problem? The problem in this example requires two answers. You want to know the change you are to receive from a $10 bill. Before you can calculate this amount though, you must determine the total cost of the item bought—that is, the sales price plus the sales tax.

How shall I proceed to solve for what I need? You solve for the total cost first:

Sales price × sales tax rate = amount of sales tax
$9.15 × 0.07 = $0.64 (rounded)

Sales price + sales tax = total cost of item

$9.15 + $0.64 = $9.79

Finally, you solve for the amount of change:

Amount of payment − total cost of item = change

$10.00 − $9.79 = $0.21

Can I check my results? Your results can best be verified by reworking the problem to verify that your calculations have been accurate. ■

| **Practice Problems** | Work the following narrative problems. |

Reminder: Analyze the problem, work the problem, check your results, and maintain a businesslike work attitude.

1. You work part-time at a bakery. Your usual schedule is five days a week, four hours a day. If you receive $3.65 an hour, what are your total earnings per week?

2. A rectangular flower bed is 60 feet long and 3 feet wide. You want to put a border around it to keep out the grass. If the border costs 10 cents a foot, what is the total cost of the border.

3. The items you purchased at the grocery store cost $1.49, $2.19, $0.89, $4.22, $3.12, and $0.77. If the tax rate is 7 percent, what is the total amount of the purchase?

ESTIMATIONS

Frequently, you will find it helpful to estimate solutions to problems before working them on the electronic calculator. Properly estimating answers will permit you to compare your machine solution with your estimation answer. This comparison will give you an indication of a problem if your estimation answer and machine solution are far apart in value or different because of the decimal placement. You should always examine a machine solution to determine if it seems realistic. If you have doubts, you may want to perform the estimation afterward just to determine if your solution is "in the ballpark."

To work with estimations, you should round each number to a significant digit (usually the largest value). The following represent rounding to the significant digit.

$1.45 will round to $1.00
278 will round to 300
0.333333 will round to 0.3
1,450 will round to 1,000

The following are suggestions for solving addition and subtraction problems.

Actual	Estimation
$1,245	$1,000
489	500
3,888	4,000
29	30
612	600
$6,263	$6,130

Notice that even though the estimation is not correct, the $6,130 estimate verifies that the $6,263 is a realistic answer. The same procedure can be used in estimating subtraction problems.

Use the following to estimate multiplication and division problems.

Find the cost of 5¾ yards of fabric that costs $3.29 per yard.

Estimation: 6 yards × $3 per yard = $18.00

Actual: 5.75 yards × $3.29 per yard = $18.92

Again, the estimation approximates the actual answer.

At a wage of $7.25 an hour, how many hours must an employee work to earn $1,015?

Estimation: $1,000 ÷ $7 = approximately 143 hours

Actual: $1,015 ÷ $7.25 = 140 hours

After rounding the estimation to the nearest hour, it is still an approximation of the actual answer.

Estimate the following answers to determine if the machine solutions are realistic. If an answer is not realistic, determine the correct answer for the problem.

1. 168 + 459 + 1,260 + 78 + 502 = 1,333
2. 8,761 + 49 + 773 + 123 + 992 = 10,698
3. The odometer read 3,468 in City A and 3,763 in City B. How many miles were driven? 295 miles

Practice Problems

4. _____

5. _____

6. _____

7. _____

8. _____

4. $12,972 - 14,026 = 854$

5. An employee worked 38 hours last week and earned $10.75 an hour. What were the gross earnings? $408.50

6. If Stock A sold for $23.375 per share and the investor bought 128 shares, how much was the purchase price of the stock? $4,800

7. If an automobile tire cost $247.50 and it had been driven 24,749 miles before being replaced, determine the cost per mile for the tire. $0.98

8. A motorist paid $10.25 for gasoline at $1.079 a gallon. How many gallons did he buy? 9.5 gallons

Operating the Ten-Key Keyboard by the Touch Method

OBJECTIVES

When you have successfully completed this chapter, you will be able to

1. Identify the following operating controls and their uses:
   — Plus (+) key
   — Total key
   — Add-mode setting
   — Clear (C) key
   — Clear entry (CE) key

2. Perform addition on the ten-key machine using the touch method.

3. Demonstrate accuracy on performance tests while using the touch method.

4. Attain confidence in your ability to use the touch method and to perform addition on the ten-key machine.

5. Approach with confidence more sophisticated procedures and work sequences.

INTRODUCTION

The touch method of entering numbers into a machine register is the same for all ten-key keyboards. The touch method permits you to use the ten-key keyboard without looking at your hands. Before studying the ten-key touch method further, there are some work preparations to be made.

Work Preparations

1. The machine should be placed on the desk to your right and at a slight angle in the position that is most comfortable to you. The desk should be clear of all materials except those you are working with. Your textbook and pencil should be directly in front of you.

2. Check the paper in the machine, making sure there is enough for your working time.

3. Check the electrical outlet to make sure the plug is in the outlet and the cord is securely fastened to the back of the machine.

Posture

A general rule in working with office machines is to sit erect, but relaxed. Specifically, you should

— Have both feet on the floor.
— Have your fingers curved and over the home-row keys.
— Have your hand follow the slant of the keyboard with your wrist just above the frame of the machine.
— With your arm bent at the elbow, have the home-row keys about an arm's length away from your body.

Figure 2.1 illustrates the correct posture for a person working with an office machine.

FIGURE 2.1   Correct Posture

TEN-KEY TOUCH METHOD

The touch method, shown in Figure 2.2, is quite similar to operating a computer keyboard in that both the ten-key machine and the computer keyboard have a home row and all reaches are made from the home row. The home row on the ten-key keyboard is the 4, 5, and 6 keys. The 4 is controlled by the index finger, the 5 by the middle finger, and the 6 by the ring finger. Figure 2.3 shows a hand in correct home-row position.

In operating the rest of the ten-key keyboard, the following points should be remembered.

1. The index finger controls the 1 and 7 keys by reaching up to strike the 7 and reaching down to strike the 1.

2. The middle finger controls the 2 and 8 keys by reaching up to strike the 8 and reaching down to strike the 2.

3. The ring finger controls the 3 and 9 keys by reaching up to strike the 9 and reaching down to strike the 3.

4. The thumb controls the 0 key.

5. The little finger controls the plus, minus, total, and other operational keys on the right side of the keyboard.

6. The operational keys on the left side of the keyboard are controlled by the index finger.

7. The electronic calculator has a decimal key that must also be controlled. The decimal key on most electronic calculators is located below either the 2 key or the 3 key and is operated by the finger that controls the 2 or the 3 key.

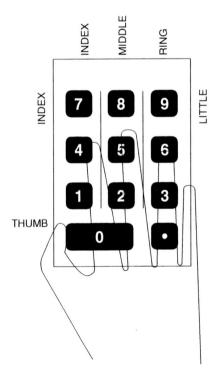

FIGURE 2.2 Ten-Key Keyboard

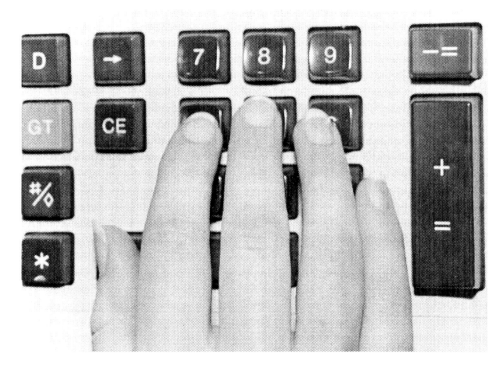

FIGURE 2.3 Home-Row Position

ADDITION

In working an addition problem on the ten-key machine, enter the first number on the keyboard, depress the + key, enter the next number on the keyboard, depress the + key, and continue this process until all numbers have been entered. To obtain the sum, depress the total key. The total key will normally be identified by the word *Total,* an asterisk (*), or a *T.*

Add-Mode

Most electronic calculators are equipped with a setting called an *add-mode.* The add-mode will be located with the round-off key or the decimal control and will be indicated by the + symbol, the word *add,* or the words *add-mode.* By setting the round-off key or decimal control on the add-mode position, the electronic calculator will print the decimal point two digits over, as would the older mechanical ten-key adding machine. If your machine does not have an add-mode setting, it will be necessary for you either to set the decimal along with the numbers or to omit the decimal point in the numbers entered and then insert it in the correct place when the sum is recorded.

Computer Calculators

Most of the current software packages contain a calculator option. The numeric ten-key keypad, located to the right of the standard typewriter keypad, becomes the major input source for the calculator. The numeric keypad is the same as the ten-key keyboard on the electronic calculator, which allows the operator to use the touch method for entering numbers. There is no *add-mode* function on most of the software packages, so you must enter a decimal every time one appears. For most computer keyboards, the *Num Lock* key must be depressed before the numeric keypad may be used. Refer to Appendix A for additional information on the computer numeric keypad or to the software support material accompanying the computer.

In working an addition problem on the ten-key keypad of a computer keyboard, enter the first number on the keyboard, depress the + key, enter the next number on the keyboard, depress the+key, and continue this process until the final number. When the final number is entered, depress the total key to obtain the sum. The total key will usually be identified by an = sign or the word *Enter*.

Locate the following parts on your machine.

1. Plus key, located on the right side of the ten-key keyboard, has a plus (+) sign on it and adds the number on the keyboard to the machine register.

2. Total key, usually located below the plus bar or below and to the right of the plus bar; has an indication of final operation such as T, *, or Total; clears machine for next operation.

3. Add-mode setting, usually where round-off key or decimal control is located, has +, add, or add-mode indication and sets calculator to act as a mechanical ten-key by automatically setting decimal at two places.

4. Clear key, various locations according to brand, clears all entries on display calculator, usually identified by C.

5. Clear entry key, various locations according to brand, clears incorrect numbers from the keyboard before any action keys are depressed, usually identified by CE; occasionally both C and CE will appear on the same key.

■ **EXAMPLE**   Work the following problem using the touch method: 55 plus 66 plus 44.

Electronic Printing Calculator	*Numeric Keypad Calculator*
Set on add-mode	Load calculator software
Depress total	Depress *Num Lock* key
Enter 55 Depress +	Depress *CE* key
Enter 66 Depress +	Enter 55 Depress +
Enter 44 Depress +	Enter 66 Depress +
Depress total	Enter 44 Depress Enter or =
Read the answer: 165	Read the answer: 165 ■

Did you use the touch method? Were you able to operate the machine without looking? Practice the example problem a few times until you are able to work it without feeling uncomfortable about entering the numbers or depressing the addition keys (+ key, total key, C key) before going on to the following problems.

Practice Problems	Complete the following home-row addition problems.

Reminder: Use the touch method. Do not look at your hands. Use correct posture at your workstation.

Note: When you have completed the problems, check your accuracy by comparing your answers to those given in Appendix C. Repeat any problems you miss.

Practice Problems

1. _____ **3,360** _____
2. _____ 572 _____
3. _____ 594 _____
4. _____ 567 _____
5. _____ 380 _____
6. _____ 506 _____
7. _____ 490 _____
8. _____ 550 _____
9. _____ 660 _____
10. _____ 780 _____
11. _____ 490 _____
12. _____ 610 _____

1.	2.	3.	4.	5.	6.
44	55	66	44	44	44
44	55	66	44	44	44
55	56	65	55	41	74
55	56	65	55	41	74
66	65	56	66	47	71
66	65	56	66	47	71
45	46	64	65	44	17
45	46	64	64	44	17
54	64	46	54	14	47
54	64	46	54	14	47

7.	8.	9.	10.	11.	12.
55	55	66	66	44	55
55	55	66	66	44	55
58	25	69	99	47	52
58	25	69	99	47	52
55	85	66	96	41	66
55	85	66	96	41	66
52	58	63	36	55	69
52	58	63	36	55	69
25	52	66	93	58	63
25	52	66	93	58	63

CORRECTIONS

When a number has been incorrectly entered on a machine, the correction is made in one of the following ways.

1. If the + key *has not* been depressed, the correction key can be depressed to remove the number from the keyboard.

2. If the error is discovered immediately after the + key has been depressed, depress the minus (−) key to remove the incorrect number. (In a later chapter, you will find that to correct any incorrect entry, you depress the opposite action key—for example, depress − to remove an incorrect + entry or depress + to remove an incorrect − entry.)

3. If other numbers have been entered after the error was made, reenter the incorrect number into the machine and depress the opposite action key. Then enter the correct number and depress the correct action key.

Find the correction mechanism on your machine and practice the methods for making corrections as given in the following examples. The first example shows the procedure for entering numbers and removing them by depressing the correction key.

■ **EXAMPLE**

Enter 4.56	Depress correction
Enter 6.54	Depress correction
Enter 5.46	Depress correction	■

The following example shows the procedure for correcting errors after the action key has been depressed.

■ **EXAMPLE**

```
   4.56
   6.54
   5.46
  16.56
```

Enter 4.56   Depress +
Enter 6.45   Depress + (error)
           Depress −
Enter 6.54   Depress +
Enter 5.64   Depress + (error)
           Depress −
Enter 5.46   Depress +
Depress total
Read the answer: 16.56   ■

The following example shows the procedure for correcting an error that is discovered after other numbers have been entered.

■ **EXAMPLE**

    5.66
    4.54
    <u>5.65</u>
  15.85

Enter 5.56   Depress +
Enter 4.54   Depress +
Enter 5.65   Depress +
(Notice when proofreading that the first number was incorrectly entered.)
Enter 5.56   Depress −
Enter 5.66   Depress +
Depress total
Read the answer: 15.85   ■

Practice Problems	
13.	<u>**35.52**</u>
14.	_44.4_
15.	_53.28_
16.	_22.28_
17.	_38.31_
18.	_30.78_
19.	_43.44_
20.	_36.71_
21.	_35.16_
22.	_41.45_

Practice Problems

Practice these reaches from the home row to the upper and lower rows.

13.	14.	15.	16.	17.
4.44	5.55	6.66	1.45	1.25
4.71	5.82	6.93	5.54	4.11
4.44	5.55	6.66	1.45	7.35
4.17	5.28	6.39	1.25	8.33
4.44	5.55	6.66	4.42	3.76
1.47	2.58	3.69	2.24	7.15
4.44	5.55	6.66	1.15	3.47
<u>7.41</u>	<u>8.52</u>	<u>9.63</u>	<u>4.78</u>	<u>2.89</u>
35.52				

18.	19.	20.	21.	22.
4.35	7.31	6.89	5.75	3.32
1.43	8.57	1.38	8.65	7.91
2.63	7.95	9.32	1.78	4.88
7.32	1.59	1.33	5.27	5.78
1.37	8.97	5.49	1.59	2.21
2.47	7.14	6.51	2.41	6.32
9.66	1.26	3.64	8.42	5.59
<u>1.51</u>	<u>4.65</u>	<u>2.15</u>	<u>1.29</u>	<u>5.44</u>

Practice Problems

23. *45*

24. *55.52*

25. *59.26*

26. *55.7*

27. *44.61*

28. *5328*

29. *5772*

30. *5994*

31. *5727*

32. *3840*

33. *5106*

34. *4950*

35. *5550*

36. *6660*

37. *7860*

38. *4950*

39. *6150*

Practice these reaches to the zero key.

23.	**24.**	**25.**	**26.**	**27.**
1.00	4.44	8.08	7.70	2.50
2.00	4.04	9.99	7.10	5.02
3.00	5.55	9.09	8.80	3.60
4.00	5.05	4.40	8.20	4.07
5.00	6.66	4.10	9.90	9.06
6.00	6.06	5.50	9.30	4.01
7.00	7.77	5.20	1.10	2.05
8.00	7.07	6.60	1.40	8.20
9.00	8.88	6.30	2.20	6.03

Practice the following, working for accuracy.

28.	**29.**	**30.**	**31.**
444	555	666	444
444	555	666	444
555	566	655	555
555	566	655	555
666	655	566	666
666	655	566	666
454	466	644	655
454	466	644	654
545	644	466	544
545	644	466	544

32.	**33.**	**34.**	**35.**
444	444	555	555
444	444	555	555
411	744	588	255
411	744	588	255
477	711	555	855
477	711	555	855
444	177	522	588
444	177	522	588
144	477	255	522
144	477	255	522

Work the following problems for accuracy.

36.	**37.**	**38.**	**39.**
666	666	444	555
666	666	444	555
699	999	477	522
699	999	477	522
666	966	411	666
666	966	411	666
633	366	555	699
633	366	555	699
666	933	588	633
666	933	588	633

Practice Problems

40.		41.		42.		43.	
	44.40		55.05		60.66		45.60
	44.40		55.05		60.66		45.60
	55.50		56.06		60.55		54.60
	55.50		56.06		60.55		54.60
	66.60		65.05		50.66		65.40
	66.60		65.06		50.66		65.40
	45.40		46.06		60.44		65.50
	45.40		46.06		60.44		65.40
	54.50		64.04		40.66		54.40
	54.50		64.04		40.66		54.40

44.		45.		46.		47.	
	44.40		44.04		50.55		55.50
	44.40		44.04		50.55		55.50
	41.10		74.04		50.88		25.50
	41.10		74.04		50.88		25.50
	47.70		71.01		50.55		85.50
	47.70		71.01		50.55		85.50
	44.40		17.07		50.22		58.80
	44.40		17.07		50.22		58.80
	14.40		47.07		20.55		52.20
	14.40		47.07		20.55		52.20

48.		49.		50.		51.	
	66.60		60.66		44.04		50.55
	66.60		60.66		44.04		50.55
	69.90		90.99		47.07		50.22
	69.90		90.99		47.07		50.22
	66.60		90.66		41.01		60.66
	66.60		90.66		41.01		60.66
	63.30		30.66		55.05		60.99
	63.30		30.66		55.05		60.99
	66.60		90.33		58.08		60.33
	66.60		90.33		58.08		60.33

40. _532.8_

41. _572.53_

42. _545.94_

43. _570.9_

44. _384_

45. _507.72_

46. _445.5_

47. _555_

48. _666_

49. _726.6_

50. _490.5_

51. _565.5_

Self-Check

1. 3016.73
2. 1,945.08
3. 143,401.79
4. 33,267.7
5. 5,300.35

| | Self-Check | Complete the following problems. Your objective is to work all the problems without error. |

1.		2.		3.		4.		5.	
	599.03		30.50		3,271.40		1,122.13		1,012.13
	465.21		172.30		335.40		16.44		834.81
	980.52		2.71		92.75		2.01		202.65
	407.63		32.20		62,543.88		2,361.61		491.05
	5.69		717.70		1,140.29		435.50		14.66
	2.11		432.10		341.20		9,158.33		42.59
	43.09		351.56		0.08		249.50		942.95
	378.95		7.76		4.77		31.20		254.31
	70.20		49.90		1,437.59		14,414.37		551.38
	64.30		148.35		74,234.43		5,476.61		953.82

Recommendation: Verify your answers by comparing them to the answers provided in Appendix B. If your answers are all correct, begin Chapter 3. If you make errors, do the Self-Check again. Should you continue to have errors, confer with your instructor for further practice and instruction.

Practice and Speed Development

OBJECTIVES

When you have successfully completed this chapter, you will be able to

1. Demonstrate speed development in operating the ten-key machine.
2. Maintain accuracy on performance tests while using the touch method.
3. Attain confidence in your ability to use the touch method, to perform addition accurately, and to demonstrate speed in keyboarding.
4. Approach with confidence more sophisticated procedures and work sequences.

INTRODUCTION

Each problem in this section has two numbers in parentheses beside the problem on the right. One number is halfway through the problem; the other is at the end. The numbers indicate the keyboarding stroke count (cumulatively). In computing keyboarding stroke count, one stroke is counted for each number entered on the keyboard, one stroke for depressing the + key, and two strokes for depressing the total key.

17	2 number-key depressions and 1 +-key depression =	3 strokes
61	2 number-key depressions and 1 +-key depression =	3 strokes
26	2 number-key depressions and 1 +-key depression =	3 strokes
63	2 number-key depressions and 1 +-key depression =	3 strokes
15	2 number-key depressions and 1 +-key depression =	3 strokes
182	1 depression of total key =	2 strokes
	Total stroke count	17

Practice Problems

1. _6378_

2. _4045_

3. _4166_

4. _3405_

Cumulative stroke counts are provided throughout Speed Development exercises in parentheses to the right of the numbers. The total stroke count is given for each set of problems.

You should first work the problems in each speed development section to familiarize yourself with what is contained in the problem set. Then take the Self-Check test by reworking the problems and timing yourself or having someone time you. After you have been timed for each Self-Check test, determine your *strokes per minute* (SPM) and record your errors as shown in the following example.

■ **EXAMPLE** If you require five minutes to work the ten problems in Speed Development 1 and have one incorrect answer, your computation would be

420 strokes ÷ 5 minutes = 84 strokes per minutes (SPM)

__84__ SPM

___1__ errors   ■

SPEED DEVELOPMENT 1

Practice Problems

Practice the following problems, maintaining accuracy while working to increase your speed. Record your answers in the blanks in the answer column.

Note: After completing the ten problems, compare your answers with those given in Appendix C. Since the numbers in the first set are whole numbers, disregard the decimal when recording your answer.

1. Set on add-mode.

2. Clear machine by depressing T or C.

1.		2.		3.		4.	
540		145		345		155	
870		507		415		140	
876		672		150		405	
986		617		526		278	
255	(20)	425	(62)	134	(104)	311	(146)
487		424		585		143	
398		366		413		205	
366		278		243		466	
782		377		637		761	
818		234		718		541	
	(42)		(84)		(126)		(168)

5.	629	6.	367	7.	783	8.	810
	464		176		345		757
	376		562		373		229
	780		192		341		858
	511 (188)		543 (230)		526 (272)		170 (314)
	505		733		757		455
	783		242		650		141
	341		165		760		225
	219		770		405		900
	246		307		611		464
	(210)		(252)		(294)		(336)

5. _4854_

6. _4087_

7. _5551_

8. _5009_

9. _2615_

10. _3534_

9.	461	10.	573
	154		103
	187		276
	103		354
	267 (356)		309 (398)
	154		687
	107		498
	378		106
	264		253
	540		375
	(378)		(420)

Self-Check	Work the preceding problems again. Attempt to complete the problems in six minutes or less with one or no incorrect answers. Compute your SPM and record your accuracy.

420 strokes ÷ _____ minutes = _____ strokes per minute
_____ SPM
_____ errors

Recommendation:　If you were able to achieve at least 70 SPM with one or no incorrect answers, proceed to the next section. If you were not able to achieve that level, repeat the ten problems, figuring your SPM and accuracy again. After this repetition, proceed to the next material and continue working for speed and accuracy.

SPEED DEVELOPMENT 2

Practice Problems	Practice the following problems, working for speed and accuracy.

Practice Problems

1. _474.3_

2. _464.06_

3. _321.14_

4. _293_

5. _547.42_

6. _550.52_

7. _676.01_

8. _474.46_

9. _349.9_

10. _536.96_

Self-Check

SPM: _____

Errors: _____

1.	45.67	2.	41.20	3.	10.45	4.	37.60
	34.12		57.67		14.10		27.09
	68.72		43.64		96.32		20.98
	45.67		99.55		12.12		14.34
	28.56 (25)		14.10 (77)		25.67 (129)		45.68 (181)
	44.00		43.87		56.29		13.33
	38.80		14.46		15.40		15.54
	47.75		78.80		30.98		12.34
	45.67		38.65		46.51		23.54
	75.34		32.12		13.30		82.56
	(52)		(104)		(156)		(208)

5.	34.21	6.	51.78	7.	89.30	8.	55.76
	95.67		64.66		70.99		39.40
	67.83		69.38		98.51		23.61
	98.41		79.53		84.05		32.31
	32.19 (233)		51.00 (285)		66.51 (337)		70.12 (389)
	24.49		75.26		69.21		65.17
	45.12		16.00		42.44		81.80
	41.95		45.76		34.67		21.21
	23.97		71.36		60.48		32.33
	83.58		25.79		59.85		52.75
	(260)		(312)		(364)		(416)

9.	40.60	10.	29.00
	17.67		22.75
	41.50		65.25
	61.00		85.50
	11.94 (441)		33.01 (493)
	44.77		62.19
	69.33		24.12
	13.12		70.80
	62.38		57.34
	20.59		87.00
	(468)		(520)

Self-Check	Work the preceding problems again. Attempt to work the problems in five minutes or less with one or no incorrect answers. Figure your SPM and record your accuracy.

520 strokes ÷ _____ minutes = _____ strokes per minute
_____ SPM
_____ errors

1. _2,1283.8_

2. _15153.75_

3. _10397.57_

4. _18575.7_

5. _15649.57_

6. _3645.1_

Recommendation: If you were able to achieve at least 100 SPM with zero or one incorrect answer, proceed to the next section. If you were not able to achieve this level, repeat the ten problems, figuring your SPM and accuracy again. After this repetition, proceed to the next material and continue working for speed and accuracy.

SPEED DEVELOPMENT 3

Practice Problems	Practice the following problems, maintaining accuracy while working to increase your speed.

1.		**2.**		**3.**	
418.20		18.90		790.13	
288.40		360.09		1,845.07	
0.42		931.25		200.80	
153.20		8,303.68		65.00	
5,203.61	(28)	50.32	(91)	624.18	(155)
730.24		167.78		231.08	
4,802.66		112.18		913.52	
9,210.83		2,610.38		208.94	
287.21		164.48		2,480.66	
189.03		2,434.69		3,038.19	
	(62)		(125)		(189)

4.		**5.**		**6.**	
56.01		4,335.50		1.90	
135.40		500.00		1,240.80	
1,468.42		87.05		0.78	
9,372.68		7,261.50		16.26	
1,987.55	(221)	398.52	(285)	346.01	(341)
1,994.00		72.06		1,425.60	
57.08		1,800.00		10.75	
484.29		57.40		7.58	
114.01		927.49		330.70	
2,906.26		210.05		861.72	
	(254)		(316)		(371)

Practice Problems

7. _3076.42_

8. _7028.32_

9. _5451.33_

10. _6305.91_

Self-Check

SPM: _____

Errors: _____

7.	1,701.00		8.	20.61	
	6.82			36.09	
	932.70			4.86	
	18.59			777.62	
	21.68	(398)		75.21	(450)
	3.04			75.01	
	2.96			4,526.17	
	180.06			146.25	
	113.45			98.64	
	96.12			1,267.86	
		(425)			(482)

9.	300.00		10.	150.19	
	80.01			3,572.16	
	2,176.60			537.20	
	72.10			84.26	
	2,176.60	(512)		106.61	(570)
	11.64			420.61	
	7.26			14.98	
	400.00			48.83	
	160.89			71.77	
	66.34			1,299.30	
		(540)			(600)

Self-Check

Work the preceding problems again. Attempt to work the problems in five minutes or less with one or no incorrect answers. Figure your SPM and record your accuracy.

600 strokes ÷ _____ minutes = _____ strokes per minute

_____ SPM

_____ errors

Recommendation: If you were able to complete the problems in five minutes or less with zero or one incorrect answer, proceed to the following self-evaluation section. If you did not achieve the expected level, repeat the ten problems, figure your SPM and accuracy, and then proceed to the Self-Evaluation Skills Posttest.

SELF-EVALUATION

Note: Beginning with this chapter and for most of the remaining chapters in this book, you will be given the opportunity to evaluate your progress after you have completed the work contained in each chapter. Recommended achievement levels for each Self-Evaluation Posttest will be given, but these may be altered by your instructor if the instruction process has been altered. The recommended uses of the Self-Evaluation Posttest are

—To evaluate progress
—To review before formal examinations
—To provide remedial practice

Skills Posttest

Complete the following ten problems in five minutes or less with one or no incorrect answers. (Do not include recording the answers in the five minutes.)

Self-Evaluation

1. _684.4_
2. _1467.78_
3. _1145.4_
4. _2746.84_
5. _1203.13_
6. _1170.97_
7. _1681.12_
8. _2407.49_

1.		2.		3.		4.	
41.54		205.44		454.65		137.66	
37.67		56.22		11.22		501.41	
5.26		1.14		55.43		350.12	
22.57		4.47		126.45		924.50	
11.65	(24)	33.75	(74)	238.90	(129)	12.89	(184)
0.87		226.70		91.56		9.25	
1.10		5.38		3.56		15.45	
11.56		44.67		91.19		90.02	
221.55		2.34		22.45		459.47	
330.66		887.67		49.99		246.07	
	(50)		(101)		(155)		(212)

5.		6.		7.		8.	
31.97		214.16		966.99		467.59	
75.79		99.75		85.76		493.86	
167.32		40.01		123.45		75.00	
83.00		8.01		2.45		11.40	
7.16	(237)	600.30	(291)	78.19	(344)	0.65	(398)
15.00		5.18		50.50		616.54	
221.40		63.00		115.00		7.50	
8.04		17.65		123.86		2.50	
12.41		20.57		49.83		189.24	
581.04		102.34		85.09		543.21	
	(265)		(318)		(373)		(426)

Self-Evaluation

9. 56 93.16

10. 5947.57

9.		10.	
391.98		924.44	
417.26		667.00	
998.91		376.89	
421.98		867.70	
721.70	(456)	899.22	(518)
329.89		566.98	
835.08		167.02	
355.10		503.65	
945.62		708.00	
275.64		266.67	
	(488)		(550)

RECOMMENDATION: If you were able to complete the Self-Evaluation Skills Posttest in five minutes or less with no more than one incorrect answer, you have satisfactorily completed Chapter 3. You are now ready to progress to the next material. If you did not satisfactorily complete this material, take the Skills Posttest again, trying for the recommended level. If you are still not able to attain the recommended level, talk with your instructor.

NOTES

PART TWO

The Electronic Calculator

The electronic calculator combines the best features of the older ten-key adding machine and the mechanical printing calculator into one machine that provides an answer in milliseconds. All four mathematical functions—adding, subtracting, multiplying, and dividing—are accomplished automatically and rapidly. A printed tape for checking is provided.

The computer calculator rapidly performs the same mathematical functions as the electronic calculator. The solutions are displayed on the screen so care must be taken in entering data and in verifying answers. Some of the command symbols differ from the electronic calculator so the user must be aware of the various symbols for the calculator software being used. Refer to Appendix A or your software support material for the symbols.

In Part Two, Chapter 4 reviews the addition and subtraction process and expands the various types of problems that can be worked on this calculator. Chapter 5 presents the multiplication process, while Chapter 6 presents the division process. Chapter 7 presents a special feature on the electronic calculator—its capability of doing multi-operation calculations with one solution process.

PART TWO

GENERIC KEYS FOR THE ELECTRONIC CALCULATOR

The following are descriptive illustrations of the keys you will need to complete this section. Read the description for each of the keys, find it on your machine, and fill in the key labeling for your machine. Use the blanks on the right for filling in the information.

1. **Plus key**   located on the right side of the ten-key keyboard; has a plus (+) sign on it.

2. **Total key**   usually located below the plus key, may be to the right; has an indication of final operation, such as T or *.

3. **Add-mode setting**   usually where round-off key or decimal control is located; has +, Add, or Add-mode indication on it.*

4. **Clear key**   various locations; may have C, All C, or similar indication.

5. **Clear-entry key**   various locations; usually has CE indication and may have C/CE on same key.

6. **Minus key**   usually above plus key; has a minus (−) sign on it.

7. **Non-add key**   various locations; has #, N, NA, or Non-add on it.*

8. **Subtotal key**   various locations; has S, ST, Sub, Subtotal, or ◊ on it.*

9. **Times key**   various locations; has times (×) symbol on it.

10. **Equals key**   various locations; has equals (=) symbol on it.

11. **Percent key**   various locations; has percent (%) symbol on it.

12. **Memory keys**   usually near equals key; usually labeled with M and math symbol to indicate positive and negative storage. MR is used for memory recall. CM or MC is used for clearing memory.

13. **Enter-dividend key**   various locations; has divide (÷) symbol on it.

1. _____

2. _____

3. _____

4. _____

5. _____

6. _____

7. _____

8. _____

9. _____

10. _____

11. _____

12. _____

13. _____

---

* These items may not be on the computer calculator.

Addition and Subtraction on the Electronic Calculator

OBJECTIVES

When you have successfully completed this chapter for the electronic printing calculator, you will be able to

1. Identify the following operating controls and their uses:
—Plus (+) key
—Minus (−) key
—Correction key
—Non-add key
—Subtotal key
—Total (T) key

2. Perform calculations on the machine in addition and subtraction using the touch method.

3. Demonstrate speed and accuracy using the touch method on performance tests.

4. Attain confidence in your ability to perform various addition and subtraction problems on the electronic calculator.

5. Advance to business application problems.

INTRODUCTION

The machine should be placed on the desk at the right and at a slight angle in the position that is most comfortable to you. Sit erect, but relaxed. Use the touch method for entering the numbers on the keyboard. Figure 4.1 shows a hand in correct home-row position. Begin by locating the following parts on your machine.

FIGURE 4.1   Hand in Proper Position on the Ten-Key Calculator

1. *Plus key*, usually on the right side of the ten-key keyboard; has a plus (+) sign on it; adds the number on the keyboard to the machine register.

2. *Minus key*, usually located above the plus bar; has a minus (−) sign on it; subtracts the number on the keyboard from the machine register.

3. *Correction key*, in various locations according to machine brand; normally has C or CE on the key; clears incorrect numbers from the keyboard before the plus or minus bar is depressed.

4. *Non-add key*, in various locations according to machine brand; normally identified by a # symbol, but may also have an N, NA, or Non-add on the key; allows the operator to enter a number for reference purposes without affecting the total of a problem.

5. *Subtotal key*, in various locations according to machine brand; normally identified by an S, ST, Sub, Subtotal, or ◊ on the key; allows the operator to take a total at any point in the problem without disturbing the final answer.

ADDITION

This material is designed to help you learn the addition procedure on the ten-key electronic calculator. The addition procedure given in the following example is the same as the one you used in Chapters 2 and 3. Practice the example problem.

Practice Problems

1. _____

2. _____

3. _____

4. _____

5. _____

6. _____

7. _____

8. _____

9. _____

10. _____

■ **EXAMPLE**

	Set decimal control on add-mode
4.56	Enter 4.56 Depress +
4.71	Enter 4.71 Depress +
5.28	Enter 5.28 Depress +
6.93	Enter 6.93 Depress +
	Depress total key
	Read the result: 21.48 ■

Addition on the computer calculator is performed in the following manner:

■ **EXAMPLE**

	Set the decimal with each number when working on the computer.
4.56	Enter 4.56 Depress +
4.71	Enter 4.71 Depress +
5.28	Enter 5.28 Depress +
6.93	Enter 6.93 Depress *Enter* or =
	Read the result: 21.48 ■

Did you use the touch method? Were you able to operate the machine without looking at your hands? Practice this problem a few times until you are able to work it without feeling uncomfortable about entering the numbers or depressing the plus and total keys. Continue with the following practice material.

| Practice Problems |

Practice the following problems using the touch method.

Reminder: Use correct posture at your workstation and do not look at your hands. Work for accuracy and repeat any problems in which you made an error.

1.	**2.**	**3.**	**4.**	**5.**
4.56	4.74	5.85	6.96	5.94
4.65	4.14	5.25	6.36	31.13
5.64	4.77	5.88	6.99	29.05
5.46	4.11	5.22	6.33	1.09
6.45	4.71	5.82	6.93	69.66
6.54	4.17	5.28	6.39	42.86
33.30	26.64	33.30	39.96	179.73

6.	**7.**	**8.**	**9.**	**10.**
68.34	77.01	1.19	9,240.03	92.46
75.77	15.97	58.21	3,173.11	693.97
265.48	1.21	747.18	25.07	63.50
0.90	60.68	49.98	326.99	806.01
282.04	734.88	16.77	591.39	74.79
4.79	40.06	730.03	84.59	2.13
697.32	929.81	1,603.36	13,441.18	1,732.86

Complete the following problems, maintaining accuracy while working to increase your speed.

Practice Problems

Note: Compare your answers with the answers given in Appendix B. Your instructor may choose to have you check your answers in a set that is more complete than the one given in Appendix C. Verify which answer source you are to use.

11.			12.			13.		
261.88			5,363.74			530.72		
43.30			14.03			8,103.77		
4,655.04			3,401.30			900.19		
9.75			19.59			596.38		
606.00	(28)		779.84	(88)		10.98	(146)	
6,804.91			22.72			111.65		
204.94			2,822.86			90.30		
13.67			266.96			4,572.06		
361.46			0.61			68.79		
7.73			95.25			3.34		
	(58)			(116)			(175)	

11. _____
12. _____
13. _____

14.			15.			16.		
7,379.30			244.88			7,752.00		
3,010.13			6,102.55			30.35		
2,490.01			445.20			769.24		
9.27			41.10			837.03		
65.72	(205)		7,110.00	(268)		70.30	(329)	
4,372.39			483.07			961.86		
706.61			3,769.80			81.63		
63.15			465.85			96.45		
441.26			88.85			569.49		
991.75			825.41			6,041.87		
	(237)			(300)			(360)	

14. _____
15. _____
16. _____
17. _____
18. _____
19. _____
20. _____

17.			18.			19.		
16.00			5,239.54			1,009.89		
736.10			3,412.18			26,115.68		
2,347.83			48.04			28.91		
6,266.53			617.76			32.68		
739.41	(391)		1,723.67	(452)		26.43	(512)	
5.87			592.44			761.40		
6,510.55			558.12			19.98		
30.90			56.58			909.44		
13.82			5,717.95			210.36		
319.97			8.51			1,110.26		
	(420)			(482)			(544)	

20.		
637.50		
2.35		
10.52		
520.93		
2,478.64	(572)	
405.16		
69.90		
0.17		
146.61		
709.13		
	(600)	

Self-Check

SPM: _____

Errors: _____

Self-Check

Work the preceding problems again. Attempt to work the problems in five minutes or less with one or no incorrect answers. Figure your SPM and record your accuracy.

600 strokes ÷ _____ minutes = _____ strokes per minute
_____ SPM
_____ errors

Recommendation: If you were able to complete the problems in five minutes or less with one or no incorrect answers, proceed to the next material. If you did not achieve the expected level, repeat the ten problems, figure your SPM and accuracy, and then proceed to the next material.

CORRECTIONS

Remember to correct your errors in the following ways.

1. If the + or − key has not been depressed, the correction key can be depressed to remove the number from the keyboard.

2. If the error is discovered immediately after the action key is depressed, depress the opposite key (depress − to remove an incorrect + entry; depress + to remove an incorrect − entry).

3. If other numbers have been entered after the error was made, reenter the incorrect number into the machine and depress the opposite action key. Then enter the correct number and depress the correct action key.

SUBTRACTION

To work a subtraction problem on the electronic calculator, enter the minuend (first number) on the keyboard, then depress the plus key; enter the subtrahend (second number) on the keyboard, then depress the minus key. To obtain the difference, depress the total key. Practice the following example problem in subtraction using the touch method.

■ **EXAMPLE**

	Set decimal control on add-mode
62.14	Enter 62.14 Depress +
−37.16	Enter 37.16 Depress −
	Depress total key
	Read the result: 24.98

■

Subtraction is performed on the computer calculator in the following manner:

■ **EXAMPLE**

	Set the decimal along with the number
62.14	Enter 62.14 Depress −
−37.16	Enter 37.16 Depress *Enter* or =
	Read the result: 24.98

■

Did you use the touch method? Were you able to operate the machine without looking at it? If you were able to answer yes to both questions, proceed with the next material. If you were not able to answer yes to both questions, review the touch method in Chapter 2, work the problem three additional times, and then proceed to the next practice problem set.

Practice Problems	Complete the following problems, maintaining accuracy and continuing to increase your speed.

21.   54.71
     −43.82
     10.89

22.   79.86
     − 15.37

23.   162.04
     − 29.81

24.   326.81
     −117.06

25.   77.62
     −55.20

26.   667.00
     −432.99

27.   260.97
     −157.23

28.   696.27
     −417.40

29.   567.82
     −121.48

30.   906.02
     −414.72

31.   2,964.80
     −1,547.26

32.   917.14
     −257.90

33.   1,948.26
     − 821.44

34.   7.89
     −2.14

35.   22.76
     −19.48

36.   426.58
     −137.49

37.   7,264.91
     −4,139.09

38.   645.19
     −387.00

39.   400.73
     −285.10

40.   941.52
     −357.81

Self-Check	Work the preceding problems again. Attempt to complete the problems in three minutes or less with two or less incorrect answers. Compute your SPM and record your accuracy.

272 strokes ÷ _____ minutes = _____ strokes per minute
_____ SPM
_____ errors

Recommendation: If you were able to achieve at least 91 SPM with two or less incorrect answers, proceed to the next material. If you were not able to achieve that level, repeat the 20 problems, figuring SPM and accuracy again. After this repetition, proceed to the next material.

Credit Balances

When subtracting numbers in which the subtrahend is larger than the minuend, the difference will be called a *credit balance*.

    14.98   minuend
−26.33   subtrahend
    11.35   difference, or credit balance

Practice Problems

21. _____**10.89**_____

22. _____

23. _____

24. _____

25. _____

26. _____

27. _____

28. _____

29. _____

30. _____

31. _____

32. _____

33. _____

34. _____

35. _____

36. _____

37. _____

38. _____

39. _____

40. _____

Self-Check

SPM: _____

Errors: _____

41. _____325.35 Cr_____

42. _____

43. _____

44. _____

45. _____

46. _____

47. _____

48. _____

49. _____

50. _____

51. _____

52. _____

53. _____

54. _____

55. _____

56. _____

Various machine brands will identify a credit balance in different ways. The electronic calculator will usually print the answer in red, but your machine may indicate credit balance in other ways. Other machine brands may indicate credit balance by printing a minus before or after the answer or a C or Cr after the answer. When a credit balance answer has been identified, it should be recorded in one of the following three ways.

$$-11.35 \qquad 11.35 \text{ Cr} \qquad (11.35)$$

| **Practice Problems** | Work the following subtraction problems. |

Reminder: Be sure to record a credit balance using one of the recommended procedures.

41.	**42.**	**43.**	**44.**
165.72	972.76	599.12	9,476.28
−491.07	−2,048.02	−837.64	−9,710.65
325.35 Cr			

45.	**46.**	**47.**	**48.**
10.98	71.53	973.84	99.80
−22.45	−80.01	−1,256.00	−136.40

49.	**50.**	**51.**	**52.**
5,168.77	71.53	9,622.40	462.76
−9,026.45	−96.03	−9,620.70	−597.20

53.	**54.**	**55.**	**56.**
110.46	4,652.13	761.28	88.02
− 87.92	−9,700.54	−645.02	−76.29

To obtain an answer to some types of problems, you will find it necessary to add and subtract several times. Practice the problem given in the following example.

■ **EXAMPLE**

	Set decimal control on add-mode	
7.98	Enter 7.98	Depress +
4.66−	Enter 4.66	Depress −
1.09	Enter 1.09	Depress +
5.32	Enter 5.32	Depress +
7.03−	Enter 7.03	Depress −
	Depress total key	
	Read the answer: 2.70	■

■ **EXAMPLE**

	Set the decimal with each number when working on the computer	
7.98	Enter 7.98	Depress −
4.66−	Enter 4.66	Depress +
1.09	Enter 1.09	Depress +
5.32	Enter 5.32	Depress −
7.03−	Enter 7.03	Depress *Enter* or = ■

(Note: The + or − key was depressed *before* entering a number; therefore, determine whether the next number to be entered is to be added or subtracted. you must depress the mathematical action key, then enter the number.)

Practice Problems	Work the following problems, indicating credit balances when it is necessary.

57. 57. _____

58. 58. _____

57. 4.98	**58.** 5.53 −	**59.** 1.79	**60.** 46.29 −
1.55	3.09	6.69	72.10
9.08 −	7.69	6.01 −	26.34 −
2.79	1.15	3.28 −	51.29
3.96 −	8.90 −	6.11	16.49

59. _____

60. _____

61. _____

61. 41.08	**62.** 129.56 −	**63.** 186.30	**64.** 1,746.29 −
46.28 −	789.08	664.88 −	8,013.51
88.16 −	341.30 −	909.13	3,718.00 −
37.89	906.73	531.70 −	9,953.18
50.05 −	541.09 −	710.44	1,068.01

62. _____

63. _____

64. _____

65. 4.98	**66.** 76.20	**67.** 1,468.25	**68.** 9.78
10.17 −	10.09	906.24	47.80 −
3.25	126.92 −	3,289.11 −	5.55
44.17	7.00	70.33	113.93
25.80	58.53 −	77.15	64.06 −

65. _____

66. _____

67. _____

69. 99.40	**70.** 17.47 −	**71.** 3.26 −	**72.** 22.38 −
203.05	36.90	394.41	5.63 −
81.45 −	830.24	0.97	182.06
72.01 −	90.18	52.00 −	4.29 −
1.73 −	922.71 −	14.78	9.11 −

68. _____

69. _____

70. _____

SUBTOTAL KEY

71. _____

A *subtotal* gives the answer to a computation at the point where you are working without disturbing the final answer. To take a subtotal on an electronic calculator, the following procedure will be used. Find the *subtotal key* on your machine, which will be indicated by an S, ST, Sub, Subtotal, or ◊. By depressing the subtotal key in an addition or subtraction problem, you will be able to obtain the answer at that point in the problem without disturbing the final answer. Practice the problem in the following example using the subtotal key on your machine.

72. _____

Practice Problems

73. _____ **272.60** _____

74. _____

75. _____

76. _____

■ EXAMPLE

17.93	Enter 17.93	Depress +
513.65	Enter 513.65	Depress +
3.22	Enter 3.22	Depress +
83.52	Enter 83.52	Depress +
618.32 S	Depress subtotal key	
	Read the answer: 618.32	

105.08	Enter 105.08	Depress +
6.87	Enter 6.87	Depress +
11.56	Enter 11.56	Depress +
74.50	Enter 74.50	Depress +
816.33 S	Depress subtotal key	
	Read the answer: 816.33	

603.87	Enter 603.87	Depress +
99.20	Enter 99.20	Depress +
4.74	Enter 4.74	Depress +
25.90	Enter 25.90	Depress +
1,550.04 T	Depress total key	
	Read the final answer: 1,550.04	

■

Practice Problems	Work the following problems, determining the subtotals and total where they are indicated.

73.	74.	75.	76.
23.47	15.33	179.17	45.86
8.69	197.53	18.00	111.78
2.56	689.70	128.69	27.37
43.75	1.55	5.25	44.40
78.47 S	S	S	S
92.10	1.59	2.05	15.29
0.39	9.20	71.64	39.38
15.36	89.84	819.26	7.49
3.67	43.92	30.57	75.13
189.99 S	S	S	S
1.33	36.51	61.21	86.65
6.94	329.07	21.12	109.62
56.62	22.93	2.09	94.69
17.72	1.26	147.89	10.75
272.60 T	T	T	T

77.	0.90	78.	547.09	79.	251.02	80.	838.09
	87.75		50.04		33.26		1.06
	15.26		602.20		36.10		185.76
	702.00		700.00		87.00		1.74
	S		S		S		S

77. _____

78. _____

79. _____

80. _____

75.48	156.21	936.74	56.74
102.05	4.25	44.59	123.15
73.10	819.64	85.77	812.00
125.64	50.08	4.91	58.63
S	S	S	S

713.57	458.10	11.19	17.18
0.58	506.68	205.02	683.04
25.43	184.35	77.71	12.70
20.10	4.50	257.20	26.86
T	T	T	T

ADDITION WITH MORE THAN TWO DIGITS AFTER THE DECIMAL POINT

The electronic calculator has been designed and programmed so that the machine will automatically place the decimals in a series of numbers as long as the decimal point is set along with the numbers being entered into the machine.

Most electronic calculators are also equipped with a decimal control mechanism of some type. The *decimal control mechanism* will be a wheel with numbers on it, a slide bar with decimal positions indicated, or a key for setting the decimal on the keyboard. You have already found this mechanism when you set your calculator on the add-mode. Find the decimal control mechanism on your machine and set it on 2. Your answers in this section will be rounded to two digits after the decimal when your decimal is set on 2. If your machine also has a 5/4 round-off switch, you will need to set it on 5/4 after setting the decimal control mechanism. The 5/4 round-off switch tells the calculator to round up if the digit is 5 or higher or to drop the digit if it is 4 or lower.

Practice the addition problem in the following example.

■ **EXAMPLE**

	Set decimal control on 2	
	Set round-off switch in 5/4 position (if applicable)	
0.72	Enter . (decimal) 72	Depress +
10.321	Enter 10. (decimal) 321	Depress +
0.002	Enter . (decimal) 002	Depress +
4.57	Enter 4. (decimal) 57	Depress +
1.2	Enter 1. (decimal) 2	Depress +
	Depress total key	
	Read the answer: 16.81	■

The machine placed the decimal point as the numbers were entered and correctly placed the decimal point in the total.

Practice Problems

81. _____ **74.97** _____

82. _____

83. _____

84. _____

85. _____

86. _____

87. _____

88. _____

89. _____

90. _____

91. _____

92. _____

93. _____

94. _____

95. _____

96. _____

Practice Problems	Work the following addition and subtraction problems.

81.	**82.**	**83.**	**84.**
6.35	10.00	3.58	6.12
27.708	1.726	6.0927	4,231.357
0.132	645.029	260.5	3.3217
5.78	0.25	247.576	5.90
35	132.427	14.1	14.558
74.97			

85.	**86.**	**87.**	**88.**
5.267	13.7921	4.1901	1.03
365.33	1.6509	10.347	0.1986
2.4756	450	93.25	211.7
12.04	40.665	0.6709	67.096
0.902	0.172	0.25	3.7104

89.	**90.**	**91.**	**92.**
8.9072	9.7018	3.25	215.23
−1.56	−6.543	−1.768	− 39.078

93.	**94.**	**95.**	**96.**
97.018	50.305	83.2	46.7325
−215.7	− 2.2963	−91.065	−38.947

CONVERTING FRACTIONS TO DECIMALS

When working with fractions on the electronic calculator, it is necessary to convert the fractions to decimals. Remember to enter the decimal along with the numbers as you did in the previous material. The following table reviews the fractions studied in Chapter 1.

Common Fraction	Decimal Equivalent	Common Fraction	Decimal Equivalent
1/4	0.25	4/5	0.8
1/2	0.5	1/8	0.125
3/4	0.75	3/8	0.375
1/3	0.333	5/8	0.625
2/3	0.667	7/8	0.875
1/6	0.167	1/10	0.1
5/6	0.833	3/10	0.3
1/5	0.2	7/10	0.7
2/5	0.4	9/10	0.9
3/5	0.6		

Practice the addition problem containing fractions given in the following example.

■ **EXAMPLE** First, convert the fractions to decimals; then enter the numbers into the machine and add.

41 3/4	41.75
77	77
6 3/8	6.375
9 4/5	9.8
59 1/6	59.167

Set decimal control on 2
Set round-off switch in 5/4 position (if applicable)

Enter 41.75   Depress +
Enter 77   Depress +
Enter 6.375   Depress +
Enter 9.8   Depress +
Enter 59.167   Depress +
Depress total key
Read the answer: 194.09   ■

Practice Problems

Complete the following addition problems. You may find it helpful to change the fractions to decimals before adding. Continue on to work the subtraction problems in the same manner.

Hint: As soon as you are able to convert fractions to decimals with ease, begin working the problems without rewriting them in decimal form.

97.	98.	99.	100.
46 3/4	17 3/10	72 3/8	71 1/10
7 1/6	91 9/10	17 7/10	22 1/3
23	88 3/5	3 1/5	7 1/4
142 1/2	1 5/6	146 1/6	90 1/6
4 5/8	126 2/3	59 4/5	43 3/5
224.04			

101.	102.	103.	104.
80 1/8	14 9/10	149 5/6	307 9/10
76 3/5	7 7/8	− 81 1/4	−112 5/8
19 1/4	46 5/6		
3 3/10	92 2/3		
56 3/4	7 7/10		

105.	106.	107.	108.
43 2/3	601 1/2	635 3/4	704 5/8
−35 4/5	−148 7/10	−519 1/6	−321 2/3

Practice Problems

97.   **224.04**

98. _____

99. _____

100. _____

101. _____

102. _____

103. _____

104. _____

105. _____

106. _____

107. _____

108. _____

NON-ADD KEY

The *non-add key* on the electronic calculator is used for numbering, coding, dating, or entering identifying information. To enter a number for these purposes, set the number on the

Practice Problems

109. _____ **278.82** _____

110. _____

111. _____

112. _____

113. _____

114. _____

115. _____

116. _____

keyboard and depress the non-add key. The number will print on the tape, but will not become a part of the answer for the problem being worked.

The non-add key is not uniformly placed on the calculator, and some calculators do not have a non-add key. If your machine has a non-add key, it will be labeled with one of the following symbols: N, NA, #, Non-add, or Print. if your machine is not equipped with a non-add key, leave out the numbers that are to be entered with the non-add key. In the following example and the following problems, all reference numbers will be identified by an N following the number.

Practice the problem given in the following example.

■ **EXAMPLE**

Set decimal control on 2
Set round-off switch in 5/4 position (if applicable)

7.34	Enter 7.34	Depress +
6.78 N	Enter 6.78	Depress non-add key
3.54	Enter 3.54	Depress +
9.01	Enter 9.01	Depress +

Depress total key
Read the answer: 19.89 ■

┌─────────────┐
│ **Practice** │ Work the following problems using the non-add key when necessary.
│ **Problems** │
└─────────────┘

Hint: You may want to use the add-mode for these problems.

109. 1.03 N	**110.** 1.04 N	**111.** 1.05 N	**112.** 1.06 N
78.25	12.59	41.38	21.37
3.39	13.89 N	28.23	96.14
93.91−	66.81−	98.13	1.36 N
46.28	22.37	12.63 N	41.63
4.56 N	3.57	15.49−	86.45
123.58	35.22	69.27	93.50−
39.36	4.73 N	58.45 N	718.66 N
67.13	732.48	93.91	23.25
14.74	82.83−	48.35	49.78−
278.82			

113. 1.07 N	**114.** 1.08 N	**115.** 1.09 N	**116.** 1.10 N
178.25	1.35	88.71	28.88
66.53−	1.25−	78.26−	89.00−
6.77 N	77.49	156.00−	10.06
376.00−	43.76	70.35	54.05
1.17 N	10.25 N	15.45	40.37−
18.07	12.38	4.58	1.76 N
70.02	16.94	9.25−	26.85−
71.64	96.41 N	132.52	94.45
72.45	97.83−	28.03 N	86.27

SELF-EVALUATION

Skills Posttest

Complete the following problems in five minutes or less with one or no incorrect answers. (Do not include recording the answers in the five minutes.)

1.	2.	3.	4.
121	9.65	46.38	26.31
413	0.41 N	58.45	93.91−
655	1.76	98.13	48.53
418	5.44	27.52	15.76 N
975	4.15	25.83	31.88
381	5.13	25.61	10.09−
991	5.79	76.68	24.83
236	5.35	95.31	1.76 N
159	1.39	91.53	10.42−
178	4.00	19.48	63.95

5.	6.	7.	8.
6.7638	83 1/10	629	24.67
121.5	41 4/5	−598	−19.48
47	6 1/3		
51.762	56 3/8		
14.98	9 1/2		

9.	10.	11.
42.69	67 3/10	7.425
−91.61	−33 4/5	−1.9891

12.

a.	b.	c.	d.
66.35	5.08−	176.94	13.44
7.18 N	26.07	70.88	99.53−
83.44	150.00	7.65 N	380.66
7.66−	7.66 N	3.47−	146.00
18.00	6.98	97.29	3.21 N
S	S	S	T

Self-Evaluation

1. _____

2. _____

3. _____

4. _____

5. _____

6. _____

7. _____

8. _____

9. _____

10. _____

11. _____

12a. _____

12b. _____

12c. _____

12d. _____

RECOMMENDATION: If you were able to complete the Self-Evaluation Skills Posttest in five minutes or less with no more than one incorrect answer, you have satisfactorily completed this segment. You are now ready to progress to the business applications problems that follow. If you did not satisfactorily complete this segment, take the Self-Evaluation Skills Posttest again, trying for the recommended level. If you are still not able to attain the recommended level, talk with your instructor.

BUSINESS APPLICATIONS: MAINTAINING CHECK REGISTERS

Business Situation

John Hutton received a letter from the neighborhood Kroger supermarket stating that his check had been returned for nonsufficient funds (NSF). After reviewing his checkbook register, he realized that the mistake was a result of incorrect subtraction. This one mistake had cost him a $25 NSF bank charge, a $25 fee charged by the merchant, and the embarrassment of having to pick up his bounced check.

A *check register* is a booklet that is used to determine the current balance in a checking account. To avoid making mistakes, be careful when determining the balance in your checkbook. Some points to remember include

1. The information needed to complete the check register should be completed *before* the check is written.

   a. The number of the check should be entered.
   b. The current date should be entered.
   c. The name of the person or company receiving the check should be written.
   d. The dollar amount of the check *or* the deposit should be placed in the proper column.
   e. The necessary addition or subtraction for determining the current balance should be carefully completed. Amounts for deposits are *added* to the previous balance; amounts for checks are *subtracted* from the previous balance.

2. After recording the above information in the check register, the check may be written.

Study the entries in the following example before completing Applications Problems 1 through 3.

■   **EXAMPLE**   John Hutton's checking account balance is $683.30. He writes check number 115 for $133.29 to pay his electric bill. He also deposits $250 in his account. What is his current balance?

CODE OR NUMBER	DATE	DESCRIPTION OF TRANSACTION	PAYMENT DEBIT OR FEE (−)	T	DEPOSIT OR CREDIT (−)	BALANCE FORWARD	
							683 30
115	1-10	To Ohio Power & Light	133 29			Pay't or Dep.	
		For January electric bill				Bal.	550 01
	1-20	To Deposit			250 00	Pay't or Dep.	
		For				Bal.	800 01

The new balance is found by subtracting the amount of the check ($133.29) from the original balance ($683.30).

The difference between recording a deposit and recording a check is that a deposit must be added to the previous balance. For example, John made a $250 deposit on January 20. This amount was added to the old balance of $550.01 to create a new balance of $800.01.   ■

Check Registers: Applications Problems 1 Through 3

Instructions	*Machine Setting*
1. Determine the balance after each entry in the check registers in Applications Problems 1 through 3. 2. Complete the equation below each check register as a method of checking your work.	1. Set decimal control on add-mode. 2. Set round-off switch in 5/4 position (if applicable).

1a. _____978.19_____

1b. _____

1c. _____

1d. _____

1e. _____

1f. _____

1g. _____

Applications Problem 1

RECORD ALL CHARGES OR CREDITS THAT AFFECT YOUR ACCOUNT

NUMBER	DATE	DESCRIPTION OF TRANSACTION	PAYMENT/DEBIT (-)	✓ T	FEE (IF ANY) (-)	DEPOSIT/CREDIT (+)	BALANCE $ 995	39
634	1-2	Detroit News	$ 17	20	$	$	a. 978	19
635	1-3	Joe Bates	24	50			b.	
636	1-3	Detroit Power & Light	50	05			c.	
	1-4	Deposit				370 00	d.	
637	1-5	Phil Hutton	124	00			e.	
	1-6	Deposit				421 50	f.	
638	1-7	Jones Office Supply	151	95			g.	

Beginning Balance +   Deposits   −   Checks   =   Balance

_____   _____   _____   _____

Applications Problems

2a. _____

2b. _____

2c. _____

2d. _____

2e. _____

2f. _____

2g. _____

2h. _____

2i. _____

Applications Problem 2

RECORD ALL CHARGES OR CREDITS THAT AFFECT YOUR ACCOUNT

NUMBER	DATE	DESCRIPTION OF TRANSACTION	PAYMENT/DEBIT (-)		✓ T	FEE (IF ANY) (-)	DEPOSIT/CREDIT (+)		BALANCE $ 1,140 30	
			$			$	$			
899	2-1	Ted Jefferson	29	95					a.	
900	2-1	Jones Lighting	34	95					b.	
901	2-2	Mathis Plants	22	30					c.	
902	2-3	Carl's Grocery	40	00					d.	
	2-4	Deposit					600	35	e.	
903	2-5	Cash	100	00					f.	
904	2-7	Washington Apts.	475	00					g.	
905	2-9	Cash	14	50					h.	
	2-9	Deposit					315	00	i.	

Beginning Balance +   Deposits   −   Checks   =   Balance

_____   _____   _____   _____

Applications Problem 3

RECORD ALL TRANSACTIONS THAT AFFECT YOUR ACCOUNT

NUMBER	DATE		DESCRIPTION OF PAYMENTS—DEBITS—FEES OR DEPOSITS—CREDITS	AMOUNT OF PAYMENT-DEBIT OR FEE (−)		T ✓	AMOUNT OF DEPOSIT OR CREDIT (+)		BALANCE FORWARD		
										625	40
233	7-1	To	South Services	178	33				Pay't or Dept.		
		For	Equipment Repair						Bal.	a.	
234	7-2	To	Bennett Shoes, Inc.	125	39				Pay't or Dept.		
		For	Replenish Stock						Bal.	b.	
235	7-3	To	Seattle Manufacturing	146	23				Pay't or Dept.		
		For	Replenish Stock						Bal.	c.	
236	7-3	To	W.F. Nelson	29	15				Pay't or Dept.		
		For	Refund						Bal.	d.	
237	7-3	To	Bill Radford	15	20				Pay't or Dept.		
		For	Refund						Bal.	e.	
	7-3	To	Deposit				1,400	00	Pay't or Dept.		
		For							Bal.	f.	
238	7-4	To	Oak Forest Printing	465	00				Pay't or Dept.		
		For	Office Forms						Bal.	g.	
239	7-5	To	Barnett Office Supply	183	29				Pay't or Dept.		
		For	Office Supplies						Bal.	h.	
240	7-5	To	Martin Consulting	235	00				Pay't or Dept.		
		For	Tax Advice						Bal.	i.	

REMINDER: RECORD AUTOMATIC PAYMENTS OR DEPOSITS ON DATE OF TRANSACTION

Beginning Balance +   Deposits   −   Checks   =   Balance

_____   _____   _____   _____

3a.  _____

3b. _____

3c. _____

3d. _____

3e. _____

3f. _____

3g. _____

3h. _____

3i. _____

BUSINESS APPLICATIONS: COMPLETING A BANK STATEMENT RECONCILIATION

Business Situation

The bank statement for Autry's Computer Store was received in the morning mail. Jill Bartlett, the firm's bookkeeper, notices that there is a difference between the balance in the checkbook and the balance on the bank statement. Last month, the bank made a $1,500 mistake. She wonders if another mistake could be the reason for the difference between the two balances.

Each month, you receive a detailed statement of transactions that affect your checking account. This statement shows the amounts subtracted from your account and the amounts added to your account. Three factors can explain the difference between the checkbook balance and the bank statement balance:

1. *Outstanding checks*—checks written that have not been paid by the bank.
2. *Deposits in transit*—deposits made that the bank has not processed.
3. *Bank charges*—charges made by the bank that you are not aware of, such as activity charges, service charges, or check printing costs.

Most banks include a form like the one in the following example to make the reconciliation process a little easier. *Notice that the directions needed for completing the reconciliation are included as part of the form.*

■   **EXAMPLE**   After receiving the monthly bank statement, the bookkeeper for Autry's Computer Store compared the statement and the firm's canceled checks. She noted the following items before attempting to reconcile the statement:

Statement balance: $5,860.06
Deposits in transit: $1,575.00
Outstanding checks: $16.00, $54.56, $43.95, $65.35, $23.45
Checkbook balance: $7,250.00
Activity charge: $8.75
Check printing: $9.50

Balance Shown		Checks Outstanding		Checkbook	
on Statement	$5,860.06	No.	Amount	Balance	$7,250.00
			16 00		
Add Deposits			54 56	Subtract (if any)	
Not Shown	1,575.00		43 95	Activity Charges	8.75
			65 35		
Subtotal	7,435.06		23 45	Subtotal	7,241.25
Subtract				Subtract (if any)	
Outstanding				Other Bank	
Checks	203.31			Charges	9.50
Balance	$7,231.75			Balance	$7,231.75
		Total	203 31		

Do the two balances agree? __X__ yes _____ no

■

Work through the preceding example to make sure you understand the addition and subtraction required to complete the bank statement reconciliation.

Bank Statement Reconciliation:
Applications Problems 4 Through 6

Instructions	*Machine Setting*
1. Complete the bank reconciliations for the businesses in the following three application problems. 2. Make sure the balance on the statement side agrees with the balance on the checkbook side.	1. Set decimal control on add-mode. 2. Set round-off switch in 5/4 position (if applicable).

**Applications
Problems**

4a. _____

4b. _____

4c. _____

4d. _____

4e. ___$3,036.25___

4f. _____

4g. _____

4h. _____

4i. _____

4j. _____

4k. _____

5a. _____

5b. _____

5c. _____

5d. _____

5e. _____

5f. _____

5g. _____

5h. _____

5i. _____

5j. _____

5k. _____

Applications Problem 4

Checking Account Data for Smythe Office Supply

Bank balance: $2,070.38
Deposits in transit: $1,250.00
Outstanding checks: $79.14, $4.60,
　　　　　　　　$68.25, $46.99, $85.15
Checkbook balance: $3,040.75
Activity charge: $4.50

Bank Balance	a. _____	Checkbook Balance	f. _____
Add Deposits Not Shown	b. _____	Subtract (if any) Activity Charges	g. _____
Subtotal	c. _____	Subtotal	h. _____
Subtract Outstanding Checks	d. _____	Subtract (if any) Other Bank Charges	i. _____
Balance	e. $3,036.25	Balance	j. _____
Do the two balances agree? k. _____ yes _____ no			

Applications Problem 5

Checking Account Data for Business Systems, Inc.

Bank balance: $1,194.14　　　　Checkbook balance: $1,145.23
Deposits in transit: $40.00　　　Activity charge: $6.20
Outstanding checks: $13.85, $34.25,　　Check printing: $12.50
　　　　　　　$12.51, $47.00

Bank Balance	a. _____	Checkbook Balance	f. _____
Add Deposits Not Shown	b. _____	Subtract (if any) Activity Charges	g. _____
Subtotal	c. _____	Subtotal	h. _____
Subtract Outstanding Checks	d. _____	Subtract (if any) Other Bank Charges	i. _____
Balance	e. _____	Balance	j. _____
Do the two balances agree? k. _____ yes _____ no			

Applications Problem 6

Checking Account Data for Bob R. Gannon, C.P.A.

Bank balance: $6,321.45

Deposits in transit: $375.00, $245.00

Outstanding checks: $875.00, $49.00,
$730.00, $125.00,
$71.29, $69.35,
$121.39

Checkbook balance: $4,929.42

Activity charge: $13.25

Check printing: $15.75

Bank Balance	a. _____	Checkbook Balance	f. _____
Add Deposits Not Shown	b. _____	Subtract (if any) Activity Charges	g. _____
Subtotal	c. _____	Subtotal	h. _____
Subtract Outstanding Checks	d. _____	Subtract (if any) Other Bank Charges	i. _____
Balance	e. _____	Balance	j. _____

Do the two balances agree? k._____ yes _____ no

6a. _____

6b. _____

6c. _____

6d. _____

6e. _____

6f. _____

6g. _____

6h. _____

6i. _____

6j. _____

6k. _____

BUSINESS APPLICATIONS:
PROCESSING CONSUMER PAYMENT CARDS

Business Situation

Last Monday, Tavia Watkins started her new job in the accounting department of the Allied Electronics Store. On Tuesday morning, her supervisor, Ann Matthews, brought in all the account cards for Allied's customers who had bought merchandise on credit or who had made payments on their accounts during the month of May. Of course, Tavia wants to complete her first assignment without any mistakes. After examining the payment cards, she realizes that all she has to do is add or subtract each entry from the customer's previous account balance.

A *payment card* provides information about a customer's account balance. Space is provided at the top of the card for the customer's name, address, credit rating, and current credit limit. Individual columns are provided for the date, the dollar amount of the customer's purchase, the amount of payment, and the new balance. *All purchases are recorded in the appropriate column and* added *to the previous balance. All payments are recorded in the appropriate column and* subtracted *from the previous balance.*

■ **EXAMPLE** On April 30, William Timberly purchased merchandise valued at $256 at the Allied Electronics Store. This purchase increased his account balance to $413.25. On May 10, Timberly made a $50 payment on this account. This transaction reduced the account balance to $363.25.

Payment Card			
William Timberly 3906 Willow Creek Tulsa, OK 72133		Credit Rating: 3A Limit: $1,000	
Date	Purchases	Payments	New Balance
20XX Apr. 1			$157.25
Apr. 30	$256.00		413.25
May 10		$ 50.00	363.25

Although the procedures required for this application are relatively easy, employees often make careless mistakes—so be careful. It is possible to check your work by completing the following formula.

Beginning Balance + Purchases − Payments = New Balance

If no mistakes have been made, the answer for the above formula should agree with the balance reported on the customer's payment card.

Customer Payment Cards:
Applications Problems 7 Through 10

Instructions	*Machine Setting*
1. Find the new balance after each transaction for the payment cards in the following four application problems. 2. Complete the equation below each payment card as a method of checking your work.	1. Set decimal control on 2 or add-mode. 2. Set round-off switch in 5/4 position (if applicable).

Applications Problem 7

<table>
<tr><td colspan="4" align="center">Payment Card</td></tr>
<tr><td colspan="2">B.H. Bennett
1908 Wyatt
Tulsa, OK 72135</td><td colspan="2">Credit Rating: 2B
Limit: $1,000</td></tr>
<tr><td>Date</td><td>Purchases</td><td>Payments</td><td>New Balance</td></tr>
<tr><td>20XX
Apr. 30</td><td></td><td></td><td>$124.35</td></tr>
<tr><td>May 1</td><td>$34.50</td><td></td><td>a.</td></tr>
<tr><td>May 2</td><td>$39.95</td><td></td><td>b.</td></tr>
<tr><td>May 3</td><td></td><td>$50.00</td><td>c.</td></tr>
<tr><td>May 10</td><td></td><td>$75.00</td><td>d.</td></tr>
<tr><td></td><td></td><td></td><td></td></tr>
</table>

Beginning Balance   +   Purchases   −   Payments   =   New Balance

e. _____   f. _____   g. _____   h. __$73.80__

7a. _____

7b. _____

7c. _____

7d. _____

7e. _____

7f. _____

7g. _____

7h. ____**$73.80**____

Applications Problems

8a. _____

8b. _____

8c. _____

8d. _____

8e. _____

8f. _____

8g. _____

8h. _____

9a. _____

9b. _____

9c. _____

9d. _____

9e. _____

9f. _____

9g. _____

9h. _____

Applications Problem 8

Payment Card			
Martin Ford 1814 N. Star Tulsa, OK 72134		Credit Rating: 2A Limit: $750	
Date	Purchases	Payments	New Balance
20XX Apr. 30			-0-
May 3	$275.00		a.
May 10	$125.90		b.
May 20	$ 63.79		c.
May 25		$300.00	d.

Beginning Balance $+$ Purchases $-$ Payments $=$ New Balance

e. _____   f. _____   g. _____   h. _____

Applications Problem 9

Payment Card			
Jim Casey 605 Windomere Tulsa, OK 72130		Credit Rating: 1A Limit: $1,000	
Date	Purchases	Payments	New Balance
20XX Apr. 30			$65.40
May 3		$65.40	a.
May 6	$265.45		b.
May 10	$ 36.70		c.
May 20	$112.49		d.

Beginning Balance $+$ Purchases $-$ Payments $=$ New Balance

e. _____   f. _____   g. _____   h. _____

Applications Problem 10

	Payment Card		
Sandra Watkins 18233 N. Cheyenne Tulsa, OK 72140		Credit Rating: 4A Limit: $1,000	
Date	Purchases	Payments	New Balance
20XX Apr. 30			$485.00
May 15	$235.80		a.
May 20		$130.00	b.
May 22	$115.47		c.
May 29		$225.00	d.
May 30		$129.50	e.

Beginning Balance   +   Purchases   −   Payments   =   New Balance

f. _____   g. _____   h. _____   i. _____

10a. _____

10b. _____

10c. _____

10d. _____

10e. _____

10f. _____

10g. _____

10h. _____

10i. _____

BUSINESS APPLICATIONS: WORKING WITH ACCOUNTING FORMS

Business Situation

At the end of each accounting period, Claudine Peterson, the accounting clerk for Jayroe Fashions, Inc., must balance the firm's accounting records to ensure that all transactions have been recorded correctly. Last month, she worked for two hours to balance the books. Finally, she found her mistake—an error in addition.

Double-entry bookkeeping is a system in which each financial transaction is recorded as two separate accounting entries to maintain the equality of debits and credits. The accounting process begins by recording daily transactions in a general journal or specialized journals, such as the cash receipts journal, cash payments journal, sales journal, and purchases journal.

In the following example, each transaction is recorded as a debit to one account and a credit to another account. On the twentieth of November, cash sales of $500 were recorded by a debit in the cash column and a credit in the sales column. All cash sales are recorded in the same manner—usually on a daily basis. On November 21, Mr. Bean made a $100 payment on his account. This transaction was recorded by a debit to cash and a credit to accounts receivable. All payments made by customers are processed in the same manner.

Study the entries in the following example before completing Applications Problems 11 through 14.

■   **EXAMPLE**   Columns are provided to record dollar amounts that affect specific accounts in the cash receipts journal below.

CASH RECEIPTS JOURNAL

Date		Explanation	Accounts Receivable Credits		Sales Credits		Cash Debits	
Nov	20	Cash Sales			500	00	500	00
	21	Collection/Bean	100	00			100	00
	25	Cash Sales			450	00	450	00
	28	Collection/Ferrel	350	00			350	00
	29	Collection/Barnes	50	00			50	00
		Totals	500	00	950	00	1,450	00

Each month, after all transactions are recorded, the accountant compares the total for all debit columns and the total for all credit columns. The proof for the cash receipts journal is illustrated in the following table.

	Proof	
	Debit Balance	*Credit Balance*
Cash debit	$1,450	
Sales credit		$ 950
Accounts receivable credit		$ 500
Totals	$1,450	$1,450

Addition is a key factor in determining the accuracy of transactions recorded throughout the month. If the debit total does not agree with the credit total, a mistake is present and must be found. ■

Accounting Forms:
Applications Problems 11 Through 14

Instructions	*Machine Setting*
1. Add all amounts in each column in Applications Problems 11 through 14. 2. Determine the total debit amount and the total credit amount for each problem. Remember, total debits should equal total credits.	1. Set decimal control on add-mode. 2. Set round-off switch in 5/4 position (if applicable).

**Applications
Problems**

Applications Problem 11

11a. _____

11b. _____

11c. _____

11d. ___**$388.97**___

11e. _____

Bartlett's Department Store
Sales Journal
Date: January 5, 20XX

Date	Customer's Name	Accounts Receivable Debit	Sales Tax Credit	Sales Income Credit
Jan 2	Jay Camp	26.20	1.25	24.95
2	Bill Wooden	92.93	4.43	88.50
3	R.K. Warden	20.99	1.00	19.99
3	James Burnett	99.23	4.73	94.50
3	Lyn Holt	62.99	3.00	59.99
3	Barb Watson	68.25	3.25	65.00
4	Bill Dodson	18.38	.88	17.50
	Totals	a. _____	b. _____	c. _____

Total Debits   d. $388.97_____   Total Credits   e. _____

Applications Problem 12

Bartlett's Department Store Purchases Journal Date: February 19, 20XX			
Date	Customer's Name	Accounts Payable Credit	Purchases Debit	Freight-in Debit

Date	Customer's Name	Accounts Payable Credit	Purchases Debit	Freight-in Debit
Feb 14	Dan Jones Company	233.60	225.00	8.60
15	Martin & Martin	1,455.16	1,429.91	25.25
15	Bacon Equipment	1,611.96	1,601.46	10.50
15	U.S. Industries	928.95	914.45	14.50
16	Cooke Wholesalers	677.65	677.65	-0-
16	Wiley Manufacturer	4,560.42	4,528.02	32.40
16	Hudson Shoe Company	1,611.30	1,611.30	-0-
17	May Fashions	3,189.67	3,165.40	24.27
Totals		a. _____	b. _____	c. _____

Total Debits d. _____   Total Credits e. _____

12a. _____

12b. _____

12c. _____

12d. _____

12e. _____

**Applications
Problems**

Applications Problem 13

13a. _____

13b. _____

13c. _____

13d. _____

13e. _____

Bartlett's Department Store
Cash Payments Journal
Date: November 15, 20XX

Date	Customer's Name	Accounts Payable Debit	Purchases Discount Credit	Cash Credit
Nov 1	Barnett Wholesale	195.00		195.00
2	H.L. Ward	1,275.00	25.50	1,249.50
3	Industrial Supply	750.00	8.50	741.50
5	Ben Carter	2,000.00	40.00	1,960.00
7	Barnes & Campbell	175.00		175.00
9	Barnett Wholesale	54.95		54.95
10	H.L. Ward	952.39	28.57	923.82
11	Furniture Company	475.75	4.76	470.99
	Totals	a. _____	b. _____	c. _____

Total Debits d. _____   Total Credits e. _____

Applications Problem 14

14a. _____

14b. _____

14c. _____

14d. _____

14e. _____

Bartlett's Department Store Cash Receipts Journal Date: April 20, 20XX				
Date	Item	Accounts Receivable Credit	Sales Credit	Cash Debit
Apr 6	Cash Sales		145.00	145.00
7	Cash Sales		130.00	130.00
9	Collection/Ferrel	79.50		79.50
9	Cash Sales		85.21	85.21
11	Collection/Cannon	43.00		43.00
12	Cash Sales		32.95	32.95
14	Collection/Miller	22.95		22.95
16	Collection/Burrough	35.60		35.60
17	Collection/Lee	24.95		24.95
	Totals	a. _____	b. _____	c. _____
	Total Debits d. _____		Total Credits e. _____	

BUSINESS APPLICATIONS: COMPLETING A PAYROLL JOURNAL

Business Situation

Today, Claudine Peterson completed the calculations for the monthly payroll. This month, she has adopted a new payroll form to help ensure accuracy. One reason for choosing a new form was a $20 error on one employee's paycheck during the last pay period. Naturally, the employee caught the mistake.

Payroll Deductions

Once total wages have been calculated, the employer must determine various *payroll deductions* before the employee's take-home pay can be determined. The employer is required by federal law to deduct federal withholding (income tax) and FICA (Social Security and Medicare) tax. In addition, some states require employers to withhold an amount for state income tax. Finally, workers often authorize employers to deduct certain payments for hospitalization, contributions to retirement plans, voluntary savings plans, and the like.

The Payroll Journal

In order to increase accuracy when preparing payrolls, most companies use a *payroll journal*. The payroll journal illustrated in the following example has a column for the employee's marital status and number of exemptions. Also, columns are provided for total wages, FICA tax, federal withholding tax, state withholding tax, various other deductions, total deductions, and net cash wages paid.

The amount of total deductions is calculated by adding the dollar amounts for FICA, federal withholding, state withholding, and other deductions. Each employee's net cash wages paid, or take-home pay, is determined by subtracting total deductions from total wages.

EMPLOYEE'S NAME For Necessary Employee Data Concerning Each Employee Refer to Inside Front Cover.	Exemptions		Total Wages	DEDUCTIONS			Other Deductions			Total Deductions	Net Cash Wages Paid
				F.I.C.A. Tax	Fed. Withholding Tax	State Withholding Tax					
Cox, Thomas	M	2	360 50	27 58	19 00					46 58	313 92
Dudley, Robert	S	1	359 00	27 46	37 00					64 46	294 54
Foster, Joan	M	3	363 50	27 81	11 00					38 81	324 69
Kaufman, Bill	S	1	375 00	28 69	40 00					68 69	306 31
Totals			1,458 00	111 54	107 00					218 54	1,239 46

■ **EXAMPLE** Thomas Cox's total wages are $360.50. FICA tax for this employee is $27.58, while the federal withholding tax is $19.00. When these two amounts are added together, total deductions amount to $46.58. Net cash wages paid can be determined by subtracting total deductions of $46.58 from total wages of $360.50. In this example, Thomas Cox's net cash wages paid are $313.92. ■

The crossfooting procedure common to most payroll journals ensures increased accuracy. Use the following procedure in order to check your work.

Step 1 Add all amounts in the net cash wages paid column to determine the *total* net cash wages paid by the employer.

Step 2 Subtract the amount in the total deductions column from the amount in the total wages column.

Step 3 Compare the two answers. If the two answers don't agree, you have made a mistake and it must be found.

Notice that the answer from Step 1 and the answer from Step 2 do agree, as illustrated in the following calculation. Thus, the accuracy of the payroll journal in the preceding example has been proven.

$$
\begin{aligned}
\text{Total Net Cash Wages Paid} &= \text{Total Wages} - \text{Total Deductions} \\
\$1{,}239.46 &= \$1{,}458.00 - \$218.54 \\
\$1{,}239.46 &= \$1{,}239.46
\end{aligned}
$$

Payroll Records: Applications Problems 15 Through 17

Instructions	*Machine Setting*
1. Determine the net cash wages paid for each employee. 2. Calculate the *totals* for the following columns: a. Total wages b. FICA tax c. Federal withholding tax d. Total deductions e. Net cash wages paid 3. Complete the formula below each payroll journal to prove the accuracy of your work.	1. Set decimal control on add-mode. 2. Set round-off switch in 5/4 position (if applicable).

Applications Problems

15a. ____$193.55____

15b. ____

15c. ____

15d. ____

15e. ____

15f. ____

15g. ____

15h. ____

15i. ____

15j. ____

15k. ____

Applications Problem 15

Employee's Name	Marital Status	Exemptions	Total Wages	FICA Tax	Fed. With.	Total Deduct.	Net Cash Wages
Brock, Bob	M	1	$215.00	$16.45	$ 5.00	$21.45	a. $193.55
Garcia, Flora	M	1	$315.00	$24.10	$20.00	$44.10	b. ____
Rice, Artha	M	1	$225.79	$17.27	$ 7.00	$24.27	c. ____
Totals			d. ____	e. ____	f. ____	g. ____	h. ____

Total Net Cash Wages Paid = Total Wages − Total Deductions

i. ____ = j. ____ − k. ____

Applications Problem 16

Employee's Name	Marital Status	Exemptions	Total Wages	FICA Tax	Fed. With.	Total Deduct.	Net Cash Wages
Appleby, Ben	M	2	$375.00	$28.69	$21.00	$49.69	a. _____
Carson, Alice	M	3	$415.00	$31.75	$19.00	$50.75	b. _____
Green, Cynthia	M	0	$380.00	$29.07	$39.00	$68.07	c. _____
Totals			d. _____	e. _____	f. _____	g. _____	h. _____

Total Net Cash Wages Paid = Total Wages − Total Deductions

i. _____ = j. _____ − k. _____

Applications Problems

16a. _____

16b. _____

16c. _____

16d. _____

16e. _____

16f. _____

16g. _____

16h. _____

16i. _____

16j. _____

16k. _____

**Applications
Problems**

Applications Problem 17

17a. _____

17b. _____

17c. _____

17d. _____

17e. _____

17f. _____

17g. _____

17h. _____

17i. _____

17j. _____

17k. _____

Employee's Name	Marital Status	Exemptions	Total Wages	FICA Tax	Fed. With.	Total Deduct.	Net Cash Wages
Haynes, Ruby	S	1	$454.00	$34.73	$52.00	$86.73	a. ___
Lacher, Nathan	M	2	$275.00	$21.04	$ 6.00	$27.04	b. ___
Richards, Louis	M	4	$570.25	$43.62	$34.00	$77.62	c. ___
Totals			d. ___	e. ___	f. ___	g. ___	h. ___

Total Net Cash Wages Paid = Total Wages − Total Deductions

i. ___ = j. ___ − k. ___

SELF-EVALUATION: PART I

Applications Posttest

INSTRUCTION	MACHINE SETTING
1. Complete the following problems in seven minutes or less with one or no incorrect answers.	1. Set decimal control on add-mode. 2. Set round-off switch in 5/4 position (if applicable).

1a. _____

1b. _____

1c. _____

1d. _____

2. _____

1. Compute a running balance for the check register that follows.

PLEASE BE SURE TO <u>DEDUCT</u> ANY PER CHECK CHARGES OR SERVICE CHARGES THAT MAY APPY TO YOUR ACCOUNT

CHECK NO	DATE	CHECKS ISSUED TO OR DESCRIPTION OF DEPOSIT	(−) AMOUNT OF CHECK		✓ T	(−) CHECK FEE (IF ANY)	(+) AMOUNT OF DEPOSIT		BALANCE 625	40
238	7-4	Oak Forest Printing	65	00					a.	
239	7-5	Barnett Office Supply	83	29					b.	
240	7-5	Martin Consulting	235	00					c.	
	7-5	Deposit					145	90	d.	

2. Calculate the total for the outstanding checks listed below.

Checks Outstanding	
No.	Amount
1204	49 95
1205	129 35
1207	36 75
1210	325 00
Total	

Self-Evaluation:
Part I

3. _____

4a. _____

4b. _____

4c. _____

3. Compute a balance for the payment card that follows.

Payment Card			
B.T. Martin 909 N. Spring Bethany, OK 73008		Credit Rating: 3A Credit Limit: $1,000	
Date	Purchases	Payments	Balance
20XX Apr. 1			$177.50
Apr. 14	$ 65.40		
Apr. 20		$54.25	
Apr. 25		$79.30	
May 4	$125.30		
May 10	$200.98		3.

4. Complete the accounting form that follows.

Date		Customer's Name	Acounts Payable Debit		Purchases Discount Credit		Cash Credit	
July	15	Hillside Offices	356	45			356	45
	17	Barton Supplies	1,560	30	31	20	1,529	10
	19	Smythe Wholesale	980	95	9	81	971	14
	22	Higgs Furniture	875	00			875	00
		Totals	a.		b.		c.	

5. Determine for the following payroll journal: (a) total wages, (b) total deductions, and (c) total net cash wages paid.

5a. _____

5b. _____

5c. _____

EMPLOYEE'S NAME	Exemptions		Total Wages	DEDUCTIONS				Other Deductions				Total Deductions		Net Cash Wages Paid	
For Necessary Employee Data Concerning Each Employee Refer to Inside Front Cover.	Fed	State		F.I.C.A. Tax	Fed. Withholding Tax	State Withholding Tax									
Lloyd, Jim	3		515 00	39 40	34 00							73 40		441 60
Matthews, Bart	2		412 00	31 52	27 00							58 52		353 48
Nelson, Betty	2		380 25	29 09	22 00							51 09		329 16
Totals			a.									b.		c.	

RECOMMENDATION: If you were able to complete Part I of the Self-Evaluation Applications Posttest in seven minutes or less with no more than one incorrect answer, proceed to Part II of the Self-Evaluation. If you did not satisfactorily complete this part of the Self-Evaluation Applications Posttest, take Part I again, trying for the recommended level. If you are still not able to attain the recommended level, talk with your instructor.

**Self-Evaluation:
Part II**

1. _____

2. _____

3a. _____

3b. _____

3c. _____

3d. _____

3e. _____

3f. _____

3g. _____

3h. _____

3i. _____

3j. _____

3k. _____

SELF-EVALUATION: PART II

Critical Thinking Problems

INSTRUCTION	MACHINE SETTING
1. Complete the following problems with one or no incorrect answers.	1. Set decimal control on 2 or add-mode. 2. Set round-off switch in 5/4 position (if applicable).

1. On July 1, 20XX, Bob Jackson had a $3,495.16 balance in his checking account. During the month of July, he wrote checks for $215.00, $175.35, $15.30, $29.80, $39.45, $10.47, and $117.21. He also made a deposit of $1,459.75. What was his checking account balance at the end of the month?

2. John Roberts received his monthly bank statement and noticed that checks in the following amounts were outstanding:

    $24.95 $112.34 $9.87 $345.90 $56.78 $12.43 $295.80

    What is the total for checks outstanding for this month?

3. As the accounting clerk for the Miles Chemical Labs, one of your responsibilities is to reconcile the firm's monthly bank statement. Your supervisor tells you the firm's checkbook balance is $40,456.78. This month's bank statement shows a balance of $36,099.36, deposits in transit of $13,250.20, checks outstanding of $8,925.48, and an activity charge of $32.70. Using the form below, reconcile this company's bank statement.

Bank Balance	a._____	Checkbook Balance	f. _____
Add Deposits Not Shown	b._____	Subtract (if any) Activity Charges	g. _____
Subtotal	c._____	Subtotal	h. _____
Subtract Outstanding Checks	d._____	Subtract (if any) Other Bank Charges	i. _____
Balance	e._____	Balance	j. _____
Do the two balances agree? k._____ yes _____ no			

4. Sally Thomas purchased the following items from Marston's Department Store: 1 shirt for $19.95; 1 pair of socks for $3.50; 1 pair of pants for $29.99; and 1 belt for $9.95. What is the total amount of her purchases?

5. Jane Austin has a charge account with a local department store. During the month of August, she made purchases of $420.78. She also made a payment of $225.00. At the beginning of the month, her balance was $315.30. The department store assessed finance charges of $4.75 at the end of the month of August. What is her balance at the end of the month?

6. On March 31, Eastern Manufacturing Company had the following totals in its Purchases Journal:

Purchases (debit):	$13,495.25
Freight-in (debit):	1,506.29
Accounts payable (credit):	15,001.54

    a. What is the total for the debit accounts?
    b. What is the total for the credit account?
    c. Does the debit total equal the credit total (yes or no)?

7. Sally Martin works 40 hours a week and is paid $7 an hour. Her employer withheld the following amounts:

    Federal withholding: $24
    FICA tax: $21.42

What was her net cash wages paid amount?

Self-Evaluation Answers:

4. _____

5. _____

6a. _____

6b. _____

6c. _____

7. _____

RECOMMENDATION: If you were able to complete Part II of the Self-Evaluation with no more than one incorrect answer, you have satisfactorily completed this chapter. You are now ready to progress to Chapter 5. If you did not satisfactorily complete Part II of the Self-Evaluation, you may want to review the material presented in the Business Applications sections of this chapter.

Multiplication on the Electronic Calculator

OBJECTIVES

When you have successfully completed this chapter for the electronic calculator, you will be able to

1. Identify the following operating controls and their uses:
   —Times (×) key
   —Equals (=) key
   —Percent (%) key
   —Accumulate keys
   —Memory keys

2. Perform simple multiplication calculations on the machine using the touch method.

3. Perform multiplication calculations on the machine using a constant multiplicand.

4. Accumulate answers from several multiplication problems.

5. Perform calculations utilizing the memory capabilities of the calculator.

6. Demonstrate speed and accuracy using the touch method while adding, subtracting, and multiplying.

7. Attain confidence in your ability to multiply on the electronic calculator.

8. Advance to business application problems.

INTRODUCTION

The machine should be placed on the desk at the right and at a slight angle in the position that is most comfortable for you. Sit erect, but relaxed. Use the touch method. Begin by locating the following parts on your machine.

1. *Times key,* in various locations according to machine brand; normally has the times (×) symbol on the key. The number entered will be maintained as a constant until another number is entered.

2. *Equals key,* normally near times key; usually has the equals (=) symbol on the key; completes the multiplication cycle.

3. *Percent key,* in various locations according to machine brand; normally has the percent (%) symbol on the key. This key will complete a multiplication problem involving a percentage, but eliminates the need for a decimal adjustment when entering the percent factor.

4. *Memory keys,* normally located near the equals key, usually to the right; normally a series of three keys: M+ or M *in* is the key used to put numbers into memory; MR or M *out* is the key used to recall a number from memory for calculation purposes; MC or M *clear* is the key used to clear all information from memory. For machines with M+, there may also be a corresponding M− key for negative input.

MULTIPLICATION KEY

Multiplication on the electronic calculator is a quick and easy procedure. Locate the times (×) key and the equals (=) key on your machine. As soon as you are familiar with the operating control locations, practice the calculation in the following example using the touch method.

■ **EXAMPLE**

16 × 8 =   Enter 16   Depress ×
                   Enter 8   Depress =
                   Read the answer: 128

Since this calculation contains only whole numbers, there is no need to set a decimal.   ■

When decimals appear in a problem, set them along with the numbers. Your calculator will print the final answer rounded to the correct number in the hundredths place (two decimal places). Practice the problem in the following example.

■ **EXAMPLE**

35.6 × 2.68 =   Set decimal control on 2
                    Set round-off switch in 5/4 position (if applicable)
                    Enter 35.6   Depress ×
                    Enter 2.68   Depress =
                    Read the answer: 95.41   ■

Multiplication on the computer calculator is performed in the following manner.

■ **EXAMPLE**

35.6 × 2.68 =   Enter 35.6   Depress *
                    Enter 2.68   Depress *Enter* or =
                    Read the answer: 95.408 rounded to 95.41   ■

Practice Problems

1. _____8,970_____

2. _____

3. _____

4. _____

5. _____

6. _____

7. _____

8. _____

9. _____

10. _____

11. _____

12. _____

13. _____75.88_____

14. _____

15. _____

16. _____

17. _____

18. _____

19. _____

20. _____

21. _____

22. _____

23. _____

24. _____

25. _____

Practice Problems

Work the following problems that have whole numbers.

1.   195
    $\times$ 46
    8,970

2.   231
    $\times$ 42

3.   699
    $\times$ 66

4.   310
    $\times$ 57

5.   992
    $\times$ 81

6.   5,707
    $\times$ 180

7.   7,192
    $\times$ 467

8.   683
    $\times$522

9.   4,021
    $\times$1,743

10.   6,190
    $\times$6,097

11.   4,564
    $\times$3,343

12.   3,754
    $\times$5,138

Work the following problems that have decimals.

13.   5.42
    $\times$ 14
    75.88

14.   4.07
    $\times$ 8.3

15.   5.53
    $\times$ 18

16.   47.9
    $\times$0.41

17.   127.7
    $\times$ 6.99

18.   24.04
    $\times$ 5.08

19.   719.05
    $\times$ 63.52

20.   86.85
    $\times$ 7.12

21.   80.805
    $\times$ 0.065

22.   67.45
    $\times$9.621

23.   5223
    $\times$0.0057

24.   67.89
    $\times$ 4.44

25.   88.668
    $\times$ 13.71

26.   344.04
    $\times$ 2.45

27.   3.98
    $\times$0.196

28.   82.197
    $\times$ 9.06

29.   1.875
    $\times$ 0.99

30.   23.777
    $\times$ 1.991

31.   33.50
    $\times$ 1.24

32.   0.1133
    $\times$ 14.68

Work the following problems that have fractions and decimals.

33.   122 1/5
    $\times$ 3/8
    45.83

34.   41 3/4
    $\times$ 6 5/6

35.   31 1/2
    $\times$ 71

36.   47 7/10
    $\times$ 7.02

37.   820
    $\times$ 12 2/3

38.   54 1/6
    $\times$ 3.92

39.   88 1/8
    $\times$ 0.654

40.   61 4/5
    $\times$14 1/3

PERCENTAGE AND PERCENT KEY

One of the most common business problems to be solved is the calculation of the portion factor in the percentage equation:

20% of 50 is 10

The arithmetic process of solving this problem is to multiply the base (50) by the rate (20%) to obtain the portion (10).

$$\begin{array}{r} 50 \\ \times\ .20 \\ \hline 10.00 \end{array}$$

Most electronic calculators have a special percent key that will eliminate the need for converting the rate (20%) into a decimal (.20). The percent key usually has the percent (%) symbol printed on the key and is used to solve percentage problems, as illustrated in the following example.

■ **EXAMPLE**

20% of 50 =   Enter 50   Depress ×
Enter 20   Depress %
Read the answer: 10

Notice that it was necessary to set the base (50) first and the rate (20%) second. ■

Note: If your calculator does not have a percent key, it will be necessary for you to convert the percent to its decimal equivalent and multiply as you would any other problem.

+---------------------+
| **Practice** | Work the following problems using the percent key.
| **Problems** |
+---------------------+

41. 15% of 68 = 10.20   **42.** 27% of 85 =   **43.** 19% of 764 =

44. 23.8% of 275 =   **45.** 99.44% of 137 =   **46.** 12 1/2% of 480 =

47. 92 1/5% of 740 =   **48.** 7/8% of 362 =

49. 1,246.8 × 44.5% =   **50.** 3,904.67 × 16 3/4% =

	Practice Problems
26.	_____
27.	_____
28.	_____
29.	_____
30.	_____
31.	_____
32.	_____
33.	45.83
34.	_____
35.	_____
36.	_____
37.	_____
38.	_____
39.	_____
40.	_____
41.	10.20
42.	_____
43.	_____
44.	_____
45.	_____
46.	_____
47.	_____
48.	_____
49.	_____
50.	_____

Practice Problems

51. _____ 352 _____

52. _____

53. _____

54. _____

55. _____

56. _____

57. _____

58. _____

59. _____

CONSTANT MULTIPLICATION

Constant multiplication involves a series of problems in which either the multiplier or the multiplicand is used as a constant—that is, it is repeated in each problem. In the following three problems, the 1.98 is the constant.

$$465 \times 1.98 =$$

$$192 \times 1.98 =$$

$$703 \times 1.98 =$$

Most electronic calculators automatically enter the constant when the number is set on the machine and the times ($\times$) key is depressed. On some machine models where this does not occur, it will be necessary to set the constant and then depress a *constant key* or bar. This action will retain a constant in the machine. If the calculator has neither of these functions, a final way of retaining a constant is to place it in memory and recall the number when it is needed.

Practice the problems in the following example using the two methods illustrated.

■ **EXAMPLE**

$$465 \times 1.98 =$$

$$192 \times 1.98 =$$

$$703 \times 1.98 =$$

Automatic Constant		*Constant Key*	
Set decimal control on 2		Set constant key	
Set round-off switch in 5/4 position (if applicable)		Enter 1.98 (constant)	Depress $\times$
		Enter 465	Depress $=$
Enter 1.98 (constant)	Depress $\times$	Read the answer: 920.70	
Enter 465	Depress $=$	Enter 192	Depress $=$
Read the answer: 920.70		Read the answer: 380.16	
Enter 192	Depress $=$	Enter 703	Depress $=$
Read the answer: 380.16		Read the answer: 1,391.94	
Enter 703	Depress $=$		
Read the answer: 1,391.94			■

Practice Problems

Work the following constant multiplication problems in groups of two or three problems.

Reminder: Set the constant with the times ($\times$) key.

51. $44 \times 8 = 352$ **52.** $44 \times 37 =$ **53.** $44 \times 1.25 =$

54. $516.04 \times 1.05 =$ **55.** $86.43 \times 1.05 =$ **56.** $97.23 \times 1.05 =$

57. $46.3 \times 5.367 =$ **58.** $46.3 \times 1.16 =$ **59.** $46.3 \times 4.801 =$

60. $648 \times 3.47 =$ **61.** $648 \times 9.62 =$ **62.** $648 \times 0.495 =$

63. $74.21 \times 44.56 =$ **64.** $482.84 \times 44.56 =$ **65.** $64.716 \times 44.56 =$

66. $9.90 \times 19 =$ **67.** $9.90 \times 27 =$ **68.** $9.90 \times 142 =$

69. $40.51 \times 72 =$ **70.** $52.61 \times 72 =$

60. _____

61. _____

62. _____

63. _____

64. _____

65. _____

| Self-Check | Work the four problems given below in two minutes or less with no incorrect answers. |

66. _____

67. _____

1.		**2.**		**3.**		**4.**	
46.25		19.42		89.65		52.97	
79.91		28.89		96.90		16.29	
74.79		25.34		26.45		15.47	
38.67		80.03		12.55		97.86	
1.02		11.31		20.40		2.87	
50.23		7.54		8.31		59.73	
19.94		50.53		51.59		32.52	
4.73		41.76		67.23		8.51	
10.51		48.74		32.17		13.23	
84.87		6.61		5.93		93.86	
23.35		90.49		91.86		54.42	
434.27	(55)	410.66	(110)	503.04	(165)	447.73	(220)

68. _____

69. _____

70. _____

Recommendation: If you are able to complete the problems in the Self-Check in two minutes or less with no incorrect answers, proceed to the next material. If you are not able to meet the goal for the Self-Check, take it again and try to improve your previous effort. If you are still unable to meet the speed and accuracy goal for the Self-Check, go back to Chapter 3 and practice the material in Speed Development 3. After practicing the material, take the Self-Check again, trying for speed and accuracy. After the third try, proceed to the next material.

1. _____

2. _____

3. _____

4. _____

ACCUMULATIVE MULTIPLICATION

Accumulative multiplication is used when a grand total of several products is needed. Most electronic calculators are equipped to store individual answers with storage keys that are labeled M+ for storing positive answers and M− for storing negative answers. Look at the following problem.

$$2 \times 3 = 6 \quad \text{product}$$
$$3 \times 3 = 9 \quad \text{product}$$
$$4 \times 2 = \underline{8} \quad \text{product}$$
$$ 23 \quad \text{grand total}$$

The following example represents the most common approach to accumulating on the electronic calculator.

■ EXAMPLE

$2 \times 3 =$ Set decimal control on 2
$3 \times 3 =$ Set round-off switch in 5/4 position (if applicable)
$4 \times 2 =$ _____   Enter 2   Depress $\times$
                         Enter 3   Depress $=$
                                    Depress M+
                         Enter 3   Depress $\times$
                         Enter 3   Depress $=$
                                    Depress M+
                         Enter 4   Depress $\times$
                         Enter 2   Depress $=$
                                    Depress M+
                         Depress total or MR
                         Read the answer: 23   ■

Some multiplication problems have answers to be subtracted. For example,

$$
\begin{array}{rll}
4 \times 6 = & 24 & \text{product} \\
3 \times 7 = & 21 & \text{product} \\
-5 \times 8 = & \underline{-40} & \text{product} \\
 & 5 & \text{grand total}
\end{array}
$$

which may also be written as

$$(4 \times 6) + (3 \times 7) - (5 \times 8) = 24 + 21 - 40 = 5$$

The following example illustrates how to work this type of problem.

■ EXAMPLE

$4 \times 6 =$ Enter 4   Depress $\times$
$3 \times 7 =$ Enter 6   Depress $=$
$-5 \times 8 =$ _____   Depress M+
                         Enter 3   Depress $\times$
                         Enter 7   Depress $=$
                                    Depress M+
                         Enter 5   Depress $\times$
                         Enter 8   Depress $=$
                                    Depress M−
                         Depress MR
                         Read the answer: 5   ■

Reminder: If the number entered into the calculator has a decimal, the decimal must be entered along with the digits of the number.

Practice Problems	Work the following accumulative multiplication problems.

71. $4 \times 6 =$
$8 \times 3 =$
$5 \times 3 =$ _____
         63

72. $78 \times 60 =$
$54 \times 81 =$
$-28 \times 56 =$ _____

73. $16 \times 451 =$
$253 \times 33 =$
$600 \times 48 =$ _____

74. $99 \times 17 =$
$321 \times 35 =$
$- 4 \times 8 =$ _____

75. $66 \times 41.3 =$
$2.46 \times 1.5 =$
$-1.23 \times 4.44 =$ _____

76. $32.5 \times 1.98 =$
$- 8.2 \times 12.50 =$
$- 5.6 \times 14.3 =$ _____

77. $19 \times 50 =$
$51.15 \times 3.7 =$
$- 0.087 \times 2.55 =$ _____

78. $0.66 \times 18.10 =$
$-481 \times 0.0098 =$
$16.101 \times 7.068 =$ _____

79. $12.12 \times 3.5176 =$
$37.09 \times 9.612 =$
$15 \times 1.22 =$ _____

80. $0.7606 \times 64 =$
$-5 \times 76.36 =$
$7.503 \times 3.505 =$ _____

81. $(3 \times 4) + (7 \times 8) - (2 \times 9) = 50$

82. $(21 \times 14) - (9 \times 81) + (17 \times 16) =$

83. $(12.2 \times 46.7) - (7.1 \times 3.9) - (10.8 \times 1.7) =$

84. $(48.29 \times 91.5) - (86.27 \times 3.754) + (55.67 \times 32) =$

85. $(87.681 \times 44.02) + (3.547 \times 3.22) - (61.007 \times 37.299) - (19.277 \times 0.0088) =$

71. _____63_____

72. _____

73. _____

74. _____

75. _____

76. _____

77. _____

78. _____

79. _____

80. _____

81. _____50_____

82. _____

83. _____

84. _____

85. _____

1. _____

2. _____

3. _____

4. _____

5. _____

6. _____

7. _____

8. _____

9. _____

10. _____

11. _____

12. _____

13. _____

14. _____

15. _____

SELF-EVALUATION

Skills Posttest

Complete the following problems in five minutes or less with one or no incorrect answers. (Do not include recording the answers in the five minutes.)

1. 54.7932
14.8
7.994
6.662
0.0043
249.06

2. 78.043
−53.9

3. 48.25
−77.3333

4. 238
× 76

5. 4.68
× 92

6. 5.91
× 63

7. 5.91
× 44

8. 5.91
×46.07

9. $91.08 \times 34.62\% =$

10. $3 \times 17 =$
$6 \times 48 =$
$33 \times 74 =$ _____

11. $1.73 \times 9.04 \ =$
$31.55 \times 0.54 \ =$
$79 \quad \times 0.066 =$ _____

12. 22.5 yds. @ \$1.79 =
3 yds. @ \$1.79 =
32 yds. @ \$1.79 =
3.5 yds. @ \$1.79 = _____

13. $225 \quad \times 10.76 =$
$- \ 62.94 \times 11.04 =$
$7.4 \ \times 14.36 =$ _____

14. $(76.014 \times 28.1) + (33.08 \times 12.99) - (52.3 \times 9.77) =$

15. $(86.743 \times 10.09) - (4.6207 \times 39.91) - (27.72 \times 0.0037) =$

RECOMMENDATION: If you were able to complete the Self-Evaluation Skills Posttest in five minutes or less with no more than one incorrect answer, you have satisfactorily completed this section of Chapter 5. You are now ready to progress to the business applications problems that follow. If you did not satisfactorily complete this section, take the Self-Evaluation Skills Posttest again, trying for the recommended level. If you are still not able to attain the recommended level, talk with your instructor.

BUSINESS APPLICATIONS:
WORKING MARKDOWN PROBLEMS

Business Situation

Joe Evans, manager of Albert's Western Wear, has decided to run a special 20 percent off sale on a group of shirts and jeans. Of course, special promotional material and advertising have been planned. In order to serve more customers, Joe's brother agrees to help out in the store, but he asks Joe to explain how to determine the 20 percent markdown on the sale items.

Markdown problems are a practical application of the Portion = Base × Rate ($P = B \times R$) formula presented in Chapter 1. When working this type of problem, you may want to use the following two steps.

Step 1   Multiply the original price (base) by the percent of markdown (rate). Notice that the percent of markdown is converted to a decimal in the example below. If your calculator has a percent (%) key, you may use that key instead. The answer is called the *markdown amount* (portion).

Step 2   Subtract the markdown amount from the original price.

■   **EXAMPLE**   A power saw originally sold for $49.50. In order to increase sales, the merchant reduced the price by 10%. What is the reduced sale price?

Step 1   Determine the markdown amount.

$$
\begin{array}{rl}
\$49.50 & \text{original price (base)} \\
\times \quad .10 & \text{percent of markdown (rate)} \\
\hline
\$\ 4.95 & \text{markdown amount (portion)}
\end{array}
$$

Step 2   Calculate the reduced sale price.

$$
\begin{array}{rl}
\$49.50 & \text{original price} \\
- \quad 4.95 & \text{markdown amount} \\
\hline
\$44.55 & \text{reduced sale price}
\end{array}
$$ ■

Alternate Method   The reduced sale price can be found by multiplying the original sale price by the *complement* of the percent of markdown. To find the complement, *mentally* subtract the percent of markdown from 100 percent. Note in the following example that the complement (90%) has been converted to a decimal (.90).

■   **EXAMPLE**   Find the reduced sale price for the power saw in the above example by the complement method.

Step 1   Mentally determine the complement.

$$
\begin{array}{rl}
100\% & \\
- \quad 10\% & \text{percent of markdown} \\
\hline
90\% & \text{complement}
\end{array}
$$

Applications Problems

1. ____85%____

2. _____

3. _____

4. _____

5. _____

Step 2 Multiply the original price by the complement.

$49.50   original price
×   .90   complement of 10%
$44.55   reduced sale price   ■

Recommendation: Review the material at the beginning of this chapter for problems with multiplication. Review the material in Chapter 4 for problems with subtraction.

Markdowns: Applications Problems 1 Through 35

Instructions	*Machine Setting*
1. Determine the complement for Group 1 problems. 2. Using the complement method, determine the reduced sale price for Group 2 problems. 3. Calculate the markdown amount for Group 3 problems. 4. Find both the markdown amount and the reduced sale price for Group 4 problems.	1. Set decimal control on 2. 2. Enter all decimals in the problem with the decimal key. 3. Set round-off switch in 5/4 position (if applicable). 4. Either convert the percent of markdown to a decimal or use your calculator's percent key. 5. If your calculator has a memory, your machine will automatically subtract the markdown amount from the original price for Group 4 problems.

Group 1: Applications Problems 1 Through 5

Reminder: Find the complement for the following percents of markdowns.

Percent of Markdown	Complement
15%	1. 85% _____
30%	2. _____
40%	3. _____
32%	4. _____
28%	5. _____

Applications Problems

6.   **$4.95**

Group 2: Applications Problems 6 Through 10

Reminder: Use the *complement* method to find the reduced sale price.

7. _____

8. _____

Albert's Western Wear			
Department: Men's Accessories			
Merchandise: Cologne		Date: 9-4-20XX	
Description	Original Price	Percent of Markdown	Reduced Sale Price
2 oz. Cologne	$ 5.50	10%	6. $4.95
4 oz. Cologne	$ 7.00	15%	7. _____
6 oz. Cologne	$ 8.50	15%	8. _____
8 oz. Cologne	$10.00	20%	9. _____
10 oz. Cologne	$12.00	25%	10. _____

9. _____

10. _____

11.   **$0.45**

12. _____

Group 3: Applications Problems 11 Through 15

Reminder: Solve for the markdown amount.

13. _____

14. _____

Albert's Western Wear			
Department: Men's Accessories			
Merchandise: After Shave		Date: 9-4-20XX	
Description	Original Price	Percent of Markdown	Markdown Amount
2 oz. After Shave	$ 4.50	10%	11. $0.45
4 oz. After Shave	$ 6.00	15%	12. _____
6 oz. After Shave	$ 7.50	15%	13. _____
8 oz. After Shave	$ 9.00	20%	14. _____
10 oz. After Shave	$11.00	25%	15. _____

15. _____

Applications Problems

16. _____$2.10_____

17. _____$18.89_____

18. _____

19. _____

20. _____

21. _____

22. _____

23. _____

24. _____

25. _____

26. _____

27. _____

28. _____

29. _____

30. _____

31. _____

32. _____

33. _____

34. _____

35. _____

Group 4: Applications Problems 16 Through 35

Reminder: You may want to review the material on using your calculator's memory presented earlier in this chapter before completing Applications Problems 16 through 35.

Albert's Western Wear				
Department: Men's Clothing Merchandise: Shirts & Jeans			Date: 9-4-20XX	
Description	Original Price	Percent of Markdown	Markdown Amount	Reduced Sale Price
Patch Vests	$20.99	10%	16. $2.10	17. $18.89
Knit Shirts	$15.50	30%	18. _____	19. _____
Leather Belts	$19.95	20%	20. _____	21. _____
Cotton Shirts	$29.00	25%	22. _____	23. _____
Silk Shirts	$44.95	30%	24. _____	25. _____
Fancy Jeans	$31.95	10%	26. _____	27. _____
Dress Jeans	$29.95	15%	28. _____	29. _____
Denim Jeans	$19.95	20%	30. _____	31. _____
Knit Jeans	$15.95	20%	32. _____	33. _____
Econo-Jeans	$12.95	30%	34. _____	35. _____

BUSINESS APPLICATIONS: CALCULATING CASH DISCOUNTS

Business Situation

Jody Martin, the accountant for the Harvard Publishing Company, has just received an invoice for $2,875 from Ros Products. Terms for the invoice are 2/10, N/30. She checks with her boss and is told that it is company policy to take advantage of cash discounts offered by suppliers.

To encourage prompt payment, many businesses give their customers a *cash discount.* Cash discount terms may be written in one of two ways. For example,

2/10, N/30   or   2/10, 1/20, N/30

In the *first* example, 2/10 means the buyer can take a 2 percent discount if the bill is paid within the first 10 days of the invoice date *or* can choose to pay the full amount if the invoice is paid between day 11 and day 30.

In the *second* example, the buyer can take a 2 percent discount if the bill is paid within 10 days of the invoice date, *or* can take a 1 percent discount if the bill is paid between day 11 and day 20, *or* can choose to pay the full amount if the bill is paid between day 21 and day 30. Note that in the second example, only *one* discount can be taken for prompt payment.

Cash discounts are a practical application of the portion formula ($P = B \times R$) presented in Chapter 1. The invoice amount (base) is multiplied by the percent of cash discount (rate). Notice that the percent of cash discount is converted to a decimal in the example below. If your calculator has a percent (%) key, you may use that key instead. The answer is called the discount amount (portion).

■ **EXAMPLE** You receive an invoice for $2,875. Terms are 2/10, N/30. You decide to pay the invoice within 10 days and take advantage of the 2 percent discount.

Step 1 Determine
the discount
amount.

	$2,875.00	invoice amount (base)
×	.02	percent of cash discount (rate)
	$57.50	discount amount (portion)

Step 2 Calculate
the amount
of payment.

	$2,875.00	invoice amount
−	57.50	discount amount
	$2,817.50	amount of payment	■

Alternate Method You can determine the amount of payment by multiplying the invoice amount by the complement of the percent of cash discount. To find the complement, mentally subtract the percent of cash discount from 100 percent.

■ **EXAMPLE** Find the amount of payment for the invoice in the above example by the complement method.

Step 1 Mentally
determine the
complement.

	100%	
−	2%	percent of cash discount
	98%	complement

Step 2 Calculate
the amount
of payment.

	$2,875.00	invoice amount
×	.98	complement of 2%
	$2,817.50	amount of payment	■

Applications Problems

36. ___**$70.00**___

37. _____

38. _____

39. _____

40. _____

> **Recommendation:** For problems with the $P = B \times R$ formula, review the material on portion, rate, and base in Chapter 1. For problems with multiplication, review the material in the first part of this chapter.

Cash Discounts: Applications Problems 36 Through 55

Instructions	*Machine Setting*
1. *Assume that all invoices are paid within 5 days after they are received.* 2. Determine the discount amount for Group 1 problems. 3. Determine the complement for Group 2 problems. 4. Using the complement method, determine the amount of payment for Group 3 problems. 5. Find both the discount amount and the amount of payment for Group 4 problems.	1. Set decimal control on 2. 2. Enter all decimals in the problem with the decimal key. 3. Set round-off switch in 5/4 position (if applicable). 4. Either convert the percent of cash discount to a decimal or use your calculator's percent key. 5. If your calculator has a memory, your machine will automatically subtract the discount amount from the invoice amount for Group 4 problems.

Group 1: Applications Problems 36 Through 40

Reminder: Find only the discount amount for Group 1 problems.

	Invoice Amount	Terms	Discount Amount
Problem 36	$3,500.00	2/10, N/30	$70.00
Problem 37	$7,850.00	3/10, N/30	_____
Problem 38	$ 549.50	1/15, N/45	_____
Problem 39	$1,799.34	2/10, N/30	_____
Problem 40	$9,850.40	3/10, N/60	_____

Group 2: Applications Problems 41 Through 45

Reminder: Find the complement for Group 2 problems.

	Terms	Complement
Problem 41	3/10, N/30	97%
Problem 42	2/10, N/30	
Problem 43	4/10, N/60	
Problem 44	1/10, N/60	
Problem 45	2/20, N/45	

Group 3: Applications Problems 46 Through 50

Reminder: Use the *complement* method to find the amount of payment.

	Invoice Amount	Terms	Amount of Payment
Problem 46	$1,400.00	2/10, N/30	$1,372.00
Problem 47	$2,700.00	3/10, N/30	
Problem 48	$4,480.00	1/10, N/30	
Problem 49	$6,685.39	1/15, N/60	
Problem 50	$8,465.42	3/20, 1/30, N/60	

Group 4: Applications Problems 51 Through 55

Reminder: You may want to review the material on using your calculator's memory presented earlier in this chapter before completing Applications Problems 51 through 55.

	Invoice Amount	Terms	Discount Amount	Amount of Payment
Problem 51	$1,540.25	3/10, N/30	a. $46.21	b. $1,494.04
Problem 52	$1,798.30	2/10, N/30	a.	b.
Problem 53	$2,610.40	1/15, N/30	a.	b.
Problem 54	$4,226.60	3/20, 2/45, N/60	a.	b.
Problem 55	$1,927.60	5/10, 3/30, N/60	a.	b.

41. _____97%_____

42. _____

43. _____

44. _____

45. _____

46. ____$1,372.00____

47. _____

48. _____

49. _____

50. _____

51a. _____$46.21_____

51b. ____$1,494.04____

52a. _____

52b. _____

53a. _____

53b. _____

54a. _____

54b. _____

55a. _____

55b. _____

BUSINESS APPLICATIONS: DETERMINING COMPOUND INTEREST AMOUNTS

Business Situation

Sandra and Don Coleman want to purchase a new home in six years, and they are trying to save enough money for the down payment. To help obtain their goal of home ownership, they decide to purchase a certificate of deposit with $10,000 they have already saved. While discussing their plans with the bank officer, they learn that their investment will earn 4 percent, compounded annually. They both realize that if the interest is allowed to compound, the value of their investment will increase. Now the big question is, How much will their investment be worth in six years?

Compound interest means that the dollar amount of interest for one time period is added to the original principal amount before the interest for the next time period is calculated.

To simplify interest calculations, most businesses use compound interest tables like the one illustrated below. Two steps are necessary to determine the compound value using an interest table when compounding occurs on an annual basis.

■   **EXAMPLE** Determine the compound value of $10,000 invested for 6 years at 4% compounded annually.

Step 1 Locate "6 years" in the interest period column, and then go across to the 4% column. The number 1.2653 is the interest factor for $1 compounded annually at 4% for six years.

Interest Period	1%	2%	3%	4%	5%	6%	7%	8%	Interest Period
1	1.0100	1.0200	1.0300	1.0400	1.0500	1.0600	1.0700	1.0800	1
2	1.0201	1.0404	1.0609	1.0816	1.1025	1.1236	1.1449	1.1664	2
3	1.0303	1.0612	1.0927	1.1249	1.1576	1.1910	1.2250	1.2597	3
4	1.0406	1.0824	1.1255	1.1699	1.2155	1.2625	1.3108	1.3605	4
5	1.0510	1.1041	1.1593	1.2167	1.2763	1.3382	1.4026	1.4693	5
6	1.0615	1.1262	1.1941	**1.2653**	1.3401	1.4185	1.5007	1.5869	6
7	1.0721	1.1487	1.2299	1.3159	1.4071	1.5036	1.6058	1.7138	7
8	1.0829	1.1717	1.2668	1.3686	1.4775	1.5938	1.7182	1.8509	8
9	1.0937	1.1951	1.3048	1.4233	1.5513	1.6895	1.8385	1.9990	9
10	1.1046	1.2190	1.3439	1.4802	1.6289	1.7908	1.9672	2.1589	10
11	1.1157	1.2434	1.3842	1.5395	1.7103	1.8983	2.1049	2.3316	11
12	1.1268	1.2682	1.4258	1.6010	1.7959	2.0122	2.2522	2.5182	12
13	1.1381	1.2936	1.4685	1.6651	1.8856	2.1329	2.4098	2.7196	13
14	1.1495	1.3195	1.5126	1.7317	1.9799	2.2609	2.5785	2.9372	14
15	1.1610	1.3459	1.5580	1.8009	2.0789	2.3966	2.7590	3.1722	15

Step 2   Multiply the $10,000 principal amount by the interest factor 1.2653.

$10,000 × 1.2653 = $12,653 (compound value after 6 years)   ■

    If the Colemans—the couple in the above Business Situation—allowed the interest on their $10,000 certificate of deposit to accumulate, they would have $12,653 at the end of six years. This money could be used to make the down payment on their new home or for any other purpose that they felt was worthwhile.

    Compounding interest on a *semiannual* (twice a year) or *quarterly* (four times a year) basis requires two additional steps.

Step 1   *Multiply* the number of years by the number of times that compounding occurs each year.

Step 2   *Divide* the interest rate by the number of times compounding occurs each year to determine the adjusted interest rate.

■   **EXAMPLE**   Determine the compound value for $6,000 compounded *semiannually* at 8 percent for four years.

Step 1   Make the adjustment required when compounding occurs on a *semiannual* basis.

4 years × 2 semiannual payments = 8 periods
8% ÷ 2 semiannual payments = 4% interest rate

Step 2   Find the interest factor for eight periods and 4 percent interest rate. The interest factor is 1.3686.

Step 3   Multiply the interest factor 1.3686 by the $6,000 principal.

$6,000 × 1.3686 = $8,211.60 (compound value after 4 years)   ■

Compound Interest:
Applications Problems 56 Through 75

Instructions	*Machine Setting*
1. Determine the interest factor for Group 1 problems. 2. Determine the compound value for Group 2 problems.	1. Set decimal control on 2. 2. Enter all decimals in the problem with the decimal key. 3. Set round-off switch in 5/4 position (if applicable).

Applications Problems

56. ___1.1249___

57. _____

58. _____

59. _____

60. _____

61. _____

62. _____

63. ___$2,720.36___

64. _____

65. _____

66. _____

67. _____

68. _____

69. _____

70. _____

71. _____

72. _____

73. _____

74. _____

75. _____

Group 1: Applications Problems 56 Through 62

Reminder: Find the interest factor for Group 1 problems.

Rate	Time	Compounded	Interest Factor
4%	3 yrs.	Annually	56. ___1.1249___
3%	2 yrs.	Annually	57. _____
6%	4 yrs.	Semiannually	58. _____
6%	2 yrs.	Semiannually	59. _____
4%	3 yrs.	Quarterly	60. _____
4%	6 yrs.	Semiannually	61. _____
4%	2 yrs.	Quarterly	62. _____

Group 2: Applications Problems 63 Through 75

Reminder: Determine the compound value for Group 2 problems.

Principal	Rate	Time	Compounded	Compound Value
$ 2,350	5%	3 yrs.	Annually	63. ___$2,720.36___
$ 6,200	6%	5 yrs.	Annually	64. _____
$ 1,350	4%	2 yrs.	Semiannually	65. _____
$ 1,800	6%	4 yrs.	Semiannually	66. _____
$ 3,375	6%	5 yrs.	Semiannually	67. _____
$ 7,500	4%	2 yrs.	Quarterly	68. _____
$ 2,500	8%	1 yr.	Quarterly	69. _____
$ 6,327	3%	6 yrs.	Annually	70. _____
$ 2,345	8%	3 yrs.	Quarterly	71. _____
$39,750	4%	3 yrs.	Quarterly	72. _____
$21,300	5%	10 yrs.	Annually	73. _____
$18,900	8%	3 yrs.	Quarterly	74. _____
$9,150	4%	5 yrs.	Semiannually	75. _____

BUSINESS APPLICATIONS: CALCULATING COMMISSIONS

Business Situation

After receiving her real estate license, Susan Matthews has just sold her first home. Naturally, she wonders how much commission she will receive.

Commission is one way to pay someone for performing a service, such as selling merchandise, real estate, or life insurance. The type of commission most people are familiar with is that paid to salespeople, agents, or brokers.

Commission is a practical application of the portion formula ($P = B \times R$) that was presented in Chapter 1. The dollar amount of commission (portion) is determined by multiplying the sales amount (base) by the percent of commission (rate). Of course, commission is paid on actual sales only. Returned goods, allowances, freight charges, and sales tax are generally not included for determining the amount of commission.

■ **EXAMPLE**   Ted Hess sold $28,000 worth of manufacturing equipment during the month of October. Ted receives a 10 percent commission on all sales. How much commission did he receive?

$28,000   sales amount (base)
$\times$ .10   percent of commission (rate)
$ 2,800   dollar amount of commission (portion)

Note that the percent of commission (10%) has been changed to .10. This step may be omitted if your calculator has a percent (%) key.   ■

Recommendation: For problems with the formula $P = B \times R$, review the material on portion, rate, and base in Chapter 1. For problems with multiplication, review the material in the first part of this chapter.

Commissions: Applications Problems 76 Through 95

Instructions	*Machine Setting*
1. Determine the dollar amount of commission for each employee in the following problems. 2. Find the total dollar amount of commission for each group of employees.	1. Set decimal control on 2. 2. Enter all decimals in the problem with the decimal key. 3. Set round-off switch in 5/4 position (if applicable). 4. Either convert the percent of commission to a decimal or use your calculator's percent key. 5. The total for each group of employees can be obtained automatically by using the memory keys described earlier in this chapter.

**Applications
Problems**

76. _____ **$340.00** _____

77. _____

78. _____

79. _____

80. _____

81. _____

82. _____

83. _____

84. _____

85. _____

Group 1: Applications Problems 76 Through 80

Reminder: Determine the dollar amount of commission and total for all sales personnel.

Rice's Quick Service Foods Department: Sandwiches For Week Ending: 9-22-20XX			
Salesperson	Sales Amount	Percent of Commission	Dollar Amount of Commission
Locke, Bill	$4,250	8%	76. <u>$340.00</u>
Handy, Ron	$3,890	7%	77. _____
Petty, Tom	$3,452	6%	78. _____
Quinn, Gale	$3,520	8%	79. _____
		TOTAL	80. _____

Group 2: Applications Problems 81 Through 85

Rice's Quick Service Foods Department: Pies For Week Ending: 9-10-20XX			
Salesperson	Sales Amount	Percent of Commission	Dollar Amount of Commission
Davis, Ed	$4,121.35	8.5%	81. _____
Burleson, Patti	$4,415.00	9.5%	82. _____
Poole, Robert	$4,402.50	8.5%	83. _____
Fraser, Jill	$4,080.30	8.4%	84. _____
		TOTAL	85. _____

Group 3: Applications Problems 86 Through 95

Hint: In this group of problems, the percent of commission is constant. Most calculators will save the first number in a multiplication problem as the constant. You may want to review the procedures for working with constants presented in this chapter.

Rice's Quick Service Foods Department: Frozen Foods For Week Ending: 11-17-20XX			
Salesperson	Sales Amount	Percent of Commission	Dollar Amount of Commission
Locke, George	$3,250	11%	86. _____
Chapman, Brad	$3,040	11%	87. _____
Timm, Harvey	$3,286	11%	88. _____
Roscoe, Henry	$3,960	11%	89. _____
Hayes, Martha	$2,875	11%	90. _____
Johnson, Mary	$3,899	11%	91. _____
Purty, Hillary	$4,120	11%	92. _____
Peoples, Sandra	$3,189	11%	93. _____
Jones, Precilla	$3,760	11%	94. _____
		TOTAL	95. _____

86. _____

87. _____

88. _____

89. _____

90. _____

91. _____

92. _____

93. _____

94. _____

95. _____

BUSINESS APPLICATIONS: WORKING WITH MARKUP—COST METHOD

Business Situation

Kathy Storey, the cost accountant for the Federated Refrigeration Company, has determined that it costs $461.50 to manufacture a new five-foot, frostless refrigerator. All other products manufactured by Federated are marked up an average of 30 percent. If the refrigerators are marked up 30 percent, what will be the manufacturer's suggested retail price for this particular model of refrigerator?

Markup (sometimes referred to as *profit*) is what keeps the manufacturer, wholesaler, or retailer in business. A markup is necessary to recover everyday expenses and cost of goods sold and to make a reasonable profit for the owners. One method of determining the suggested retail price of an article is based on cost of the article. Most small stores, wholesalers, and manufacturers use this method.

Cost markup is a practical application of the portion formula ($P = B \times R$) that was presented in Chapter 1. When using the cost method, the markup amount (portion) is determined by multiplying the cost (base) by the percent of markup (rate).

■ **EXAMPLE** Determine the manufacturer's suggested retail price for a frostless refrigerator that originally cost $461.50 when the percent of markup is 30 percent.

Step 1 Determine the markup amount.

$$
\begin{array}{rl}
\$461.50 & \text{cost (base)} \\
\times \quad .30 & \text{percent of markup (rate)} \\
\hline
\$138.45 & \text{markup amount (portion)}
\end{array}
$$

(Note that 30% is converted to .30. If your calculator has a percent [%] key, you may choose to use that instead.)

Step 2 Calculate the suggested retail price.

$$
\begin{array}{rl}
\$461.50 & \text{cost} \\
+ \quad 138.45 & \text{markup amount} \\
\hline
\$599.95 & \text{suggested retail price}
\end{array}
$$

■

Alternate Method Often, only the suggested retail price is needed. To obtain the suggested retail price using a one-step procedure, multiply the cost by the percent of markup + 100 percent.

■ **EXAMPLE** Note that the same figures are used to demonstrate that the suggested retail price is the same, regardless of the method used.

$$
\begin{array}{rl}
\$461.50 & \text{cost} \\
\times \quad 1.30 & \text{percent of markup} + 100\% \\
\hline
\$599.95 & \text{suggested retail price}
\end{array}
$$

(Again, notice that 130% is converted to 1.30. If your calculator has a percent [%] key, you may choose to use that instead.)

■

Recommendation: For problems with multiplication, review the material in the first part of this chapter. For problems with the $P = B \times R$ formula, review the material in Chapter 1.

Markup—Cost Method:
Applications Problems 96 Through 110

96. ___$32.50___

Instructions	*Machine Setting*
1. Using the cost method of markup, determine the markup amount for Group 1 problems. 2. Using the cost method of markup, calculate the suggested retail price for Group 2 problems. 3. Using the cost method of markup, calculate both the markup amount and the suggested retail price for Group 3 problems.	1. Set decimal control on 2. 2. Enter all decimals in the problem with the decimal key. 3. Set round-off switch in 5/4 position (if applicable). 4. Either convert the percent of markup to a decimal or use your calculator's percent key. 5. If your calculator has a memory, your machine will automatically add the markup amount to the original cost for Group 3 problems.

97. _____

98. _____

99. _____

100. _____

Group 1: Applications Problems 96 Through 100

Reminder: Calculate the markup amount for Group 1 problems.

Federated Refrigeration Company			
Department: Refrigerators		Merchandise: Small Refrigerators	
Description	Cost	Percent of Markup	Markup Amount
1.3 cu. ft. Ref.	$130.00	25%	96. $32.50 _____
1.7 cu. ft. Ref.	$150.00	30%	97. _____
2.5 cu. ft. Ref.	$240.00	35%	98. _____
3.5 cu. ft. Ref.	$310.00	40%	99. _____
5.0 cu. ft. Ref.*	$445.00	45%	100. _____
*With Icemaker			

Applications Problems

101. _$384.40_

102. _____

103. _____

104. _____

105. _____

106a. _$28.50_

106b. _$123.49_

107a. _____

107b. _____

108a. _____

108b. _____

109a. _____

109b. _____

110a. _____

110b. _____

Group 2: Applications Problems 101 Through 105

Reminder: Calculate the suggested retail price for Group 2 problems.

Federated Refrigeration Company			
Department: Freezers		Merchandise: Home Use	
Description	Cost	Percent of Markup	Suggested Retail Price
6.0 cu. ft. Freezer	$310.00	24%	101. $384.40
7.5 cu. ft. Freezer	$330.00	25%	102. _____
9.0 cu. ft. Freezer	$350.00	27%	103. _____
11.0 cu. ft. Freezer	$385.00	30%	104. _____
13.0 cu. ft. Freezer*	$410.00	38%	105. _____
*With Icemaker			

Group 3: Applications Problems 106 Through 110

Reminder: Calculate the markup amount and suggested retail price for Group 3 problems.

Federated Refrigeration Company				
Department: Air Conditioners		Merchandise: Window/Central		
Description	Cost	Percent of Markup	Markup Amount	Suggested Retail Price
5,000 Window Unit*	$ 94.99	30%	106. a. $28.50	b. $123.49
6,000 Window Unit*	$115.25	34%	107. a. _____	b. _____
7,500 Window Unit*	$129.30	36%	108. a. _____	b. _____
11,500 Window Unit*	$199.40	25%	109. a. _____	b. _____
13,500 Window Unit*	$256.35	28%	110. a. _____	b. _____
*Units Listed According to BTU Rating				

SELF-EVALUATION: PART I

Applications Posttest

INSTRUCTION	MACHINE SETTING
1. Complete the following problems in eight minutes or less with one or no incorrect answers.	1. Set decimal control on 2. 2. Enter all decimals in the problem with the decimal key. 3. Set round-off switch in 5/4 position (if applicable).

1a. _____

1b. _____

1c. _____

1d. _____

1e. _____

1f. _____

1. Calculate the markdown amount and the reduced sale price for the problems below.

Original Price	Percent of Markdown	Markdown Amount	Reduced Sale Price
$14.95	15%	a. _____	b. _____
$29.50	20%	c. _____	d. _____
$19.95	25%	e. _____	f. _____

2a. _____

2b. _____

2c. _____

2d. _____

2e. _____

2f. _____

2. Determine the discount amount and the amount of payment for the problems below. *Assume that all invoices are paid within 5 days after they are received.*

Invoice Amount	Terms	Discount Amount	Amount of Payment
$1,534.60	2/10, N/30	a. _____	b. _____
$ 875.35	3/10, N/30	c. _____	d. _____
$3,490.50	1/10, N/30	e. _____	f. _____

3a. _____

3b. _____

3c. _____

3. Complete the compound interest problems below. Refer to the compound interest table in the Business Applications: Determining Compound Interest Amounts section.

Principal	Rate	Time	Compounded	Compounded Value
$3,220.70	6%	1 yr.	Semiannually	a. _____
$3,670.50	6%	3 yrs.	Annually	b. _____
$6,700.12	4%	2 yrs.	Quarterly	c. _____

**Self-Evaluation:
Part I**

4a. _____

4b. _____

4c. _____

5a. _____

5b. _____

5c. _____

5d. _____

5e. _____

5f. _____

4. Determine the dollar amount of commission for the sales figures below.

Sales Amount	Percent of Commission	Dollar Amount of Commission
$2,340.00	12%	a. _____
$3,450.75	11%	b. _____
$4,112.90	13%	c. _____

5. Using the cost method of markup, calculate the markup amount and the suggested retail price for the following problems.

Cost	Percent of Markup	Markup Amount	Suggested Retail Price
$ 2.00	49%	a. _____	b. _____
$11.00	18%	c. _____	d. _____
$22.52	33%	e. _____	f. _____

RECOMMENDATION: If you were able to complete Part I of the Self-Evaluation Applications Posttest in eight minutes or less with no more than one incorrect answer, proceed to Part II of the Self-Evaluation. If you did not satisfactorily complete Part I of the Self-Evaluation Applications Posttest, take it again, trying for the recommended level. If you are still not able to attain the recommended level, talk with your instructor.

SELF-EVALUATION: PART II

Critical Thinking Problems

INSTRUCTION	MACHINE SETTING
1. Complete the following problems with one or no incorrect answers.	1. Set decimal control on 2. 2. Set round-off switch in 5/4 position (if applicable).

1. Houston Lumber & Hardware Supply is sponsoring a 20 percent off promotional sale for all merchandise in the store. You are considering the purchase of a cordless electric drill that was originally priced at $109.95.

   a. What is the markdown amount?

   b. What is the reduced sale price?

2. Pay-less Printing Company purchases all of its printing supplies from Seattle Wholesale Supply. Its last purchase consisted of paper, ink, and corrugated boxes. The purchase totaled $3,211. Last week, Pay-less Printing received an invoice from Seattle Wholesale for the entire amount with terms of 2/10, N/60. Assume that Pay-less Printing pays the invoice within 10 days.

   a. What is the discount amount?

   b. What is the amount of payment?

3. Martha and John Evans are trying to save enough money to purchase a new car. Last year, they put $12,000 in a certificate of deposit that pays 4 percent interest compounded semiannually. At the end of four years, what is the compound value of this investment?

Note: You may want to use the interest table presented earlier in this chapter.

Self-Evaluation:
Part II

1a. _____

1b. _____

2a. _____

2b. _____

3. _____

Self-Evaluation:
Part II

4. _____

5. _____

6a. _____

6b. _____

4. Albert Bennett is a salesperson for the Martindale Foundry. Last month, he sold steel products valued at $240,500. He is paid a 2 percent commission on all sales. How much commission did Mr. Bennett earn last month?

5. Plumbing Fixture Supply, Inc., received a shipment of marble bathtubs. The firm's accountant said that the company should sell the marble tubs for $649.50 each. The tubs cost Plumbing Fixture Supply $389.20 each. If the tubs are sold at the price that the accountant recommends, what is the dollar amount of profit the firm will earn on each marble tub?

6. As salesperson for Hundley Pottery Company, you are responsible for pricing merchandise before it is sold to the customer. Your supervisor tells you to price a new shipment of 12-inch clay pots. The original cost for each pot is $3.60, and the firm uses a standard 40 percent markup (based on cost).

    a. What is the markup amount?

    b. What is the suggested retail price?

RECOMMENDATION: If you were able to complete Part II of the Self-Evaluation with no more than one incorrect answer, you have satisfactorily completed this chapter. You should talk with your instructor before progressing to new material. If you did not satisfactorily complete this segment, take the Self-Evaluation again, trying for the recommended level. If you are still not able to attain the recommended level, talk with your instructor.

Division on the Electronic Calculator

OBJECTIVES

When you have successfully completed this chapter on the electronic calculator, you will be able to

1. Identify the enter-dividend (÷) key and its use.
2. Perform calculations in division on the machine using the touch method.
3. Perform division calculations on the machine using a constant divisor.
4. Accumulate answers from several division problems.
5. Demonstrate speed and accuracy while adding, subtracting, multiplying, and dividing.
6. Attain confidence in your ability to divide on the electronic calculator.
7. Advance to business applications problems.

INTRODUCTION

Proper desk arrangement and correct posture should be maintained. Use the touch method. Begin your work by locating the enter-dividend key on your machine. This key appears in various locations according to machine brand; normally, the divide (÷) symbol is shown on the key. It is used to enter the dividend in the machine register.

Practice Problems

1. _____2.89_____

2. _____

3. _____

4. _____

5. _____

6. _____

7. _____

8. _____

9. _____

10. _____

11. _____

12. _____

13. _____

14. _____

15. _____

16. _____

17. _____

18. _____

19. _____

20. _____

DIVISION

The electronic calculator is quick and accurate in obtaining a quotient in division. Locate the enter-dividend ($\div$) key on your machine. The basic steps in working a division problem on this calculator are illustrated in the following example.

■ EXAMPLE

$144 \div 6 =$ Set decimal control on 2
Set round-off switch in 5/4 position (if applicable)
Enter 144   Depress $\div$
Enter 6   Depress $=$
Read the answer: 24   ■

In the division problem in the preceding example, the quotient is a whole number (24) with no remainder. In most division problems, however, the quotient will be a whole number plus part of another. For the work contained in this chapter, we round all the quotients to hundredths (two digits after the decimal point). Practice the problem in the following example, remembering to set the decimal along with the individual digits when a number has a decimal.

■ EXAMPLE

$46.235 \div 14.8 =$ Enter 46.235   Depress $\div$
Enter 14.8   Depress $=$
Read the answer: 3.12   ■

Division on the computer calculator is performed in the following manner.

■ EXAMPLE

$46.235 \div 14.8 =$ Enter 46.235   Depress /
Enter 14.8   Depress *Enter* or $=$
Read the answer: 3.12 rounded to two digits   ■

Practice Problems

Work the following division problems, recording your answer to hundredths.

1. $52 \div 18 = 2.89$ **2.** $79 \div 16 =$ **3.** $256 \div 38 =$

4. $1,848 \div 161 =$ **5.** $584 \div 38 =$ **6.** $298 \div 76 =$

7. $788 \div 22 =$ **8.** $1,922 \div 245 =$ **9.** $34,208 \div 130 =$

10. $31,455 \div 907 =$ **11.** $28.59 \div 24 =$ **12.** $23.5 \div 5.5 =$

13. $138.7 \div 95.83 =$ **14.** $61.2 \div 0.425 =$ **15.** $2,705.66 \div 348.56 =$

16. $25.9 \div 0.007 =$ **17.** $81.09 \div 62.9 =$ **18.** $2.059 \div 0.0783 =$

19. $2.007 \div 37.7 =$ **20.** $8.7 \div 2.355 =$

CONSTANT DIVISION

Constant division involves a series of problems where the divisor is the same for each problem. The electronic calculator has the ability to retain a divisor for repeat division. The following example shows how to work division problems when the same divisor is used several times as a constant.

■ EXAMPLE

$78.4 \div 14.17 =$	Set decimal control on 2
$91.65 \div 14.17 =$	Set round-off switch in 5/4 position (if
$29.17 \div 14.17 = $ _____	applicable)
	Enter 78.4 Depress ÷
	Enter 14.17 Depress =*
	Read the answer: 5.53
	Enter 91.65 Depress =
	Read the answer: 6.47
	Enter 29.17 Depress =
	Read the answer: 2.06 ■

21. ____17.22____

22. _____

23. _____

24. _____

25. _____

26. _____

27. _____

28. _____

29. _____

30. _____

> **Practice Problems**

Work the following constant division problems in groups of three or four problems.

21. $91.77 \div 5.33 = 17.22$ **22.** $126 \div 5.33 =$ **23.** $46.82 \div 5.33 =$

24. $102.68 \div 4.06 =$ **25.** $99.43 \div 4.06 =$ **26.** $2.036 \div 4.06 =$

27. $19.26 \div 0.57 =$ **28.** $7.68 \div 0.57 =$ **29.** $46.1 \div 0.57 =$

30. $1.225 \div 0.57 =$

ACCUMULATIVE DIVISION

Accumulative division is used when you wish to obtain a grand total of several quotients. The accumulative keys used for multiplication are used to accumulate division quotients also. Remember that the M+ key is used for positive number storage and the M− key is used when storing negative answers. The following example represents the most common approach to accumulating quotients on the electronic calculator.

---

*When the = key is depressed after 14.17, the number entered with the = sign remains in the machine as a constant divisor until a new division series is started and the ÷ key is used again.

Practice Problems

31. _____12.29_____

32. _____

33. _____

34. _____

35. _____

36. _____

37. _____

38. _____

39. _____

40. _____

■ **EXAMPLE** If your calculator has the M+ and M− keys, the problem is worked in the following manner.

18 ÷ 3 =	Enter 18 Depress ÷
36.24 ÷ 9.2 =	Enter 3 Depress =
− 3.05 ÷ 2 =	Depress M+
−14.7 ÷ 7.5 = _____	Enter 36.24 Depress ÷
	Enter 9.2 Depress =
	Depress M+
	Enter 3.05 Depress ÷
	Enter 2 Depress =
	Depress M−
	Enter 14.7 Depress ÷
	Enter 7.5 Depress =
	Depress M−

Depress MR
Read the answer: 6.45 ■

Practice Problems	Work the following accumulative division problems.

31. 16 ÷ 4 =
26 ÷ 5 =
34 ÷ 11 = _____
  12.29

32. 43 ÷ 26 =
87 ÷ 19 =
47 ÷ 9 = _____

33. 47.1 ÷ 8.2 =
97.4 ÷ 36.5 =
10.5 ÷ 26.1 = _____

34. 90.47 ÷ 37.6 =
88.35 ÷ 9.47 =
73.01 ÷ 14.29 = _____

35. 14.73 ÷ 31.5 =
−40.87 ÷ 19.3 =
720.49 ÷ 93.07 = _____

36. 126.75 ÷ 4.327 =
−37.715 ÷ 53.333 =
−75.26 ÷ 25.47 = _____

37. 776.23 ÷ 128.65 =
3.4769 ÷ 0.0057 =
−976 ÷ 847.3 = _____

38. (3.907 ÷ 4.876) − (9.375 ÷ 0.097) + (14 ÷ 7) + (16.07 ÷ 1.9) =

39. (1,746.05 ÷ 816.4) + (47.07 ÷ 0.096) − (472.99 ÷ 13.67) − (55.1 ÷ 7.69) =

40. (66.67 ÷ 3.735) − (129.003 ÷ 2.413) + (5.993 ÷ 17.54) − (163.008 ÷ 87.14) =

Self-Check		
Self- Check	Work the four problems given below in two minutes or less with no in- correct answers.	1. _____
		2. _____
		3. _____
		4. _____

1.	76.43	2.	13.98	3.	46.52	4.	99.01
	44.31		80.19		67.58		7.95
	3.45		10.00		59.08		7.01
	58.68		18.42		2.02		89.65
	25.72		3.54		21.82		10.59
	95.45		2.05		58.05		11.32
	9.54		10.26		12.13		20.80
	80.79		11.18		4.00		15.79
	31.79		84.03		30.33		22.90
	20.06		91.52		79.89		40.88
	63.51		44.50		60.26		96.48
	509.73 (55)		369.67 (110)		441.68 (165)		422.38 (220)

Recommendation: If you are able to complete the problems in the Self-Check in two minutes or less with no incorrect answers, proceed to the Self-Evaluation Skills Posttest. If you were not able to meet the goal for the Self-Check, take it again and try to improve your previous effort. If you are still unable to meet the goal of speed and accuracy for the Self-Check, go back to Chapter 3 and practice the material in Speed Development 3. After practicing the material, take the Self-Check again for speed and accuracy. After the third try, proceed to the Self-Evaluation Skills Posttest.

Self-Evaluation

1. _____

2. _____

3. _____

4. _____

5. _____

6. _____

7. _____

8. _____

9. _____

10. _____

11. _____

12. _____

13. _____

14. _____

15. _____

SELF-EVALUATION

Skills Posttest

Complete the following problems in five minutes or less with one or no incorrect answers. (Do not include recording the answers in the five minutes.)

1.
560.10
157.30
425.50
268.70
_____ S
530.10
854.40
195.10
526.30

2.
854.10
-734.65

3.
317
$\times 476$

4.
9.32
$\times 0.0021$

5. $(3.1 \times 5.11) - (21 \times 98) + (96.1 \times 37.6) =$

6. $876 \div 37 =$

7. $455.125 \div 9.125 =$

8. $260.667 \div 384 =$

9. $164.57 \div 0.035 =$

10. $87.612 \div 23.5 =$

11. $54.125 \div 23.5 =$

12. $31.76 \div 23.5 =$

13. $(78 \div 59) + (21 \div 43) - (10 \div 6) =$

14. $(2.82 \div 0.06) + (14.9 \div 0.04) - (555 \div 56) =$

15. $(176.8 \div 6.11) - (19.23 \div 9.17) + (67.13 \div 11.16) - (25.50 \div 68.7) =$

RECOMMENDATION: If you were able to complete the Self-Evaluation Skills Posttest in five minutes or less with no more than one incorrect answer, you have satisfactorily completed this section of Chapter 6. You are now ready to progress to the business applications problems that follow. If you did not satisfactorily complete this section, take the Self-Evaluation Skills Posttest again, trying for the recommended level. If you are still not able to attain the recommended level, talk with your instructor.

BUSINESS APPLICATIONS: WORKING WITH MARKUP—RETAIL METHOD

Business Situation

John Palmer, a sophomore at Southern Illinois University, has just obtained a part-time job at Contemporary Fashions. He is responsible for receiving new merchandise and then pricing the merchandise before it is placed on the sales floor. John's supervisor has shown him how to determine the sales price once, but John still feels uneasy about the correct procedure. He doesn't want to make a lot of mistakes the first day.

In Chapter 5, the cost markup method of calculating the sales price for merchandise was explained. A second and *different method*—the retail markup method—is presented in this business application. *Retail markup* is a variation of the $B = P \div R$ formula presented in Chapter 1. When using the retail method, the *R* (rate) is the *complement* of the percent of markup. To find the complement, mentally subtract the percent of markup from 100 percent. Then the retail price (base) is determined by dividing the cost (portion) by the complement (rate).

■   **EXAMPLE**   John Palmer receives a shipment of sports coats. Each coat costs the store $150. John knows that there must be a 40 percent markup based on the retail method.

Step 1 Mentally determine the complement of the percent of markup.

$$\begin{array}{rl} 100\% & \\ -\;\;40\% & \text{percent of markup} \\ \hline 60\% & \text{complement} \end{array}$$

Step 2 Divide cost by the complement.

$150.00 (cost) $\div$ .60 (complement) = $250.00 (retail sale price)

The 60 percent has been changed to the decimal .60. This step may be omitted if your machine has a percent key.

Note: When you use the retail method, your answer represents the retail price. If you need to know the dollar amount of markup, subtract the cost from the retail sale price.

Step 3 Subtract the cost from the retail sale price.

$$\begin{array}{rl} \$250.00 & \text{retail sale price} \\ -150.00 & \text{cost} \\ \hline \$100.00 & \text{amount of markup} \end{array}$$ ■

Recommendation: If you did not obtain the correct answer for the sample problem, determine whether the difficulty is in Step 1, Step 2, or Step 3. For problems with Step 1 and Step 3, review the subtraction process in Chapter 4. For problems with Step 2, review the division process presented in this chapter.

Applications Problems

1. ___75%___

2. ___

3. ___

4. ___

5. ___

6. ___

7. ___

Markup—Retail Method:
Applications Problems 1 Through 20

Instructions	*Machine Setting*
1. For all problems in this assignment, use the *retail* method of markup.	1. Set decimal control on 2.
2. Determine the complement for Group 1 problems.	2. Enter all decimals in the problem with the decimal key.
3. Calculate both the complement and the retail sale price for Group 2 problems.	3. Set round-off switch in 5/4 position (if applicable).
4. Find the complement, retail sale price, and amount of markup for Group 3 problems.	4. Either convert the complement to a decimal or use your calculator's percent key.
	5. For problems in Group 3, you may want to use your machine's memory system to find the amount of markup.

Group 1: Applications Problems 1 Through 7

Reminder: Find the complement for Group 1 problems.

Cost	Percent of Markup	Complement
$11.99	25%	1. _75%_
$18.19	30%	2. ___
$14.92	35%	3. ___
$13.50	37%	4. ___
$11.19	39%	5. ___
$10.75	41%	6. ___
$10.33	43%	7. ___

Group 2: Applications Problems 8 Through 12

Reminder: Determine the complement and retail sale price for Group 2 problems.

Contemporary Fashions				
Department: Clothing				Merchandise: Coats
Description	Cost	Percent of Markup	Complement	Retail Sale Price
Cotton Coats	$12.99	35%	8.a. 65%	b. $19.98
50% Wool Coats	$20.39	32%	9.a. _____	b. _____
Plaid Coats	$23.03	36%	10.a. _____	b. _____
Denim & Fur	$22.39	30%	11.a. _____	b. _____
Fun Fur	$43.19	28%	12.a. _____	b. _____

8a. _____65%_____

8b. _____$19.98_____

9a. _____

9b. _____

10a. _____

10b. _____

11a. _____

11b. _____

12a. _____

12b. _____

Applications Problems

13a. _____52%_____

13b. ___$10.00___

13c. ___$4.80___

14a. _____

14b. _____

14c. _____

15a. _____

15b. _____

15c. _____

16a. _____

16b. _____

16c. _____

17a. _____

17b. _____

17c. _____

18a. _____

18b. _____

18c. _____

19a. _____

19b. _____

19c. _____

20a. _____

20b. _____

20c. _____

Group 3: Applications Problems 13 Through 20

Reminder: Calculate the complement, retail sale price, and markup amount for Group 3 problems.

Contemporary Fashions

Department: Clothing | Merchandise: Shirts/Sweaters

Description	Cost	Percent of Markup	Complement	Retail Sale Price	Markup Amount
Knit Vest	$ 5.20	48%	13.a. 52%	b. $10.00	c. $4.80
Knit Vest	$ 5.94	46%	14.a. ___	b. ___	c. ___
Sweater	$ 7.20	40%	15.a. ___	b. ___	c. ___
Sweater	$ 8.12	42%	16.a. ___	b. ___	c. ___
Sweater/Blend	$14.00	30%	17.a. ___	b. ___	c. ___
Knit Sweater	$17.50	20%	18.a. ___	b. ___	c. ___
Knit Pullover	$20.00	35%	19.a. ___	b. ___	c. ___
Knit Coat	$31.40	40%	20.a. ___	b. ___	c. ___

BUSINESS APPLICATIONS: CALCULATING PERCENT OF INCREASE/DECREASE

Business Situation

Just one month ago, the Markley Chemical Company held its monthly sales meeting. Each salesperson was challenged by the vice-president of marketing to increase sales by 20 percent during the next month. Now, at the end of the month, it is time to measure the dollar amount of increase and to determine whether each salesperson achieved the 20 percent sales objective.

Management frequently compares current sales, expenses, and profits with amounts for the same items from previous accounting periods. By studying the results, managers can determine trends and make more intelligent decisions. Both the dollar amount of increase or decrease and the percent of increase or decrease can be determined by following the steps below.

Step 1   Determine the dollar amount of change by subtracting the smaller amount from the larger amount. *(If the amount for the previous period is smaller than the current amount, there is an increase. If the previous amount is larger than the current amount, there is a decrease.)*

Step 2   Divide the dollar amount of change by the amount for the *earlier* period.

Step 3   Mentally convert your decimal answer to a percent by moving the decimal two places to the right and adding a percent sign.

■   **EXAMPLE**   Determine the dollar amount of change and the percent of increase if chemical sales in July were $7,500 and sales in August were $8,800.

Step 1   Determine the dollar amount of change.

$8,800   August sales
– 7,500   July sales
$1,300   amount of change (increase)

Step 2   Divide the dollar amount of change by the amount of sales for the *earlier* period.

$1,300 ÷ $7,500 = .1733
amount   earlier
  of   sales
change

Step 3   Mentally convert your answer to a percent by moving the decimal two places to the right and adding a percent sign.

.17.33 becomes 17.33%, the percent of increase   ■

Note that this type of problem is a practical application of the $R = P \div B$ formula presented in Chapter 1. The amount of change represents the portion (P), and the sales amount for the *earlier* period is the base (B). Also, note that the answer (R) .1733 has been changed to 17.33% in Step 3. This step may be omitted if your calculator has a percent key.

Applications Problems

21a. ___$4,000___

21b. ___increase___

22a. _____

22b. _____

23a. _____

23b. _____

24a. _____

24b. _____

25a. _____

25b. _____

In this example, there was a $1,300 increase in chemical sales. This increase represents a 17.33 percent increase in sales when compared to the sales of the previous month. It should be pointed out that percent of increase and decrease calculations can be the basis for many management decisions. And although the actual calculation is a simple one, the information it provides can be the basis for the decisions that managers must make to keep a firm on track toward obtaining its goals and objectives. In this example, monthly sales did increase, but the sales force did not achieve the 20 percent sales increase the vice-president of marketing had wanted. Now the vice-president of marketing, individual sales managers, and each salesperson must take steps to increase the firm's sales revenues.

Practice the example problem on page 125 to see if you can find the dollar amount of change and the percent of increase.

> **Recommendation:** If you did not obtain the correct answer, determine whether the difficulty is Step 1, Step 2, or Step 3. For problems with Step 1, review the material in Chapter 4. For problems with Step 2, review the division process in this chapter. For problems with Step 3, review the material in Chapter 1.

Percent of Increase/Decrease: Applications Problems 21 Through 35

Instructions	Machine Setting
1. Find the dollar amount of change and indicate whether this amount is an increase or a decrease for Group 1 problems.	1. Set decimal control on 2 for Step 1 (dollar amount of change).
2. Determine the dollar amount of change and percent of increase or decrease for Group 2 and Group 3 problems. Also indicate whether your answers represent an increase or a decrease.	2. Set decimal control on 4 for Step 2. 3. Set round-off switch in 5/4 position (if applicable). 4. Either convert the decimal answer in Step 2 to a percent or use your calculator's percent key.

Group 1: Applications Problems 21 Through 25

Reminder: Determine the dollar amount of change and indicate whether this amount is an increase or decrease.

Markley Chemical Supply				
Subject: Salary Expense				Date: January 15, 20XX
Department	2008 Expense	2007 Expense	Dollar Amount of Change (Step 1)	Increase or Decrease
Sales	$53,500	$49,500	21.a. $4,000	b. Increase
Personnel	$22,300	$20,300	22.a. _____	b. _____
Administration	$47,950	$49,600	23.a. _____	b. _____
Production	$74,220	$79,500	24.a. _____	b. _____
Research	$18,500	$19,800	25.a. _____	b. _____

Group 2: Applications Problems 26 Through 30

Reminder: Calculate the dollar amount of change and percent of increase or decrease. Also, indicate whether this amount is an increase or decrease for problems in Group 2 and Group 3.

Markley Chemical Supply

Subject: Gasoline Expense

Date: January 15, 20XX

Department	2008 Expense	2007 Expense	Dollar Amount of Change (Step 1)	Percent of Increase or Decrease (Steps 2 & 3)	Increase or Decrease
Sales	$5,400	$4,900	26.a. $500	b. 10.20%	c. Increase
Delivery	$8,900	$7,300	27.a.	b.	c.
Administration	$1,025	$1,950	28.a.	b.	c.
Production	$1,835	$1,720	29.a.	b.	c.
Research	$1,575	$1,311	30.a.	b.	c.

Applications Problems

26a. _____$500_____

26b. _____10.20%_____

26c. _____Increase_____

27a. _____

27b. _____

27c. _____

28a. _____

28b. _____

28c. _____

29a. _____

29b. _____

29c. _____

30a. _____

30b. _____

30c. _____

Applications Problems

Group 3: Applications Problems 31 Through 35

31a. _____

31b. _____

31c. _____

32a. _____

32b. _____

32c. _____

33a. _____

33b. _____

33c. _____

34a. _____

34b. _____

34c. _____

35a. _____

35b. _____

35c. _____

Markley Chemical Supply

Subject: Sales—Chemical Cleaner   Date: January 15, 20XX

Product Code	2008 Sales	2007 Sales	Dollar Amount of Change (Step 1)	Percent of Increase or Decrease (Steps 2 & 3)	Increase or Decrease
X-70 HD	$24,830	$21,950	31.a. _____	b. _____	c. _____
X-72 HD	$39,250	$36,725	32.a. _____	b. _____	c. _____
X-74 HD	$22,790	$25,860	33.a. _____	b. _____	c. _____
X-76 HD	$40,980	$42,250	34.a. _____	b. _____	c. _____
Z-12	$19,832	$17,811	35.a. _____	b. _____	c. _____

BUSINESS APPLICATIONS: ANALYZING STATEMENTS OF FINANCIAL POSITION

Business Situation

Joe Mariano, chief accountant for Marston Manufacturing, has just received a call from the corporate president, Mr. Marston. It seems that Mr. Marston needs more information for an upcoming board meeting. Although he has a current statement of financial position, the president wants a more in-depth analysis of the statement.

A *statement of financial position* is one of the most essential accounting reports used by business today. (The term *balance sheet* is preferred by some accountants.) This statement is prepared at the end of the accounting period, which usually covers one year. Most firms also have statements of financial position prepared semiannually, quarterly, or monthly. Three accounting terms must be defined before examining a statement of financial position in detail.

1. *Assets* are usually defined as something a firm owns—its cash, inventory, machinery, land, buildings, etc. Normally, assets are classified as either current or fixed assets. *Current assets* are those converted to cash within one year or less. Items held or used for longer than one year are called *fixed assets.*

2. *Liabilities* are a firm's debts. *Current liabilities* are obligations that will be repaid within one year or less. A firm's *long-term liabilities* are repaid over a longer period of time.

3. *Owner's equity* refers to the money, land, buildings, equipment, or other items of value an owner has invested in a business.

The relationship among assets, liabilities, and owner's equity forms the basis for a firm's statement of financial position. That is, the statement must show that the firm's assets are equal to its liabilities plus owners' equity.

■   **EXAMPLE**   Exhibit 6-1 illustrates the statement of financial position for Marston Manufacturing, Inc., and shows dollar amounts for assets, liabilities, and owner's equity.   ■

Notice that assets ($224,000) = liabilities ($58,000) + owner's equity ($166,000). This equation ensures that there are no mathematical errors in the statement of financial position.

Many managers find it is easier to interpret a statement of financial position when the dollar amounts are converted to percents. As shown in the following example, the percent for each individual asset can be found by dividing the dollar amount of an individual asset by the total dollar amount for assets.

■   **EXAMPLE**   Determine the percent of total assets for the cash account when the cash balance is $45,000 and the total amount for assets is $224,000.

Step 1   Divide the individual asset amount by the total amount for assets.

$45,000 (cash) ÷ $224,000 (total amount for assets) = .201

EXHIBIT 6-1 Statement of Financial Position for Marston Manufacturing, Inc.

<table>
<tr><th colspan="3">Marston Manufacturing, Inc.
Statement of Financial Position
December 31, 20XX</th></tr>
<tr><td></td><td>*Amount*</td><td>*Percent*</td></tr>
<tr><td>Assets</td><td></td><td></td></tr>
<tr><td>Current Assets</td><td></td><td></td></tr>
<tr><td>Cash</td><td>$ 45,000</td><td>20.1%</td></tr>
<tr><td>Accounts Receivable</td><td>23,000</td><td>10.3%</td></tr>
<tr><td>Supplies</td><td>24,000</td><td>10.7%</td></tr>
<tr><td>Total Current Assets</td><td>$ 92,000</td><td>41.1%</td></tr>
<tr><td>Fixed Assets</td><td></td><td></td></tr>
<tr><td>Building & Land</td><td>$ 97,000</td><td>43.3%</td></tr>
<tr><td>Equipment</td><td>35,000</td><td>15.6%</td></tr>
<tr><td>Total Fixed Assets</td><td>$132,000</td><td>58.9%</td></tr>
<tr><td>Total Assets</td><td>$224,000</td><td>100.0%</td></tr>
<tr><td>Liabilities</td><td></td><td></td></tr>
<tr><td>Current Liabilities</td><td></td><td></td></tr>
<tr><td>Accounts Payable</td><td>$ 21,500</td><td>9.6%</td></tr>
<tr><td>Notes Payable</td><td>12,000</td><td>5.4%</td></tr>
<tr><td>Total Current Liabilities</td><td>$ 33,500</td><td>15.0%</td></tr>
<tr><td>Long-Term Liabilities</td><td></td><td></td></tr>
<tr><td>Mortgage Payable</td><td>$ 24,500</td><td>10.9%</td></tr>
<tr><td>Total Liabilities</td><td>$ 58,000</td><td>25.9%</td></tr>
<tr><td>Owner's Equity</td><td></td><td></td></tr>
<tr><td>Common Stock</td><td>$125,500</td><td>56.0%</td></tr>
<tr><td>Retained Earnings</td><td>40,500</td><td>18.1%</td></tr>
<tr><td>Total Owner's Equity</td><td>$166,000</td><td>74.1%</td></tr>
<tr><td>Total Liabilities and Owner's Equity</td><td>$224,000</td><td>100.0%</td></tr>
</table>

Step 2 Mentally convert your answer to a percent by moving the decimal two places to the right and adding a percent sign.

.201 becomes 20.1%

The second step may be omitted if you use your calculator's percent key. ∎

Note that this type of problem is a practical application of the $R = P \div B$ formula presented in Chapter 1. The dollar amount for each individual asset account represents the portion (P), and the total dollar amount for assets represents the base (B).

It is also possible to find the percent for each individual liability and owner's equity account by dividing the individual dollar amount for each account by the total dollar amount for liabilities and owner's equity.

■ **EXAMPLE** Determine the percent of total liabilities and owner's equity for the accounts payable account when the accounts payable balance is $21,500 and the total amount for liabilities and owner's equity is $224,000.

Step 1 Divide the individual amount by the total amount for liabilities and owner's equity.

$21,500 (acct. pay.) ÷ $224,000 (total amt. for liab. and o.e.) = .096

Step 2 Mentally convert your answer to a percent by moving the decimal two places to the right and adding a percent sign.

.096 becomes 9.6%

Again, the second step may be omitted if you use your calculator's percent key. ■

Practice both example problems until you are able to work them without feeling uncomfortable about entering the numbers or depressing the keys on your calculator.

Recommendation: If you did not obtain the correct answer for the sample problems, determine whether the difficulty is in Step 1 or Step 2. For problems with Step 1, review the division process presented at the beginning of this chapter. For problems with Step 2, review the material on converting decimals to percents in Chapter 1.

Statements of Financial Position:
Applications Problems 36 Through 65

Instructions	*Machine Setting*
1. Determine the percent of total assets for each individual asset account included on the two statements of financial position. 2. Determine the percent of total liabilities and owner's equity for each individual liability or owner's equity account included on each statement of financial position. 3. Convert all answers to percents.	1. Set decimal control on 3. 2. Set round-off switch in 5/4 position (if applicable). 3. The total asset amounts and the total liability and owner's equity amounts are constant. Most calculators will save the second number in division as a constant.

Applications
Problems

Group 1: Applications Problems 36 Through 50

36. _____15.9%_____

37. _____

38. _____

39. _____

40. _____

41. _____

42. _____

43. _____

44. _____

45. _____

46. _____

47. _____

48. _____

49. _____

50. _____

Marcello's Italian Restaurants, Inc. Statement of Financial Position December 31, 20XX		
	Amount	*Percent*
Assets		
Current Assets		
Cash	$ 21,500	36. 15.9% _____
Supplies	12,900	37. _____
Total Current Assets	$ 34,400	38. _____
Fixed Assets		
Building	$ 75,700	39. _____
Equipment	15,400	40. _____
Land	9,300	41. _____
Total Fixed Assets	$ 100,400	42. _____
Total Assets	$ 134,800	100.0%
Liabilities		
Current Liabilities		
Accounts Payable	$ 21,850	43. _____
Notes Payable	5,400	44. _____
Total Current Liabilities	$ 27,250	45. _____
Long-Term Liabilities Mortgage Payable	$ 49,500	46. _____
Total Liabilities	$ 76,750	47. _____
Owner's Equity		
Common Stock	$ 52,400	48. _____
Retained Earnings	5,650	49. _____
Total Owner's Equity	$ 58,050	50. _____
Total Liabilities and Owner's Equity	$ 134,800	100.0%

Group 2: Applications Problems 51 Through 65

Management Consultants, Inc. Statement of Financial Position December 31, 20XX		
	Amount	*Percent*
Assets		
Current Assets		
Cash	$ 13,500	51. _____
Notes Receivable	4,000	52. _____
Accounts Receivable	11,900	53. _____
Supplies	5,200	54. _____
Total Current Assets	$ 34,600	55. _____
Fixed Assets		
Building	$ 92,800	56. _____
Equipment	8,320	57. _____
Land	11,400	58. _____
Total Fixed Assets	$ 112,520	59. _____
Total Assets	$ 147,120	100.0%
Liabilities		
Current Liabilities		
Accounts Payable	$ 13,250	60. _____
Notes Payable	9,900	61. _____
Total Liabilities	$ 23,150	62. _____
Owner's Equity		
Common Stock	$ 100,000	63. _____
Retained Earnings	23,970	64. _____
Total Owner's Equity	$ 123,970	65. _____
Total Liabilities and Owner's Equity	$ 147,120	100.0%

51. _____

52. _____

53. _____

54. _____

55. _____

56. _____

57. _____

58. _____

59. _____

60. _____

61. _____

62. _____

63. _____

64. _____

65. _____

BUSINESS APPLICATIONS: ANALYZING INCOME STATEMENTS

Business Situation

Both Mary and Don Collins looked forward to the next meeting with their accountant. They knew their small business, Collins Landscaping Products, Inc., had sold more merchandise last year than in previous years. What they didn't realize was that although sales were up, so were expenses. After a half-hour meeting with their accountant, they realized there is more to operating a successful business than simply selling merchandise.

Owners and managers of a business use income statements to determine whether a business is profitable. An *income statement* is a summary of a firm's revenues and expenses during a specified accounting period. Normally, income statements are prepared on an annual basis, but they may also be prepared on a quarterly, semiannual, or monthly basis.

■ **EXAMPLE** Exhibit 6-2 illustrates an income statement for Collins Landscaping Products, Inc.

EXHIBIT 6-2 Income Statement for Collins Landscaping Products, Inc.

Collins Landscaping Products, Inc. Income Statement for Year Ended December 31, 20XX	Amount	Percent
Net Sales	$129,000	100.0%
Cost of Goods Sold		
Inventory, January 1	$ 11,500	8.9%
Purchases	50,400	39.1%
Merchandise Available for Sale	$ 61,900	48.0%
Less Inventory, December 31	10,750	8.3%
Cost of Goods Sold	$ 51,150	39.7%
Gross Profit	$ 77,850	60.3%
Operating Expenses		
Salary	$ 35,200	27.3%
Rent	5,400	4.2%
Depreciation	4,320	3.3%
Utilities	3,970	3.1%
Supplies Used	2,150	1.7%
Miscellaneous	1,345	1.0%
Total Operating Expenses	$ 52,385	40.6%
Net Income Before Taxes	$ 25,465	19.7%

The profit or loss amount reported on a firm's income statement is based on the following formula.

revenue − cost of goods sold − expenses = net income before taxes ■

As shown in Exhibit 6-2, this firm had net sales of $129,000. When cost of goods sold ($51,150) and total operating expenses ($52,385) are deducted from net sales, net income before taxes of $25,465 remains.

Many business owners and managers find it is easier to interpret an income statement when dollar amounts are converted to percents. The percent for each individual account can be found by dividing the dollar amount for each individual account by the total dollar amount for net sales, as shown in the next example.

■ **EXAMPLE** Determine the percent of net sales for the January 1 inventory account when net sales are $129,000 and the January 1 beginning inventory amount is $11,500.

Step 1 Divide the individual amount by the total amount for net sales.

$11,500 (beg. inv.) ÷ $129,000 (total amount for net sales) = .089

Step 2 Mentally convert your answer to a percent by moving the decimal two places to the right and adding a percent sign.

.089 becomes 8.9%

The second step may be omitted if you use your calculator's percent key. ■

For this example, January 1 inventory represents 8.9 percent of net sales. This type of problem is actually a practical application of the $R = P ÷ B$ formula presented in Chapter 1. In this case, the January 1 inventory dollar amount is the portion, while the net sales figure represents the base. The answer is the rate.

Recommendation: If you did not obtain the correct answer for the sample problem, determine whether the difficulty is Step 1 or Step 2. For problems with Step 1, review the division process presented in this chapter. For problems with Step 2, review the material on converting decimals to percents in Chapter 1.

Income Statement:
Applications Problems 66 Through 95

Instructions	*Machine Setting*
1. Determine the percent of net sales for each individual account included on the two income statements that follow. 2. Convert all answers to percents.	1. Set decimal control on 3. 2. Set round-off switch in 5/4 position (if applicable). 3. The total net sales amount is constant. Most calculators will save the second number in a division problem as a constant.

**Applications
Problems**

Group 1: Applications Problems 66 Through 75

66. _____48.5%_____

67. _____

68. _____

69. _____

70. _____

71. _____

72. _____

73. _____

74. _____

75. _____

Alex Freeman, Inc. Income Statement for Year Ended December 31, 20XX		
	Amount	*Percent*
Revenue		
Sales	$184,700	100.0%
Operating Expenses		
Salary	$ 89,650	66. 48.5%____
Rent	22,540	67. _____
Advertising	15,340	68. _____
Utilities	4,490	69. _____
Depreciation	14,600	70. _____
Insurance	6,200	71. _____
Supplies Used	12,540	72. _____
Miscellaneous	1,689	73. _____
Total Operating Expenses	$167,049	74. _____
Net Income Before Taxes	$ 17,651	75. _____

Applications
Problems

Group 2: Applications Problems 76 Through 95

Bryson's Antique Shop Income Statement for Year Ended December 31, 20XX		
	Amount	*Percent*
Revenue		
Gross Sales	$220,000	76. _____
Less Sales Returns	2,100	77. _____
Less Sales Discounts	900	78. _____
Net Sales	$217,000	100.0%
Cost of Goods Sold		
Inventory, January 1	$35,400	79. _____
Purchases	110,850	80. _____
Merchandise Available for Sale	$146,250	81. _____
Less Inventory, December 31	21,970	82. _____
Cost of Goods Sold	$124,280	83. _____
Gross Profit	$92,720	84. _____
Operating Expenses		
Salary	$42,625	85. _____
Rent	7,600	86. _____
Advertising	3,500	87. _____
Utilities	3,050	88. _____
Depreciation	3,185	89. _____
Insurance	2,215	90. _____
Supplies Used	4,420	91. _____
Delivery	3,650	92. _____
Miscellaneous	1,198	93. _____
Total Operating Expenses	$71,443	94. _____
Net Income Before Taxes	$21,277	95. _____

Applications
Problems

76. _____

77. _____

78. _____

79. _____

80. _____

81. _____

82. _____

83. _____

84. _____

85. _____

86. _____

87. _____

88. _____

89. _____

90. _____

91. _____

92. _____

93. _____

94. _____

95. _____

BUSINESS APPLICATIONS: CALCULATING DEPRECIATION— STRAIGHT LINE

Business Situation

Martha and Bob Finley, owners of Finley's Art and Frame Shop, have just purchased a new delivery truck. Their accountant explains that they must depreciate the cost of the new truck over a five-year period. Later, as they are going over the company books, they notice that the accountant has included a $4,000 depreciation expense for the first year. Their question is, How did the accountant determine the depreciation expense?

Depreciation is an accounting method used to spread the cost of a fixed asset over the time period during which it will be used. One method of determining depreciation expense is called the *straight-line* method, which deducts the same amount of money for each year that a piece of equipment is used. Three essentials are needed when the straight-line method is used. They are

The **original cost** of the article
The **estimated salvage value** of the equipment
The **estimated life** of the equipment

Once these three factors have been determined, the following formula is used to determine the dollar amount of annual depreciation expense.

$$\frac{\text{original cost} - \text{estimated salvage value}}{\text{estimated life}} = \text{annual depreciation expense}$$

■ **EXAMPLE 1** Finley's Art and Frame Shop purchased a new delivery truck for an original cost of $22,500. The truck has an estimated salvage value of $2,500 and an estimated life of 5 years.

$$\frac{\text{original cost} - \text{estimated salvage value}}{\text{estimated life}} = \text{annual depreciation expense}$$

$$\frac{\$22,500 - \$2,500}{5} = \text{annual depreciation expense}$$

$$\frac{\$20,000}{5} = \text{annual depreciation expense}$$

$$\$4,000 = \text{annual depreciation expense} \quad ■$$

The *book value* for any asset is found by subtracting the annual depreciation expense from the original cost or previous year's book value. For the delivery truck in Example 1, first-year book value is $18,500.

■ **EXAMPLE 2**

$22,500	original cost
− 4,000	annual depreciation expense
$18,500	first-year book value

■

The book value for the second, third, fourth, and fifth years is found by subtracting another year's depreciation expense from the previous year's book value.

■   **EXAMPLE 3**   The following table shows the annual depreciation expense and book value over a five-year period for the delivery truck purchased by Finley's Art and Frame Shop.   ■

Year	Annual Depreciation Expense	Book Value
1	$4,000	$18,500
2	$4,000	$14,500
3	$4,000	$10,500
4	$4,000	$6,500
5	$4,000	$2,500

Notice that one of the advantages of using the straight-line method of depreciation is that the annual depreciation expense is the same each year. The formulas presented below may be used to verify depreciation and book value calculations.

total   **=**   **annual**   **×**   **year**
depreciation expense   **depreciation expense**   **of depreciation**

book value = original cost − total depreciation expense

Practice the example problems until you feel comfortable with the procedures for determining annual depreciation expense and book value for the delivery truck.

Recommendation: If you did not obtain the correct answers, you may want to review the subtraction process presented in Chapter 4 and the division process presented in this chapter.

Depreciation—Straight Line: Applications Problems 96 Through 113

Instructions	Machine Setting
1. Find the annual depreciation expense for Group 1 problems. 2. Determine the annual depreciation expense, total depreciation, and book value at the end of the specified year for Group 2 problems.	1. Set decimal control on 2. 2. Enter all decimals in the problem with the decimal key. 3. Set round-off switch in 5/4 position (if applicable).

Applications Problems

96.   **$700.00**

97. _____

98. _____

99. _____

100. _____

101. _____

102. _____

103. _____

104. _____

105. _____

Group 1: Applications Problems 96 Through 105

Reminder: Find the annual depreciation expense for Group 1 problems.

Straight-Line Depreciation			
Original Cost	Estimated Salvage Value	Estimated Life (Years)	Annual Depreciation Expense
$5,000	$100	7	96. $700.00
$9,700	$500	4	97.
$8,000	$350	8	98.
$3,985	$ 0	9	99.
$6,610	$500	5	100.
$4,950	$200	7	101.
$5,250	$625	6	102.
$8,755	$650	8	103.
$2,450	$230	10	104.
$4,562	$160	5	105.

Group 2: Applications Problems 106 Through 113

Hint: You may want to use the formulas for total depreciation expense and book value presented in this business application for Group 2 problems.

Straight-Line Depreciation

Original Cost	Estimated Salvage Value	Estimated Life (Years)	Year of Depreciation	Annual Depreciation Expense	Total Depreciation	Book Value at End of Specified Year
$2,000	$ 0	5	1st	106. a. $400	b. $400	c. $1,600
$4,250	$200	4	2nd	107. a.	b.	c.
$2,150	$100	5	3rd	108. a.	b.	c.
$7,700	$250	7	2nd	109. a.	b.	c.
$9,500	$300	6	3rd	110. a.	b.	c.
$5,510	$ 0	8	2nd	111. a.	b.	c.
$2,635	$150	7	4th	112. a.	b.	c.
$8,980	$675	8	2nd	113. a.	b.	c.

Applications Problems

106a. ____ $400 ____

106b. ____ $400 ____

106c. ____ $1,600 ____

107a. _____

107b. _____

107c. _____

108a. _____

108b. _____

108c. _____

109a. _____

109b. _____

109c. _____

110a. _____

110b. _____

110c. _____

111a. _____

111b. _____

111c. _____

112a. _____

112b. _____

112c. _____

113a. _____

113b. _____

113c. _____

1a. _____

1b. _____

1c. _____

1d. _____

1e. _____

1f. _____

2a. _____

2b. _____

2c. _____

2d. _____

2e. _____

2f. _____

2g. _____

2h. _____

2i. _____

SELF-EVALUATION: PART I

Applications Posttest

INSTRUCTION	MACHINE SETTING
1. Complete the following problems in eight minutes or less with one or no incorrect answers.	1. Set decimal control on 2 unless instructed to use another decimal setting. 2. Set round-off switch in 5/4 position (if applicable). 3. Enter all decimals in the problem with the decimal key.

1. Using the *retail method* of markup presented in this chapter, calculate the complement and retail sale price for the problems below.

Cost	Percent of Markup	Complement	Retail Sale Price
$47.96	20%	**a.** _____	**b.** _____
$11.99	25%	**c.** _____	**d.** _____
$7.19	28%	**e.** _____	**f.** _____

2. Compute the amount of change and percent of increase or decrease for the problems below. Also, in the last column, indicate if your answers represent an increase or a decrease.

2007	2006	Amount of Change	Percent of Inc./Dec.	Inc./Dec.
$14,500	$13,775	**a.** _____	**b.** _____	**c.** _____
$29,650	$24,970	**d.** _____	**e.** _____	**f.** _____
$ 8,935	$10,244	**g.** _____	**h.** _____	**i.** _____

3. Compute the percent of total assets for the individual accounts listed below (use three decimals).

Individual Account	Total Assets	Percent of Total Assets
$22,400 (Cash)	$144,800.00	a. _____
$11,300 (Supplies)	$139,650.35	b. _____
$89,500 (Building)	$215,789.40	c. _____

4. Determine the percent of net sales for the individual accounts listed below (use three decimals).

Individual Account	Net Sales	Percent of Net Sales
$54,800 (Purchases)	$135,679.00	a. _____
$34,678 (Salary Expense)	$142,675.00	b. _____
$ 5,678 (Utilities Expense)	$129,671.35	c. _____

5. Using the straight-line method of depreciation, calculate the annual depreciation expense for the following problems.

Original Cost	Estimated Life	Estimated Salvage Value	Annual Depreciation Expense
$954.40	6 years	$200	a. _____
$875.00	4 years	$100	b. _____
$789.50	8 years	$0	c. _____

3a. _____

3b. _____

3c. _____

4a. _____

4b. _____

4c. _____

5a. _____

5b. _____

5c. _____

RECOMMENDATION: If you were able to complete Part I of the Self-Evaluation Applications Posttest in eight minutes or less with no more than one incorrect answer, proceed to Part II. If you did not satisfactorily complete this part of the Self-Evaluation Applications Posttest, take Part I again, trying for the recommended level. If you are still not able to attain the recommended level, talk with your instructor.

Self-Evaluation: Part II

1. _____

2a. _____

2b. _____

3a. _____

3b. _____

SELF-EVALUATION: PART II

Critical Thinking Problems

INSTRUCTION	MACHINE SETTING
1. Complete the following problems with one or no incorrect answers.	1. Set decimal control on 2 unless instructed to use another decimal setting. 2. Set round-off switch in 5/4 position (if applicable).

1. Mitchell's Department Store received a shipment of men's sport coats. The manufacturer's suggested retail price is $219.95. The wholesale cost for each coat is $136.70. If the coats are sold at the suggested retail price, how much profit will the store earn on each coat?

2. Robert Hundley is a sales associate for ABC Appliance Store. As part of his job description, he is responsible for pricing merchandise that is later sold to retail customers. A new shipment of microwave ovens just arrived. The unit cost for each microwave oven is $186.75. Robert's boss tells him to mark up each oven 25 percent based on the retail method.

    a. What is the retail sale price for each oven?

    b. What is the markup amount for each oven?

3. Betty Moreland, manager for Boots and More, is concerned because retail sales seem to be falling. She decides to compare sales for this month with sales for the same month last year. After reviewing the firm's income statements, she determines that sales for March 2007 were $34,500. Sales for March 2006 were $30,956. Use three decimal places to determine percent of change.

    a. What is the amount of change?

    b. What is the percent of change?

4. Last year Waterview Candy Company invested $365,400 in a new manufacturing facility. Now, after a year of declining sales, the president of the company is concerned that the company may have too much money invested in the building. The company has total assets of $987,567. What percent of total assets does the building represent? Use two decimal places.

5. In 2007, Seattle Janitorial Supply had utility expenses of $38,043. During the same year, the company had net sales of $2,161,538. What percent of net sales do utility expenses represent? Use three decimal places.

6. Bill Everman, president of Everman Auto Parts, just purchased a new delivery vehicle that costs $16,800. He estimates that the truck will last for five years and should have a salvage value of $1,000. Assume that the firm uses the straight-line method of depreciation.

    a. What is the annual depreciation expense?

    b. What is the book value for the delivery truck at the end of the third year?

4. _____

5. _____

6a. _____

6b. _____

RECOMMENDATION: If you were able to complete Part II of the Self-Evaluation with no more than one incorrect answer, you have satisfactorily completed this chapter and are ready to progress to Chapter 7. If you did not satisfactorily complete Part II of the Self-Evaluation, you may want to review the material presented in the business applications sections of this chapter.

Multiple Operations on the Electronic Calculator

OBJECTIVES

When you have successfully completed this chapter, you will be able to

1. Identify the sequence to be followed in solving a multiple operation problem.
2. Follow the correct sequence and perform calculations on your calculator involving multiple operations.
3. Attain confidence in your ability to perform various multiple operation calculations on the electronic calculator.
4. Advance to business application problems.

INTRODUCTION

Many business activities involve the combination of several mathematical functions to obtain an answer. For instance, the determining of interest on a note will use both multiplication and division in arriving at a final answer. The term used to identify a situation in which you will use more than one mathematical function is *multiple operations*.

MULTIPLE OPERATIONS

Calculations involving multiple operations are to be performed in the following sequence of steps.

Step 1 Perform calculations within parentheses.

Step 2 Perform multiplication and division calculations from left to right.

Step 3 Perform addition and subtraction calculations from left to right.

The example problem illustrates the sequence for solving a fairly difficult multiple operation problem.

■ **EXAMPLE**

$$4.6 + (9.3 \times 7.6) + 4.7 \times 1.3 - (7.1 + 3.8) - 96.5 \div 5 - 18.1 =$$

Step 1 Perform all calculations contained within parentheses.

$$4.6 + (9.3 \times 7.6) + 4.7 \times 1.3 - (7.1 + 3.8) - 96.5 \div 5 - 18.1 =$$

$$4.6 + \quad (70.68) \quad + 4.7 \times 1.3 - \quad (10.9) \quad - 96.5 \div 5 - 18.1 =$$

Step 2 Perform all multiplication and division calculations from left to right.

$$4.6 + (70.68) + 4.7 \times 1.3 - (10.9) - 96.5 \div 5 - 18.1 =$$

$$4.6 + (70.68) + \quad 6.11 \quad - (10.9) - \quad 19.3 \quad - 18.1 =$$

Step 3 Perform all addition and subtraction calculations from left to right.

$$4.6 + (70.68) + 6.11 - (10.9) - 19.3 - 18.1 = 33.09 \qquad ■$$

In reality, very few business application solutions require multiple operations of this level of difficulty, but the sequence should be followed in solving all multiple operation problems.

Practice Problems	Complete the following multiple operation problems using the proper sequence of steps for solving. Remember to use the touch method of operating your machine. Round your *final* answer to two digits after the decimal (hundredths).

1. $4 \times 5 \times 6 = 120$

2. $4 \times 5 \times 6 \div 7 =$

3. $71.2 \div 6.3 \times 5.02 =$

4. $3.5 \times 16.1 \div 8.2 \times 1.7 =$

5. $66 - 3.5 \times 3.5 - 16.2 =$

6. $46.7 \div 8.4 \times 0.98 - 3.34 =$

7. $9.24 \times 1.83 - 7.52 \times 0.05 =$

8. $73.1 - 3.03 \div 0.1 + 8.19 =$

Practice Problems

9. _____

10. _____

11. _____

12. _____

13. _____

14. _____

15. _____

9. $62.6 \div 4 \times 9.2 - 88.16 =$

10. $5.40 \times 5.7 + 6.53 - 2.46 \times 7 + 43.2 \div 2.5 =$

11. $83.59 - 5.32 + 9.09 + 39.12 - 29.76 \div 0.3 =$

12. $16.49 - (7.4 \times 1.1) + 63 \div 7 + (8.4 - 3.2) =$

13. $45 \times (3.47 \times 2) - 147.1 \div 10 - 80.08 =$

14. $(77.28 \div 4) \times (4 \times 0.07) - 16.2 \div 2.4 + 21.13 =$

15. $4.77 - 7.79 + 27.56 \div 2 + (7.13 - 4.15) + 4.15 =$

SELF-EVALUATION

Skills Posttest

| Complete the following problems in five minutes or less with one or no incorrect answers. |

1. 4.96
    2.18
    0.07
    4.39
    29.044
    15.706
    0.375

2. 8.992
    -10.461

3. 72 1/5
    -46 1/4

4. 3.14
    $\times 7.62$

5. 26.406
    $\times\ 7.13$

6. $5.448 \div 2.779 =$

7. $4 \times 28 \times 50 =$

8. $6.35 \times 25.93 \times 58.08 =$

9. $0.41 \times 6.071 \times 0.733 =$

10. $82.4 \div 12.6 \times 9.44 =$

11. $9.68 \times 3.65 - 7.13 \times 0.092 =$

12. $5.88 \times 2.76 + 8.39 - 9.24 \times 4 + 36.8 \div 7.2 =$

13. $59.4 \div 4 \times 8.6 - 72.493 =$

14. $34.90 - (3.7 \times 4.8) + 75 \div 25 + (8.5 - 3.9) =$

15. $(19.32 \div 3) \times (4 \times 0.08) - 12 \div 0.024 \times 63.92 =$

Self-Evaluation

1. _____

2. _____

3. _____

4. _____

5. _____

6. _____

7. _____

8. _____

9. _____

10. _____

11. _____

12. _____

13. _____

14. _____

15. _____

RECOMMENDATION: If you were able to complete the Self-Evaluation Skills Posttest in five minutes or less with no more than one incorrect answer, you have satisfactorily completed this section of Chapter 7. You are now ready to progress to the business applications problems that follow. If you did not satisfactorily complete this section, take the Self-Evaluation Skills Posttest again, trying for the recommended level. If you are still not able to attain the recommended level, talk with your instructor.

BUSINESS APPLICATIONS: CALCULATING DEPRECIATION—DECLINING BALANCE

Business Situation

Recently, Carla Martinez, owner of Carla's Home Furnishings, met with her accountant to go over her present financial situation. The accountant suggested that she opt for the declining-balance method of determining depreciation expense. Until now, she had always used the straight-line method of depreciation: now, after talking with her accountant, she has decided to change to this new method because of the advantages it offers.

In addition to the straight-line method of depreciation described in Chapter 6, the *declining-balance method* is used by a number of businesses as a method of increasing depreciation expense during the first few years of use. Normally, the maximum depreciation for accounting purposes is *twice* the straight-line rate when the declining-balance method is used.

The depreciation rate needed when using the declining-balance method is obtained by dividing 100 percent by the number of years the equipment will be used by the business. If the maximum depreciation amount is desired, this depreciation rate is multiplied by two (twice the straight-line rate). Then the original cost of the equipment is multiplied by the new depreciation rate.

■   **EXAMPLE**   Determine the first-year depreciation expense for a delivery truck that has an original cost of $20,000 and an estimated life of five years.

Step 1   Divide 100 percent by the estimated life.

$$\frac{100\%}{5} = 20\%$$

Step 2   Multiply the answer from Step 1 by two (*twice the straight-line rate*).

$20\% \times 2 = 40\%$ declining-balance rate

Step 3   Multiply the original cost by the declining-balance rate from Step 2.

$20,000	original cost
$\times$ .40	declining-balance rate
$ 8,000	first-year depreciation expense

■

Note that 40 percent has been converted to .40. This step may be omitted if you use your calculator's percent key.

The *first-year book value* for the delivery truck is found by subtracting the first-year depreciation expense ($8,000) from the original cost ($20,000).

$20,000 - $8,000 = $12,000   first-year book value

To determine the *second-year depreciation expense,* the first-year book value ($12,000) is multiplied by the depreciation rate obtained in Step 2 (40%).

$12,000 $\times$ .40 = $4,800   second-year depreciation expense

The *second-year book value* is calculated by subtracting the second-year depreciation expense ($4,800) from the first-year book value ($12,000).

$12,000 - $4,800 = $7,200

The above steps are repeated for each year of estimated life. The declining-balance method of depreciation does not use an estimated salvage value except as a dollar amount that the book value cannot fall below.

The table below demonstrates the dollar difference when depreciation expense is determined by the straight-line method and the declining-balance method.

Original cost of a new commercial copier: $12,000
Estimated life: 5 years
Estimated salvage value: $1,000

Year	Straight Line	Declining Balance
1	$ 2,200	$ 4,800.00
2	$ 2,200	$ 2,880.00
3	$ 2,200	$ 1,728.00
4	$ 2,200	$ 1,036.80
5	$ 2,200	$ 555.20*
	$11,000	$11,000.00

Try the example to see if you can obtain the depreciation expense amounts and the book values for the first two years.

Recommendation: If you did not obtain the correct answers, determine which part of the problem is causing difficulty. Possible problem areas to review are division in Chapter 6, multiplication in Chapter 5, and subtraction in Chapter 4.

Depreciation—Declining Balance: Applications Problems 1 Through 20

Instructions	Machine Setting
1. Using the declining-balance method, determine depreciation rate, first-year depreciation expense, and first-year book value for Group 1 problems. 2. For Group 2 problems, determine first-year depreciation expense, first-year book value, and second-year depreciation expense.	1. To determine the declining-balance rate, use four decimal places. 2. To determine each year's depreciation expense and book value, use two decimal places. 3. Enter all decimals in the problem with the decimal key. 4. Set round-off switch in 5/4 position (if applicable). 5. Either convert the depreciation rate to a decimal or use your calculator's percent key.

---

*Fifth-year depreciation is limited to $555.20, or the amount necessary to reduce the fifth-year book value to the estimated salvage value of $1,000.

Applications Problems

1a.	**40%**
1b.	**$1,320.00**
1c.	**$1,980.00**
2a.	
2b.	
2c.	
3a.	
3b.	
3c.	
4a.	
4b.	
4c.	
5a.	
5b.	
5c.	
6a.	
6b.	
6c.	
7a.	
7b.	
7c.	
8a.	
8b.	
8c.	
9a.	
9b.	
9c.	
10a.	
10b.	
10c.	
11a.	**$600.00**
11b.	**$900.00**
11c.	**$360.00**

Group 1: Applications Problems 1 Through 10

Reminder: Find the depreciation rate, first-year depreciation, and first-year book value for Group 1 problems.

Depreciation: Declining-Balance Method				
Original Cost	Estimated Life (Years)	Depreciation Rate	First-Year Depreciation	First-Year Book Value
$3,300	5	1.a. 40%	b. $1,320.00	c. $1,980.00
$4,200	8*	2.a. _____	b. _____	c. _____
$2,890	4	3.a. _____	b. _____	c. _____
$4,850	8*	4.a. _____	b. _____	c. _____
$1,370	10	5.a. _____	b. _____	c. _____
$6,725	8*	6.a. _____	b. _____	c. _____
$1,839	5	7.a. _____	b. _____	c. _____
$3,800	6*	8.a. _____	b. _____	c. _____
$4,900	8*	9.a. _____	b. _____	c. _____
$3,380	7*	10.a. _____	b. _____	c. _____

*Remember to use four decimal places when determining the declining-balance rate.

Group 2: Applications Problems 11 Through 20

Reminder: Find the first-year depreciation first-year book value, and second-year depreciation for Group 2 problems.

Depreciation: Declining-Balance Method					
Original Cost	Estimated Life (Years)	Year of Depreciation	First-Year Depreciation	First-Year Book Value	Second-Year Depreciation
$1,500	5	2nd	11.a. $600.00	b. $900.00	c. $360.00
$7,645	4	2nd	12.a. _____	b. _____	c. _____
$6,420	6*	2nd	13.a. _____	b. _____	c. _____
$7,900	5	2nd	14.a. _____	b. _____	c. _____
$1,800	4	2nd	15.a. _____	b. _____	c. _____
$1,275	7*	2nd	16.a. _____	b. _____	c. _____
$5,000	6*	2nd	17.a. _____	b. _____	c. _____
$7,250	10	2nd	18.a. _____	b. _____	c. _____
$2,100	6*	2nd	19.a. _____	b. _____	c. _____
$8,235	4	2nd	20.a. _____	b. _____	c. _____

*Remember to use four decimal places when determining the declining-balance rate.

Applications
Problems

12a. _____

12b. _____

12c. _____

13a. _____

13b. _____

13c. _____

14a. _____

14b. _____

14c. _____

15a. _____

15b. _____

15c. _____

16a. _____

16b. _____

16c. _____

17a. _____

17b. _____

17c. _____

18a. _____

18b. _____

18c. _____

19a. _____

19b. _____

19c. _____

20a. _____

20b. _____

20c. _____

BUSINESS APPLICATIONS: WORKING WITH SERIES (CHAIN) DISCOUNTS

Business Situation

Joe Ward, owner of Appliances Unlimited, has just received a new catalog from one of his suppliers. The catalog contains pictures and descriptions of new appliances currently available. The catalog also contains suggested retail prices. Of course, Joe is concerned about what he will charge the customer, but he also wants to know his wholesale price and how much profit he can earn on each appliance.

Often manufacturers and wholesalers advertise their products by sending store owners a catalog that describes new merchandise. The prices given in the catalog are suggested retail prices (the prices that customers pay). In order to determine the wholesale price, the retailer must deduct *one or more discounts* from the suggested retail price. This method has at least two advantages.

1. The *retail* customer can often see a picture and description of merchandise when the retailer is temporarily out of stock. While looking at the catalog, the customer sees the suggested retail price, but not the wholesale price.

2. By inserting a new discount sheet in the back of the catalog, manufactures can change wholesale prices without printing another catalog, thus reducing printing costs.

Most often, geographic location, seasonal fluctuation, quantity purchased, and competition account for changes in the number and size of discounts offered by a manufacturer or wholesaler to a retailer.

■   **EXAMPLE: Discount Method**   The suggested retail price for a computer is $500. The retailer is given discounts of 20%, 15%, and 10% and must determine the wholesale price for the computer.

Step 1	$500	**Step 2**	$500	**Step 3**	$400
	× .20		− 100		× .15
	$100		$400		$ 60

Step 4	$400	**Step 5**	$340	**Step 6**	$340
	− 60		× .10		− 34
	$340		$ 34		$306 wholesale price ■

You may also use the complement of each discount rate to work a series discount problem. To determine each complement, mentally subtract each discount from 100 percent. Again, multiplication is used to calculate the final wholesale price.

■   **EXAMPLE: Complement Method**   Use the same suggested retail price and discounts as in the first example ($500 less 20, 15, and 10 percent).

Step 1
$500   suggested retail price
× .80   complement of 20% discount
$400

Step 2
$400
× .85   complement of 15% discount
$340

Step 3
$340
× .90   complement of 10% discount
$306   wholesale price   ■

By using *multifactor multiplication,* it is possible to omit a number of the steps presented in the previous examples. Notice in the example below that the problem is entered from left to right exactly as you read it. When you depress the equals (=) key, the wholesale price of $306 will appear.

■   **EXAMPLE**

suggested retail price		complements				wholesale price
$500	×	.80	×	.85	×	.90 = $306 ■

All percents have been converted to decimals in the previous example. You may use the percent key, but you will not be able to use the multifactor procedure outlined above.

Regardless of the method used to calculate the wholesale price, the amount of profit can be determined by subtracting the wholesale price from the manufacturer's suggested retail price.

■   **EXAMPLE**   The suggested retail price for a computer is $500. The retailer determines a wholesale price of $306 when discounts of 20, 15, and 10 percent are given. The profit is $194, as calculated below.

$500   suggested retail price
− 306   wholesale price
$194   amount of profit   ■

Choose either the discount method or the complement method and try the example problems to see if you obtain the correct wholesale price and amount of profit.

Recommendation: If you did not obtain the right answers, determine which part of the problem is causing the difficulty. Some possible problem areas to review are multiplication in Chapter 5, subtraction in Chapter 4, changing percents to decimals in Chapter 1, and using complements as discussed in this Business Application.

Series (Chain) Discounts:
Applications Problems 21 Through 35

<table>
<tr><td colspan="2">Instructions</td></tr>
</table>

Instructions	*Machine Setting*
1. For Group 1 problems, determine the wholesale price. 2. For Group 2 and Group 3 problems, determine the wholesale price and the amount of profit.	1. Set decimal control on 2. 2. Enter all decimals in the problem with the decimal key. 3. Set round-off switch in 5/4 position (if applicable). 4. You may want to use the procedure for multifactor calculations presented in this chapter.

Group 1: Applications Problems 21 Through 25

Reminder: Find the wholesale price for Group 1 problems.

Appliances Unlimited		
Merchandise: Televisions		Date: March 15, 20XX
Manufacturer's Suggested Retail Price	Discounts	Wholesale Price
$750	20%, 10%	21. $540.00
$695	10%, 10%	22.
$595	25%, 5%	23.
$498	25%, 10%	24.
$375	15%, 10%	25.

21. _____$540.00_____

22. _____

23. _____

24. _____

25. _____

Applications Problems

26a. ___$567.76___

26b. ___$131.24___

27a. _____

27b. _____

28a. _____

28b. _____

29a. _____

29b. _____

30a. _____

30b. _____

31a. _____

31b. _____

32a. _____

32b. _____

33a. _____

33b. _____

34a. _____

34b. _____

35a. _____

35b. _____

Group 2: Applications Problems 26 Through 30

Reminder: Find the wholesale price and amount of profit for problems in Group 2 and Group 3.

Appliances Unlimited				
Merchandise: Commercial Video Recorders			Date: February 15, 20XX	
Manufacturer's Suggested Retail Price	Discounts		Wholesale Price	Amount of Profit
$699	10%, 5%, 5%		26.a. $567.76	b. $131.24
$649	20%, 10%, 2%		27.a. _____	b. _____
$599	15%, 10%, 5%		28.a. _____	b. _____
$549	15%, 8%, 5%		29.a. _____	b. _____
$499	20%, 10%, 8%		30.a. _____	b. _____

Group 3: Applications Problems 31 Through 35

Appliances Unlimited				
Merchandise: Commercial Washing Machines/Dryers			Date: April 2, 20XX	
Manufacturer's Suggested Retail Price	Discounts		Wholesale Price	Amount of Profit
$699.75	20%, 18%, 4%		31.a. _____	b. _____
$649.99	25%, 10%, 2%		32.a. _____	b. _____
$629.98	20%, 10%, 5%		33.a. _____	b. _____
$597.00	10%, 10%, 10%		34.a. _____	b. _____
$575.00	10%, 10%, 10%		35.a. _____	b. _____

BUSINESS APPLICATIONS: COMPLETING INVOICES

Business Situation

Before payment is made for merchandise delivered to Heritage Office Supply, Susan Mathews must check the accuracy of a detailed invoice that accompanies the merchandise. She must determine if the extension amounts are correct. In addition, she must recheck the calculations necessary to determine the wholesale price. Finally, she must find the total if the cash discount is taken. Only after the invoice has been double-checked for accuracy is a check written to pay for the merchandise.

An *invoice* is a document prepared by the seller that requests payment for goods and services purchased by the customer. An invoice is a combination of an accumulative multiplication problem, a series discount problem, and a cash discount problem. Three steps are needed to complete an invoice.

Step 1 The subtotal for all merchandise must be calculated.

Step 2 The series (chain) discount must be applied to the subtotal for merchandise obtained in Step 1.

Step 3 The cash discount terms must be applied to the wholesale price obtained in Step 2.

INVOICE

FROM ___ Heritage Office Supply, 515 North Star Road ___

___ Dallas, TX 75243 ___

February 21 ___ 20 __ XX __

TO ___ North Printing Company ___

ADDRESS ___ 1312 North Central Expressway ___

CITY ___ Richardson, TX 75081 ___

TERMS ___ 2/10, N/30 ___ ORDER NO. ___ 3470-A ___

Quantity	Description	Unit Cost		Total	
135	Note Pads—4 columns	1	99	268	65
140	Desk Calendars	2	95	413	00
100	Pencil Holders	3	50	350	00
		Subtotal		1,031	65
		Less 5%, 10%		149	59
		Wholesale Price		882	06
		Less 2/10, N/30		17	64
		Invoice Total		864	42

CASH DISCOUNT

SERIES DISCOUNT

MULTIPLICATION EXTENSION

The secret of working with invoices is breaking the invoice into its three component parts. First, the total for each type of merchandise must be calculated. This can be accomplished by multiplying the quantity for each item by the unit cost. Of course, the amount for each individual item must be added to determine the subtotal for all merchandise purchased.

Second, the series (chain) discount must be applied to the subtotal. Most people normally use the complement of each discount to complete this step. Notice in the example below that the numbers are entered from left to right, exactly as you read them, and all complements have been converted to decimals. *When you depress the equals (=) key, the wholesale price will appear.*

■   **EXAMPLE**

subtotal   complements   wholesale price

$1,031.65   ×   .95   ×   .90   = $882.06

The answer ($882.06) is the wholesale price for all of the merchandise purchased.   ■

The amount of discount is determined by subtracting the wholesale price from the subtotal of all merchandise purchased.

■   **EXAMPLE**

$1,031.65   subtotal
−   882.06   wholesale price
$ 149.59   amount of discount   ■

Third, the cash discount is applied to the *wholesale price* of $882.06. Notice that the terms of the cash discount are included in the top section of the invoice. The cash discount terms 2/10, N/30 mean that the customer is entitled to a 2 percent discount if the invoice is paid within 10 days of the invoice date. Notice that 2 percent has been converted to a decimal in the example below.

■   **EXAMPLE**

$882.06   wholesale price
×   .02   percent of cash discount
$ 17.64   amount of cash discount   ■

The invoice total is found by subtracting the amount of cash discount from the wholesale price.

■   **EXAMPLE**

$882.06   wholesale price
−   17.64   amount of cash discount
$864.42   invoice total   ■

Naturally, in order to save the amount of cash discount, the invoice must be paid within the specified time.

Try to complete the sample invoice one step at a time to review the process. Did you obtain the correct answer?

Recommendation: If you did not obtain the correct answer, possible problem areas for review are multiplication in Chapter 5, subtraction in Chapter 4, series discounts in this chapter, and cash discounts in Chapter 5.

Invoices: Applications Problems 36 Through 39

Instructions	*Machine Setting*
1. Determine the dollar amount for each item ordered on the following invoices.	1. Set decimal control on 2.
	2. Enter all decimals in the problem with the decimal key.
2. Add all individual item totals to determine the subtotal for all merchandise purchased.	3. Set round-off switch in 5/4 position (if applicable).
3. Complete the portion of the invoice that deals with series discounts.	4. If your calculator has a memory, your calculator will automatically store extension answers.
4. Calculate the amount of cash discount. *Assume that all invoices are paid within five days of the invoice date.*	5. You may want to use the procedure for multifactor multiplication presented in this chapter when working with the series discounts on each invoice.
5. Determine the invoice total for each problem.	

Applications Problems

36a. _____

36b. _____

36c. _____

36d. _____

36e. _____

36f. _____

36g. _____

36h. _____ $251.99

Applications Problem 36

INVOICE

FROM___ Heritage Office Supply, 515 North Star Road ___

Dallas, TX 75243

February 21   XX
20_____

TO___ Martin Clothing Stores ___

ADDRESS___ 167 Oak Cliff Boulevard ___

CITY___ Dallas, TX 75206 ___

TERMS___ 2/10, N/30 ___   ORDER NO.___ 1329-86 ___

Quantity	Description	Unit Cost		Total	
144	Ball Point Pens		49	a.	
96	Mechanical Pencils	1	25	b.	
72	Mechanical Pencils	1	75	c.	
		Subtotal		d.	
		Less 10%, 5%, 5%		e.	
		Wholesale Price		f.	
		Less 2/10, N/30		g.	
		Invoice Total		h. $251	99

Applications Problem 37

INVOICE

FROM ___ Heritage Office Supply, 515 North Star Road _____

Dallas, TX 75243

_____ February 21 ___ XX
_____ 20 _____

TO ___ Jones Equipment Company _____

ADDRESS ___ 727 North Saner _____

CITY ___ Dallas, TX 75216 _____

TERMS ___ 2/10, N/30 _____ ORDER NO. ___ AZ-3343 _____

Quantity	Description	Unit Cost		Total	
8	2-Drawer Files	89	50	a.	
5	4-Drawer Files	159	95	b.	
5	4-Drawer Files (Legal)	159	98	c.	
		Subtotal		d.	
		Less 10%, 5%, 5%		e.	
		Wholesale Price		f.	
		Less 2/10, N/30		g.	
		Invoice Total		h.	

37a. _____

37b. _____

37c. _____

37d. _____

37e. _____

37f. _____

37g. _____

37h. _____

**Applications
Problems**

Applications Problem 38

38a. _____

38b. _____

38c. _____

38d. _____

38e. _____

38f. _____

38g. _____

38h. _____

INVOICE

FROM ___ Heritage Office Supply, 515 North Star Road

Dallas, TX 75243

February 21 ___ 20 ___ XX

TO ___ Movie Supplies, Inc.

ADDRESS ___ 3247 East Broadway

CITY ___ Mesquite, TX 75132

TERMS ___ 2/10, N/30   ORDER NO. ___ 3456-C

Quantity	Description	Unit Cost		Total	
3	Calculators	89	50	a.	
2	Computer Systems—104AD	495	98	b.	
2	Automatic Copiers	298	50	c.	
		Subtotal		d.	
		Less 10%, 5%, 5%		e.	
		Wholesale Price		f.	
		Less 2/10, N/30		g.	
		Invoice Total		h.	

Applications Problem 39

INVOICE

FROM_____ Heritage Office Supply, 515 North Star Road

Dallas, TX 75243

February 21 _____ XX
_____ 20_____

TO_____ Cass Production Company

ADDRESS_____ 2980 South Central Expressway

CITY_____ Dallas, TX 75222

TERMS_____ 2/10, N/30   ORDER NO._____ AZ-2901

Quantity	Description	Unit Cost		Total	
12	Desk Chairs	129	95	a.	
6	Desks—1830U	325	00	b.	
10	File Units—131U	129	00	c.	
		Subtotal		d.	
		Less 10%, 5%, 5%		e.	
		Wholesale Price		f.	
		Less 2/10, N/30		g.	
		Invoice Total		h.	

39a. _____

39b. _____

39c. _____

39d. _____

39e. _____

39f. _____

39g. _____

39h. _____

BUSINESS APPLICATIONS: CALCULATING SIMPLE INTEREST

Business Situation

Ted Harvey knew there was normally a charge for borrowing money and 11 percent sounded like a reasonable charge, but when he determined the dollar amount, he was astounded. The car that he wanted would cost an additional $3,450 if he paid for it over a 36-month period.

Interest is a dollar charge that is paid for the use of borrowed money. The dollar amount of interest is found by multiplying the principal (*P*) by the rate (*R*) by the time (*T*). This can be expressed in the following formula.

$$P \times R \times T = \text{Interest}$$

The amount of money borrowed is the *principal*. The *rate* is the percent of the principal that is charged as interest. The *time* is the period for which the money is borrowed and may be expressed in days, months, or years. If the time is expressed in days, the number of days must be placed over the number of days in one year. Usually, interest is computed on the basis of a 360-day or a 365-day year. The 360-day method is referred to as the *ordinary-interest* method. A 365-day method is referred to as the *exact-interest* method.

■   **EXAMPLE**   Find the interest on a loan for $1,525.57 at 11% for 175 days using the ordinary-interest method.

principal × rate ×   time   = interest
$1,525.57 × .11 × 175/360 = $81.58   ■

By using the multifactor or chain feature on your calculator, it is possible to omit a number of steps necessary to solve the above problem. Notice in the example below that the problem is entered from left to right, exactly as you read it. When you depress the equals (=) key, the interest amount of $81.58 will appear.

■   **EXAMPLE**

principal × rate ×   time   = interest
$1,525.57 × .11 × 175 ÷ 360 = $81.58   ■

The interest rate (11%) has been changed to a decimal. By converting the percent to a decimal, it is possible to use the multifactor features on your calculator. You may also use your calculator's percent key, but you will not be able to use the multifactor procedure outlined above.

One additional step may be necessary when working simple interest problems. Both the borrower and the lender are concerned about the total dollar amount that must be repaid. This amount can be determined by adding the interest to the principal amount, as shown in the following example.

■   **EXAMPLE**

    $1,525.57   principal
+ $81.58   interest
    $1,607.15   total amount to be repaid (principal + interest)   ■

Try the example problems to see if you can obtain the correct answers.

Recommendation: If you did not obtain the correct answers, determine which part of the problem is causing the difficulty. Possible problem areas for review are multifactor operations, presented in the first part of this chapter, and addition, presented in Chapter 4.

40a. _____ $90.00 _____

40b. _____ $1,590.00 _____

41a. _____

41b. _____

42a. _____

42b. _____

43a. _____

43b. _____

44a. _____

44b. _____

Simple Interest: Applications Problems 40 Through 49

Instructions	*Machine Setting*
1. Determine the interest amount and repayment amount for Group 1 and Group 2 problems. 2. Use a 360-day ordinary year for problems in Group 1. 3. Use a 365-day exact year for problems in Group 2.	1. Set decimal control on 2. 2. Enter all decimals in the problem with the decimal key. 3. Set round-off switch in 5/4 position (if applicable). 4. You may want to use the procedure for multifactor calculations presented in the first part of this chapter.

Group 1: Applications Problems 40 Through 44

Reminder: Use an ordinary 360-day year for these problems.

Simple Interest				
Principal	Rate	Time	Interest	Repayment Amount
$1,500	12%	180 Days	40.a. $90.00	b. $1,590.00
$1,060	14%	250 Days	41.a. _____	b. _____
$2,950	9%	210 Days	42.a. _____	b. _____
$5,950	10%	300 Days	43.a. _____	b. _____
$2,230	9%	90 Days	44.a. _____	b. _____

Applications Problems

45a. _____

45b. _____

46a. _____

46b. _____

47a. _____

47b. _____

48a. _____

48b. _____

49a. _____

49b. _____

Group 2: Applications Problems 45 Through 49

Reminder: Use an exact 365-day year for these problems.

Simple Interest				
Principal	Rate	Time	Interest	Repayment Amount
$2,945	12½%	120 Days	45.a. _____	b. _____
$3,270	15%	150 Days	46.a. _____	b. _____
$8,904	15%	340 Days	47.a. _____	b. _____
$ 981	11 ½%	95 Days	48.a. _____	b. _____
$7,715	15¼%	135 Days	49.a. _____	b. _____

BUSINESS APPLICATIONS: CALCULATING DISTRIBUTION OF EXPENSE

Business Situation

Jane Storey, the accountant for Phillips Chemical Supply, has made a careful check of janitorial expenses for the past month. At the end of the month, she concludes that it has cost the company $1,500 for janitorial service. Now she must find a method of distributing this expense among the Sales Department, the Manufacturing Department, and the General Office.

Usually, there is no direct method of distributing expenses like janitorial service, general repair expense, utility expense, or overhead costs. Accountants are often forced to estimate what each department's share of dollar expense should be. In the following example, the space each department occupies is the basis for distribution of the expense because of the relationship between square footage and the janitorial expense.

■ **EXAMPLE** During the month of April, Phillips Chemical Supply had janitorial expenses totaling $1,500. A total of 2,800 square feet is divided between three departments, as illustrated below.

	Square Feet	*Distribution of Expense*
Office	800	_____
Manufacturing	1,500	_____
Sales	500	_____
	2,800	$1,500 janitorial expense

Step 1 *Find the percent of space for each department by dividing each department's square footage by the total square footage.* Use the float (F) decimal setting and then round your answers to six decimals for Step 1. Notice that the total square footage (2,800) is constant because it is used more than once. Most calculators will save the *second* number, or constant, in a *division* problem to eliminate reentering this number.

Office	800 sq. ft. ÷ 2,800 sq. ft. = .285714
Manufacturing	1,500 sq. ft. ÷ 2,800 sq. ft. = .535714
Sales	500 sq. ft. ÷ 2,800 sq. ft. = .178571

Step 2 *Multiply the janitorial expense by the answer for each department obtained in Step 1.* Use two decimal places for your answer in Step 2 because you are working with dollars and cents. Notice that the janitorial expense ($1,500) is constant because it is used more than once. Most calculators will save the *first* number, or constant, in a *multiplication* problem to eliminate reentering this number.

Office	$1,500 × .285714 = $428.57
Manufacturing	$1,500 × .535714 = $803.57
Sales	$1,500 × .178571 = $267.86 ■

To check your work, add the individual answers in Step 2. Sometimes this total will not agree with the total expense you started with. If there is a slight difference, most people will add a few pennies to or subtract a few pennies from the largest departmental expense. The amount added or subtracted is usually shown in parentheses beside the amount for the largest department and will force the expense amounts for individual departments to equal the total expense you started with.

Practice both steps of the example to see if you can obtain the correct answers.

Recommendation: If you did not obtain the correct answers for the example, determine whether the difficulty is with Step 1 or Step 2. For problems determining the answer for Step 1, review the material on division in Chapter 6. For problems determining each department's dollar share of expense (Step 2), review the material on multiplication presented in Chapter 5.

Applications Problems

50. _____

51a. ___.492308___

51b. ___$2,001.72___

52a. _____

52b. _____

53a. _____

53b. _____

Distribution of Expense:
Applications Problems 50 Through 63

Instructions	Machine Setting
1. Find the total square footage for each problem presented in Groups 1 through 3. 2. Determine the dollar distribution of expense for each department in each group of problems.	1. Set decimal control on float (F) and then round answers to 6 for Step 1. 2. Set decimal control on 2 for Step 2. 3. Enter all decimals in the problem with the decimal key. 4. Set round-off switch in 5/4 position (if applicable). 5. The total square footage (Step 1) and total dollar expense (Step 2) are constant. Most calculators will save the first number in multiplication and the second number in division. 6. If your calculator has a memory, your machine will automatically add your answers to double-check the accuracy of your work in Step 2.

Group 1: Applications Problems 50 Through 53

Hawkins Clothing Emporium			
Department	Square Footage	Step 1 (Round Answers to 6 Decimals)	Step 2 Dollar Distribution of Expense (2 Decimals)
Jeans	800	51.a. _.492308_	b. $2,001.72
Shirts	450	52.a. _____	b. _____
Shoes	375	53.a. _____	b. _____
	50. _____ (Total Square Footage)		$4,066 Janitorial Expense

Group 2: Applications Problems 54 Through 57

All Star Discount Drugs, Inc.			
Department	Square Footage	Step 1 (Round Answers to 6 Decimals)	Step 2 Dollar Distribution of Expense (2 Decimals)
Cosmetics	275	55.a. _____	b. _____
Hair Supplies	150	56.a. _____	b. _____
Pharmaceutical	325	57.a. _____	b. _____
	54. _____ (Total Square Footage)		$4,560 Natural Gas Expense

54. _____

55a. _____

55b. _____

56a. _____

56b. _____

57a. _____

57b. _____

Applications Problems

58. _____

59a. _____

59b. _____

60a. _____

60b. _____

61a. _____

61b. _____

62a. _____

62b. _____

63a. _____

63b. _____

Group 3: Applications Problems 58 Through 63

The Extra Touch—Men's Apparel			
Department	Square Footage	Step 1 (Round Answers to 6 Decimals)	Step 2 Dollar Distribution of Expense (2 Decimals)
Belts	200	59.a. _____	b. _____
Socks	230	60.a. _____	b. _____
Jewelry	215	61.a. _____	b. _____
Cologne	150	62.a. _____	b. _____
Accessories	85	63.a. _____	b. _____
	58. _____ (Total Square Footage)		$8,050 Overhead Expense

SELF-EVALUATION: PART I

Applications Posttest

INSTRUCTION	MACHINE SETTING
1. Complete the following problems in eight minutes or less with one or no incorrect answers.	1. Set decimal control on 2 unless instructed to use another decimal setting. 2. Enter all decimals in the problem with the decimal key. 3. Set round-off switch on the 5/4 position (if applicable).

1. Using the declining-balance method of depreciation, determine the depreciation rate, first-year depreciation amount, and first-year book value.

Original Cost	Estimated Life (Years)	Depreciation Rate	First-Year Depreciation	First-Year Book Value
$3,260.00	5 years	a. _____	b. _____	c. _____
$ 975.00	4 years	d. _____	e. _____	f. _____
$2,150.00	10 years	g. _____	h. _____	i. _____

2. Determine the wholesale price for the problems below.

Manufacturer's Suggested Retail Price	Less Discounts	Wholesale Price
$ 850.00	30%, 10%, 5%	a. _____
$3,465.35	20%, 15%, 10%	b. _____
$5,925.50	10%, 10%, 10%	c. _____

1a. _____

1b. _____

1c. _____

1d. _____

1e. _____

1f. _____

1g. _____

1h. _____

1i. _____

2a. _____

2b. _____

2c. _____

**Self-Evaluation:
Part I**

3a. _____

3b. _____

3c. _____

3d. _____

3e. _____

3f. _____

4a. _____

4b. _____

4c. _____

4d. _____

4e. _____

4f. _____

3. Determine the *total* for the invoice below.

	NUMBER: 3478-A
SOLD TO: Heritage Office Supply 167 Richfield Plaza Dallas, TX 75430	DATE: 1-14-20XX
	TERMS: Cash

Quan- tity	Description	Unit Cost	Amount
160	Calc. Stands	2.09	a.
175	File Folders	2.34	b.
80	Staplers	2.45	c.
	Subtotal		d.
	Less 25%, 10%, 5%		e.
	Invoice Total		f.

4. Calculate the amount of simple interest and repayment amount in the problems below. (Use an ordinary 360-day year for these problems.)

Principal	Interest Rate	Time	Interest	Repayment Amount
$1,525.70	11%	180 days	a. _____	b. _____
$4,590.00	10%	205 days	c. _____	d. _____
$13,210.00	9½%	180 days	e. _____	f. _____

5. Determine the dollar distribution of expense in the following problem.

Department	Square Footage	(round answers to 6 decimals)	Dollar Distribution of Expense (2 decimals)
Belts	260 sq. ft.	a. _____	b. _____
Socks	290 sq. ft.	c. _____	d. _____
Ties	325 sq. ft.	e. _____	f. _____
	875 sq. ft.	1.00	$1,850 rent expense

5a. _____

5b. _____

5c. _____

5d. _____

5e. _____

5f. _____

RECOMMENDATION: If you were able to complete Part I of the Self-Evaluation Applications Posttest in eight minutes or less with no more than one incorrect answer, proceed to Part II of the Self-Evaluation. If you did not satisfactorily complete this part of the Self-Evaluation Applications Posttest, take Part I again, trying for the recommended level. If you are still not able to attain the recommended level, talk with your instructor.

Self-Evaluation:
Part II

1a. _____

1b. _____

1c. _____

1d. _____

1e. _____

2. _____

3a. _____

3b. _____

4a. _____

4b. _____

SELF-EVALUATION: PART II

Critical Thinking Problems

INSTRUCTION	MACHINE SETTING
1. Complete the following problems with zero or one incorrect answer.	1. Set decimal control on 2. 2. Set round-off switch in 5/4 position (if applicable).

1. Reynold's Delivery Service recently purchased a new delivery truck. The original cost of the truck was $18,500. The firm's accountant estimates that the truck will be used for 5 years. Use the declining-balance method of depreciation.

   a. What is the first-year depreciation amount?

   b. What is the first-year book value?

   c. What is the second-year depreciation amount?

   d. What is the second-year book value?

   e. What is the third-year depreciation amount?

2. Michael's Art & Frame recently purchased some frames for use in the business. They purchased 15 gold-leaf frames at $49.95, 5 bronze frames at $22.40, 8 aluminum frames at $11.60, and 14 wooden frames at $8.62. What is the total amount of their purchase?

3. On March 1, A-1 Module Furniture, Inc., ordered 22 coffee tables. Three weeks later the merchandise was delivered along with the invoice from the supplier. The suggested retail price for this merchandise was $4,290 less terms of 25, 15, and 10 percent.

   a. What is the wholesale price for this shipment of merchandise?

   b. What is the total amount of discount for this shipment of merchandise?

4. On May 10, Jenkins Transfer and Storage received an invoice from Kansas Office Supply. The invoice totaled $310.40. Kansas Office Supply offers customers terms of 2/10, N/30. Assume the cash discount is taken.

   a. What is the cash discount amount?

   b. What is the amount that Jenkins Transfer and Storage should pay Kansas Office Supply if Jenkins pays the invoice within the discount period?

5. Matthew Jones just borrowed $3,875 from his local bank. The bank charges 12.5 percent interest on loans that are repaid within one year. One hundred eighty days later Mr. Jones decides to repay the short-term loan. Use the exact 365-day year for this problem.

   a. What is the amount of interest that must be paid?

   b. What is the amount that is repaid to the bank?

6. The Jackson Retail Emporium consists of six different departments. Square footage allotments for each department are as follows: (1) Women's clothing: 1,200 sq. ft.; (2) Men's clothing: 1,000 sq. ft.; (3) Children's clothing: 1,420 sq. ft.; (4) Infants' clothing: 870 sq. ft.; (5) Accessories: 480 sq. ft.; and (6) Office area: 240 sq. ft. What is the total amount of square footage that the Jackson Retail Emporium occupies?

7. Total overhead expense for the Arizona Outlet Mall is $22,500. Total square footage for this mall is 18,500 sq. ft. The shoe store occupies 1,480 sq. ft. What is the shoe store's dollar share of the overhead expense?

5a. _____

5b. _____

6. _____

7. _____

RECOMMENDATION: If you were able to complete Part II of the Self-Evaluation with no more than one incorrect answer, you have satisfactorily completed this chapter. You should talk with your instructor before progressing to new material. If you did not satisfactorily complete this Self-Evaluation, take it again, trying for the recommended level. If you are still not able to attain the recommended level, talk with your instructor.

PART THREE

Advanced Business Applications

In the rapidly changing workplace of today, the ability to identify a problem, choose between alternatives, perform the alternative chosen, and evaluate the results is essential for success. The material in Chapters 8 and 9 provides you with the opportunity to further develop your employment skills. It also provides you with the opportunity to develop and use the critical thinking skills that will be important to you in your selected profession.

PART THREE

The Woodside Apartments simulation in Chapter 9 is designed to enable you to gain practical on-the-job experience in the classroom setting. The material can be used by anyone who has access to a calculator or a computer and can follow instructions. The skills required to complete the typical business machines course are reinforced when the Woodside Apartments simulation is used as a conclusion or capstone activity.

Developing Keyboarding and Critical Thinking Skills

OBJECTIVES

When you have successfully completed this chapter, you will be able to

1. Develop your keyboarding skills with additional practice.
2. Demonstrate increasing speed and accuracy in your keyboarding skills.
3. Advance to additional experiences in business applications problems.
4. Utilize the critical thinking skills of identifying, reasoning, interpreting, making decisions, and applying learning in problem-solving situations.
5. Attain confidence in your ability to use the ten-key office machine, calculate the needed information, and use critical thinking skills in problem solving.

INTRODUCTION

Additional keyboarding skills, problem-solving challenges, and self-evaluation materials are provided in this chapter. They are there to help you increase and expand the skills, abilities, and learning you have already attained. Moreover, the material in this chapter will provide you with the challenge of developing your decision-making ability and your critical thinking skills.

KEYBOARDING OPERATIONS

This is a brief review of the mathematical functions on the calculator. For more detailed information, refer to Chapters 4, 5, 6, and 7. For further information on the computer calculator, review Appendix A.

Addition

	Set decimal control on add-mode	
4.56	Enter 4.56	Depress +
4.71	Enter 4.71	Depress +
5.28	Enter 5.28	Depress +
<u>6.93</u>	Enter 6.93	Depress +
	Depress total key	
	Read the answer:	21.48

Subtraction

	Set decimal control on add-mode	
34.19	Enter 34.19	Depress +
−26.57	Enter 26.57	Depress −
	Depress total key	
	Read the answer:	7.62

Multiplication

	Set decimal control on 2	
	Set round-off switch in 5/4 position (if applicable)	
$24.6 \times 3.5 =$	Enter 24.6	Depress $\times$
	Enter 3.5	Depress =
	Read the answer:	86.10

Division

	Set decimal control on 2	
	Set round-off switch in 5/4 position (if applicable)	
$56.9 \div 15.27 =$	Enter 56.9	Depress $\div$
	Enter 15.27	Depress =
	Read the answer:	3.73

Multiple Operations

$$4.6 + (.93 \times 7.6) + 47 \times 1.3 - (7.1 + 3.8) - 96.5 \div 5 - 18.1 = 24.47$$

Remember to solve multiple operation problems in the following sequence:

1. Perform all calculations contained within parentheses first.
2. Perform all multiplication and division calculations from left to right.
3. Perform all addition and subtraction calculations from left to right.

Practice Problems

Complete the following problems using the touch method. Use correct posture at your workstation and do not look at your hands. As you complete each section of problems, check your answers with the answers given in Appendix B. Work for accuracy and repeat any problem in which you made an error.

Practice Problems

1. _____ **1,732.45**

2. _____

3. _____

4. _____

5. _____

6. _____

7. _____

8. _____

9. _____

10. _____

11. _____

12. _____

13. _____

14. _____

15. _____

16. _____

17. _____

18. _____

19. _____

20. _____

21. _____

1.
```
    51.24
   310.07
    48.07
    70.25
   444.61
   808.21
 1,732.45
```

2.
```
    83.40
     0.04
    16.08
    88.84
   749.00
    11.86
```

3.
```
   914.08
   604.46
    93.33
    57.32
   292.06
    18.15
```

4.
```
 4,675.46
   734.93
   164.73
 2,953.59
 9,321.11
    73.00
```

5.
```
    40.67
   119.03
 7,329.94
   786.67
    59.22
 4,789.99
```

6.
```
   616.85
  −334.52
```

7.
```
 7,120.48
 −  683.77
```

8.
```
   313.13
  −171.78
```

9.
```
   109.05
  −  66.03
```

10.
```
 8,537.41
 −6,238.00
```

11.
```
   602.06
 ×  58.33
```

12.
```
   571.43
 ×0.3333
```

13.
```
   142.97
 ×  6.538
```

14.
```
   181.85
 ×  41.34
```

15. $51.2 \div 0.068 =$

16. $68.31 \div 33.71 =$

17. $9.7053 \div 0.0668 =$

18. $62.6 \div 4 \times 9.2 - 88.16 =$

19. $5.40 \times 5.7 + 6.53 - 2.46 \times 7 + 43.2 \div 2.5 =$

20. $83.59 - 5.32 + 9.09 + 38.12 - 29.76 \div 0.3 =$

21. $16.49 - (7.4 \times 1.1) + 63 \div 7 + (8.6 - 3.2) =$

SELF-EVALUATION

Skills Posttest

Self-Evaluation

1. _____

2. _____

3. _____

4. _____

5. _____

6. _____

7. _____

8. _____

9. _____

10. _____

11. _____

12. _____

13. _____

14. _____

15. _____

Complete the following problems in five minutes or less with one or no incorrect answers.

1.   5.84
4.51
0.65
6.72
53.175
44.099
0.825

2.   5.658
-23.782

3.   84 1/4
-32 1/3

4.   2.56
$\times 3.48$

5.   35.105
$\times$ 4.32

6. $3.476 \div 1.529 =$

7. $5 \times 17 \times 39 =$

8. $7.41 \times 12.13 \times 27.97 =$

9. $0.23 \times 1.076 \times 0.522 =$

10. $65.7 \div 31.06 \times 8.12 =$

11. $9.47 \times 2.36 - 6.98 \times 0.071 =$

12. $4.91 \times 2.35 + 7.56 - 8.64 \times 3 + 41.8 \div 6.1 =$

13. $67.2 \div 4 \times 7.5 - 61.76 =$

14. $21.06 - (4.9 \times 2.6) + 75 \div 15 + (9.3 - 4.7) =$

15. $(19.32 \div 6) \times (3 \times 0.09) - 12 \div 2.4 + 37.49 =$

RECOMMENDATION: If you were able to complete the Self-Evaluation Skills Posttest in five minutes or less with no more than one incorrect answer, you have satisfactorily completed this section. You are now ready to progress to the business applications problems that follow. If you did not satisfactorily complete this section, take the Self-Evaluation Skills Posttest again, trying for the recommended level. If you are still not able to attain the recommended level, talk with your instructor.

BUSINESS APPLICATIONS: FINDING STATISTICAL AVERAGES

Business Situation

William Kenner, Inc., is a firm that sells electrical supplies to builders and contractors in the state of Colorado. Last year the firm's sales increased to $3.3 million. During the same twelve-month period, profits increased to just over $400,000. Mr. Kenner states that the increase in both sales and profits would not have been possible had it not been for the extraordinary effort of the firm's sales force. Each of the firm's sixteen salespeople sold an average of $206,250 in electrical supplies last year.

One way that managers can obtain the information that they need is by computing average sales, average profits, and average expenses. By studying these averages, they can then determine trends and make more informed decisions. In fact, averages are used more extensively than any other statistical measure in business today. In addition to averages, two other statistical measures—the median and the mode—are examined.

The *average* of a set of numbers is the total of all the values divided by the number of items.

■   **EXAMPLE**   Calculate the average profits for the Presto Print Shop for three consecutive years. Profits for 2005 were $24,580, profits for 2006 were $28,560, and profits for 2007 were $35,631.

Step 1   Determine the total profit for all three years.

    2005: $24,580
    2006:   28,560
    2007:   35,631
    Total profit: $88,771

Step 2   Divide the total profit by the number of years.

    $88,771 ÷ 3 = $29,590.33   average yearly profits   ■

Two other statistical measures used in business today are the median and the mode. The *median* of a set of numbers is the value that appears at the exact middle of the numbers *when they are arranged in order from the smallest value to the largest.* The *mode* of a set of numbers is the value that appears most frequently in the set. The determination of these two statistical measures is illustrated in the following example.

■ **EXAMPLE** Determine the median and the mode for the following monthly salaries. (*Note:* Dollar amounts are arranged from the smallest salary value to the largest.)

Employee	Monthly Salary
Jones	$1,350
Barnes	1,575
Martin	1,575
Chandler	1,650
Peterson	1,825
Jackson	2,000
Roberts	2,150

The *median* is the value that appears at the exact middle of the numbers *when they are arranged in order.*

$1,350
1,575
1,575
1,650 ⟵——— $1,650 is the median.
1,825
2,000
2,150

Note that the median amount ($1,650) is positioned in the middle, with three salary amounts smaller than the median and three salary amounts larger than the median.

The *mode* is the value that appears most frequently in a set of numbers.

$1,350
1,575 ⟵——— $1,575 is the mode because it occurs two times.
1,575 ↙
1,650
1,825
2,000
2,150   ■

Practice the example problems in this section to see if you can obtain the correct average, median, and mode.

Recommendation: If you did not obtain the correct answers for the example problems, determine whether the difficulty is the concepts presented in this section or the division process. For problems with the concepts of average, median, or mode, review the material presented in this application. For problems with division, review the material in Chapter 6.

**Applications
Problems**

1. _____

2. _____

3. _____

4. _____

Statistical Averages:
Applications Problems 1 Through 12

Instructions	*Machine Setting*

1. Determine the total for the sales amounts, expense amounts, or profit amounts in each group of problems.
 2. For each group of problems, calculate
   a. the average
   b. the median
   c. the mode
	1. Set decimal control on 2.
	 2. Enter all decimals in the problem with the decimal key.
	 3. Set round-off switch in 5/4 position (if applicable).

Group 1: Applications Problems 1 Through 4

Comet Woodworks, Inc.

Insurance Expense

2003:	$5,470.50	2006:	$6,650.20
2004:	5,470.50	2007:	6,890.25
2005:	6,089.72		

1. What is the total amount that this firm paid for insurance during this five-year period?

2. What is the average?

3. What is the median?

4. What is the mode?

Group 2: Applications Problems 5 Through 8

Texas Lighting Design

Salary Expense

2001: $32,450.40	2005: $38,560.30
2002: 34,000.00	2006: 40,560.24
2003: 34,000.00	2007: 46,573.20
2004: 34,000.00	

5. What is the total amount that this firm paid for salaries during this seven-year period?

6. What is the average?

7. What is the median?

8. What is the mode?

Group 3: Applications Problems 9 Through 12

Hint: Be sure to arrange all amounts in order from the smallest to largest amounts.

Richardson Cleaners and Laundry

Monthly Sales

January: $3,540.30	May: $3,045.29
February: 3,540.30	June: 2,975.40
March: 3,865.43	July: 4,560.23
April: 2,678.34	

9. What is the total amount that this firm received in sales for this seven-month period?

10. What is the average?

11. What is the median?

12. What is the mode?

5. _____

6. _____

7. _____

8. _____

9. _____

10. _____

11. _____

12. _____

BUSINESS APPLICATIONS: CALCULATING DIVIDEND YIELD AND STOCK EARNINGS

Business Situation

Like most couples, Jo and Bob Kaufman were trying to get ahead. Although they had managed to save $10,000 during the last three years, they felt they should have accumulated more. The fact that their savings account had earned over $1,000 interest during the three-year period was little consolation. Why, inflation during the same period was almost 5 percent. Jo suggested that maybe they should look at other investments, like common stock, but Bob was scared. Jo agreed that investing in stocks seemed more complicated and required more evaluation.

Calculating Dividend Yield

Calculating dividend yield is one method of evaluating the return on stocks when compared with other investment alternatives. The *current dividend yield* for a stock investment is found by dividing the dividend amount by the current market value of a share of stock.

■   **EXAMPLE**   From the following information, determine the current dividend yield for Albertson's—a large retailer that sells both groceries and health products.

Albertson's

Current market value: $36
Annual dividend amount: $0.76

Step 1   Divide the annual dividend amount by the current market value:

$0.76 \div $36 = 0.021$

Step 2   Mentally convert the decimal to a percent:

$0.021 = 2.1\%$ ■

Determining Earnings from the P–E Ratio

Before a company can pay stockholders a dividend, it must earn a profit. One indicator—the P–E ratio (price-to-earnings ratio)—is used by investors to evaluate a firm's profitability and its ability to continue paying dividends. The *P–E ratio* is included in most local newspapers and has three fundamental uses.

1. You can keep a record of your stock's P–E ratio over a period of time. A *lower* P–E ratio indicates *higher* earnings in relation to the current market value of the stock. A *higher* P–E ratio indicates *lower* earnings in relation to the current market value of the stock.

2. You can compare the P–E ratio for one corporation with those of other corporations within the same industry. Again, a lower P–E ratio may indicate higher earnings when compared with the current market value of the stock.

3. You can use the P–E ratio to estimate what the current earnings are for a corporation. To find the estimated earnings, divide the stock's current market value by the P–E ratio.

■   **EXAMPLE**   From the following information, determine the estimated earnings for Abbot Labs.

Abbot Labs
_____

Current market value per share: $56
P–E ratio: 52

Calculation: $56 ÷ 52 = $1.08   ■

In the example just given, we can estimate that Abbot Labs earned approximately $1.08 per share during the past 12 months. Practice the example problems to review the material on current dividend yield and earnings per share. Did you obtain the correct answers?

> **Recommendation:**   If you did not obtain the correct answers, you may want to review the material on division presented in Chapter 6. You may also want to review the material on changing decimals to percents presented in Chapter 1.

Dividend Yield and Stock Earnings: Applications
Problems 13 Through 28

Instructions	*Machine Setting*
1. For Group 1 problems, calculate the current dividend yield when given the dividend amount and the current market value. 2. For Group 2 problems, find the approximate per share earnings when given the current market value and the P–E ratio.	1. Set decimal control on 3 for problems in Group 1. 2. Set decimal control on 2 for problems in Group 2. 3. Enter all decimals in the problem with the decimal key. 4. Set round-off switch in 5/4 position (if applicable). 5. For Group 1 problems, either convert your answer to a percent or use your calculator's percent key.

Applications Problems

13. _____2.8%_____

14. _____

15. _____

16. _____

17. _____

18. _____

19. _____

20. _____

21. _____$2.29_____

22. _____

23. _____

24. _____

25. _____

26. _____

27. _____

28. _____

Group 1: Applications Problems 13 Through 20

Reminder: Use 3 decimal places.

13. Applied Industrial Technology
Dividend amount: $0.48
Current market value: $17
Dividend yield: _2.8%_

14. Hershey Chocolates
Dividend amount: $1.21
Current market value: $67
Dividend yield: _____

15. Alcan
Dividend amount: $0.60
Current market value: $35
Dividend yield: _____

16. Bassett Furniture
Dividend amount: $0.80
Current market value: $14
Dividend yield: _____

17. Eastman Kodak
Dividend amount: $1.80
Current market value: $31
Dividend yield: _____

18. Coca-Cola
Dividend amount: $0.72
Current market value: $50
Dividend yield: _____

19. Kellogg Foods
Dividend amount: $1.01
Current market value: $30
Dividend yield: _____

20. Wal-Mart
Dividend amount: $0.28
Current market value: $57
Dividend yield: _____

Group 2: Applications Problems 21 Through 28

Reminder: Use 2 decimal places.

21. Exxon Mobil
Current market value: $39
P–E ratio: 17
Per share earnings: _$2.29_

22. Microsoft
Current market value: $67
P–E ratio: 58
Per share earnings: _____

23. Kimberly Clark
Current market value: $59
P–E ratio: 18
Per share earnings: _____

24. Franklin Electric
Current market value: $81
P–E ratio: 19
Per share earnings: _____

25. Oneida Ltd.
Current market value: $12
P–E ratio: 31
Per share earnings: _____

26. Pep Boys
Current market value: $18
P–E ratio: 27
Per share earnings: _____

27. Home Depot
Current market value: $51
P–E ratio: 43
Per share earnings: _____

28. Chevron/Texaco
Current market value: $89
P–E ratio: 12
Per share earnings: _____

BUSINESS APPLICATIONS: WORKING WITH INVENTORY VALUATION

Business Situation

Joan Morgan, the accountant for Hill's Stereo and Video Shoppes, Inc., has been working on an improved inventory system. Joan estimates it cost the company $168,000 to physically count the merchandise in fourteen different stores throughout the United States. As she pointed out to top management, this cost is too high when each store's average inventory is only $276,500.

Inventory valuation—that is, the procedure used to determine the dollar amount of inventory available for sale—can be a time-consuming and expensive procedure for an ongoing business. There are two solutions to this problem. First, some firms physically count all merchandise in the store at least once a year. This method is called the *periodic* inventory method. Other companies maintain what is commonly called a *perpetual* inventory system. The perpetual method provides up-to-date inventory information at any time. When the perpetual system is used, business firms generally use an electronic cash register that is coupled to a computer to maintain perpetual inventory records.

Regardless of the method used to maintain inventory records, the accountant must take this information and calculate the total dollar value of inventory before financial statements can be completed. There are two widely used methods of determining the dollar value of inventory: (1) specific identification and (2) average cost. The following information will be used to illustrate each method.

Inventory for Stereo Television Model No. 698-ITB

Date of Purchase	Quantity	Unit Cost	Total Cost
Beginning inventory	5	$630	$ 3,150
April 23, 20XX	10	$660	$ 6,600
June 15, 20XX	8	$680	$ 5,440
August 18, 20XX	12	$710	$ 8,520
October 29, 20XX	6	$730	$ 4,380
	41		$28,090

Specific Identification Method

The *specific identification method,* as the name implies, is used where each item in a group of merchandise can be identified. Identification is based on a model number, serial number, date of purchase, or purchase price. This method is normally used where a company maintains perpetual inventory records at actual cost and where the number of individual sales for each item is small. Merchandise in this category is usually referred to as "big ticket" items, those that cost a lot of money, such as appliances, jewelry, fur coats, and automobiles.

■   **EXAMPLE**   Of seven televisions remaining at the end of a financial period, the specific identification inventory method indicated that three of the units had been purchased on April 23 at a cost of $660 each, two units had been purchased on August 18 at a cost of $710 each, and two units had been purchased on October 29 at a cost of $730 each. The accountant must determine the dollar value of the seven televisions still available for sale.

April 23, 20XX   3 @ $660 = $1,980
August 18, 20XX   2 @ $710 = $1,420
October 29, 20XX   2 @ $730 = $1,460
                   total cost = $4,860   ■

Average Cost Method

Unlike the specific identification method, the *average cost method* does not attempt to identify specific units that remain unsold. Instead, this method uses a *weighted average* for all remaining merchandise. The average is calculated by dividing the total cost of all merchandise by the total number of units purchased by the business firm during an accounting period.

■   **EXAMPLE**   If we use the information for the stereo televisions, the average cost method results in a total cost of $4,795.84 for the seven unsold televisions.

Step 1 $\text{average cost} = \dfrac{\text{total cost of all units}}{\text{total number of available units}}$

$\text{average cost} = \dfrac{\$28,090}{41}$

$\text{average cost} = \$685.12$

Step 2   total cost = number of units remaining $\times$ average unit cost

total cost =   7 $\times$ $685.12

total cost = $4,795.84   ■

Comparison of Inventory Methods

When choosing a method to value ending inventory, an accountant considers several factors. For example, the specific identification method is the most accurate method, but is normally used only with high-priced items. When individual items are inexpensive and there are many items, the average cost method is used. The average cost method is also accurate, since each individual unit is valued at a weighted average. Each inventory method results in a different total cost for ending inventory, as illustrated below.

Specific identification $4,860.00
Average cost $4,795.84

Try the example problem presented with each inventory method. Did you obtain the correct answers? If you did not obtain the correct answers, review the material in the preceding examples before trying to work the problems that follow. You may also want to review multiplication presented in Chapter 5 and division presented in Chapter 6.

Inventory Valuation:
Applications Problems 29 Through 40

29. _____

30. _____

31. $1,717.50

32. _____

Instructions	Machine Setting
1. In each problem, add the numbers in the quantity column. 2. In each problem, add the numbers in the total cost column. 3. Determine the total cost using the specific identification method and the average cost method for the following problems.	1. Set decimal control on 2. 2. Enter all decimals in the problem with the decimal key. 3. Set round-off switch in 5/4 position. 4. If your calculator has a memory, your machine will automatically add up individual answers when the specific identification method is used.

Group 1: Applications Problems 29 Through 32

Note: Assume that there are 210 blank video tape packages remaining in the Boston Video Shop.

Video Blank Tapes Model No. VHS—3 Pack			
Date of Purchase	Quantity	Unit Cost	Total Cost
Beginning Inventory	125	$7.50	$ 937.50
January 23, 20XX	250	$8.50	$2,125.00
April 20, 20XX	150	$8.75	$1,312.50
June 18, 20XX	100	$8.00	$ 800.00
September 30, 20XX	150	$7.50	$1,125.00
November 25, 20XX	130	$8.25	$1,072.50
	29. _____		30. _____

31. ____$1,717.50____   Specific Identification—100 units were purchased on April 20; 35 units were purchased on June 18; 75 units were purchased on September 30.

32. _____   Ending Inventory—Average Cost Method

Applications Problems

33. _____

34. _____

35. _____

36. _____

37. _____

38. _____

39. _____

40. _____

Group 2: Applications Problems 33 Through 36

Note: Assume that there are 30 cleaning kits remaining in the Boston Video Shop.

Video Recorder Cleaning Kits No. 39A			
Date of Purchase	Quantity	Unit Cost	Total Cost
Beginning Inventory	15	$11.50	$172.50
January 22, 20XX	10	$11.00	$110.00
March 10, 20XX	20	$10.75	$215.00
May 19, 20XX	35	$11.25	$393.75
July 29, 20XX	15	$12.25	$183.75
November 8, 20XX	10	$13.50	$135.00
	33. _____		34. _____

35. _____   Specific Identification—20 units were purchased January 22; 15 units were purchased March 10; 10 units were purchased July 29.

36. _____   Ending Inventory—Average Cost Method

Group 3: Applications Problems 37 Through 40

Note: Assume that there are 22 DVD players remaining in the Boston Video Shop.

Commercial DVD Players Model No. SY—40			
Date of Purchase	Quantity	Unit Cost	Total Cost
Beginning Inventory	15	$465.00	$6,975.00
February 12, 20XX	5	$485.50	$2,427.50
May 20, 20XX	5	$510.30	$2,551.50
July 2, 20XX	10	$520.00	$5,200.00
August 15, 20XX	5	$535.75	$2,678.75
October 28, 20XX	10	$650.00	$6,500.00
	37. _____		38. _____

39. _____   Specific Identification—15 units were purchased February 12; 7 units were purchased July 2; 10 units were purchased October 28.

40. _____   Ending Inventory—Average Cost Method

BUSINESS APPLICATIONS: CALCULATING FINANCIAL RATIOS

Business Situation

Sandra Garner opened her interior design business three years ago. The first two years she kept all the accounting records. During the third year, she decided that she was too busy to do everything, so she hired a certified public accountant (CPA). After the CPA kept the books for one accounting period, Sandra was given a current statement of financial position and an income statement. In addition, she also received some financial ratios that the CPA thought would help her manage her business more effectively.

A firm's statement of financial position and income statement (both discussed in Chapter 6) answer a variety of questions about the firm's ability to do business and stay in business, its profitability, its value as an investment, and its ability to repay its debts. Even more information can be obtained by using the information contained in a firm's financial statements to calculate financial ratios. A *financial ratio* is a number that shows the relationship between two elements on a firm's financial statements. Many different financial ratios can be formed, but in this section we examine three specific ratios—current ratio, net profit margin, and inventory turnover—that are particularly relevant for all businesses.

■   **EXAMPLE**   To help illustrate each of the three ratios, the following financial data are used.

Current assets	$160,500
Current liabilities	78,000
Net income after taxes	34,160
Net sales	485,000
Cost of goods sold	363,780
Average inventory	38,700 ■

Current ratio   A firm's *current ratio* is computed by dividing current assets by current liabilities. Based on the example data,

$$\text{current ratio} = \frac{\text{current assets}}{\text{current liabilities}} = \frac{\$160,500}{\$\ 78,000} = 2.06$$

This calculation means that this firm has $2.06 of current assets for every $1 of current liabilities. With a current ratio of 2.06, this firm should have no difficulty paying its current liabilities. *The average current ratio for all industries is 2.0, but it varies greatly from industry to industry.* A low current ratio (less than 2.0) can be improved by repaying current liabilities, by converting current liabilities to long-term liabilities, or by increasing the firm's cash balance by reducing dividend payments to stockholders.

Net profit margin *Net profit margin* is a financial ratio that is calculated by dividing net income after taxes by net sales. For the example data,

$$\text{net profit margin} = \frac{\text{net income after taxes}}{\text{net sales}} = \frac{\$\ 34,160}{\$485,000} = .07 = 7\%$$

The net profit margin indicates how effectively the firm is transforming sales into profits. Today, *the average net profit margin for all business firms is between 4 and 5 percent.* With a net profit margin of 7 percent, this firm is above average. A low net profit margin (less than 4 or 5 percent) can be increased by reducing expenses or by increasing sales.

Inventory turnover A firm's *inventory turnover* is the number of times the firm sells and replaces its inventory in one year. It is approximated by dividing the cost of goods sold in one year by the average value of the inventory. Based on the example data,

$$\text{inventory turnover} = \frac{\text{cost of goods sold}}{\text{average inventory}} = \frac{\$363,780}{\$\ 38,700} = 9.40$$

This firm sells and replaces its merchandise inventory 9.40 times each year, or about once every 39 days (365 days ÷ 9.40 = 39 days). *The average inventory turnover for all firms is about 9 times per year, but turnover rates vary widely from industry to industry.* A low inventory turnover (less than 9 times per year) can be improved by ordering merchandise in smaller quantities at more frequent intervals.

Try the sample problems for current ratio, net profit margin, and inventory turnover to see if you can obtain the correct answers.

Recommendation: If you did not obtain the correct answers, you may want to review the material on division presented in Chapter 6.

Financial Ratios: Applications Problems 41 Through 52

Instructions	*Machine Setting*
1. For each of the firms below, calculate a current ratio, net profit margin, and inventory turnover. 2. Beside each ratio calculation, indicate if this firm is above average, average, or below average.	1. Set decimal control on 2. 2. Set round-off switch in 5/4 position (if applicable).

Group 1: Applications Problems 41 Through 43

Exotic Pool Company			
Financial Data			
Current assets	$90,325	Net sales	$524,760
Current liabilities	$60,970	Cost of goods sold	$135,850
Net income after taxes	$67,430	Average inventory	$10,450

41. The current ratio is __1.48__

_____ above average
_____ average
__X__ below average

42. The net profit margin is _____

_____ above average
_____ average
_____ below average

43. The inventory turnover is _____

_____ above average
_____ average
_____ below average

Group 2: Applications Problems 44 Through 46

Boston Leather & Suitcase, Inc.			
Financial Data			
Current assets	$375,900	Net sales	$3,880,850
Current liabilities	$145,200	Cost of goods sold	$2,328,000
Net income after taxes	$135,800	Average inventory	$297,142

44. The current ratio is _____

_____ above average
_____ average
_____ below average

45. The net profit margin is _____

_____ above average
_____ average
_____ below average

46. The inventory turnover is _____

_____ above average
_____ average
_____ below average

41. __1.48/below__

42. _____

43. _____

44. _____

45. _____

46. _____

**Applications
Problems**

47. _____

48. _____

49. _____

50. _____

51. _____

52. _____

Group 3: Applications Problems 47 Through 49

All-American Woodworking, Inc.			
Financial Data			
Current assets	$149,500	Net sales	$1,895,000
Current liabilities	$48,513	Cost of goods sold	$793,905
Net income after taxes	$99,487	Average inventory	$75,610

47. The current ratio is _____

_____ above average
_____ average
_____ below average

48. The net profit margin is _____

_____ above average
_____ average
_____ below average

49. The inventory turnover is _____

_____ above average
_____ average
_____ below average

Group 4: Applications Problems 50 Through 52

Barton Manufacturing Company			
Financial Data			
Current assets	$19,540	Net sales	$875,200
Current liabilities	$11,555	Cost of goods sold	$410,400
Net income after taxes	$24,511	Average inventory	$14,750

50. The current ratio is _____

_____ above average
_____ average
_____ below average

51. The net profit margin is _____

_____ above average
_____ average
_____ below average

52. The inventory turnover is _____

_____ above average
_____ average
_____ below average

BUSINESS APPLICATIONS: EXAMINING CORPORATE TAXATION

Business Situation

Future Technology, Inc., is a small, rapidly growing corporation that produces hardware components used in personal computers. The company has been in business for three years. The first two years the company lost money, but the third year it earned a profit of $425,000. Now the accountant must calculate the amount of corporate tax and then send a check to the federal government.

A *corporation* is an artificial being, invisible, intangible, and existing only in contemplation of the law. In other words, a *corporation* is an artificial person created by law with most of the legal rights of a real person. These rights include the right to start and operate a business, to own or sell property, to borrow money, to sue or be sued, and to enter into binding contracts. The corporation is also responsible for paying federal income tax on any profit it earns.

Corporations pay federal income tax only on their *taxable income,* which is the amount of *profit* that remains after deducting all legal business expenses from net sales. Current corporate tax rates are illustrated in Table 8.1.

TABLE 8.1 Corporate Tax Rates

Over–	But not over–	Tax is:	Of the amount over–
$0	$50,000	15%	$0
50,000	75,000	$7,500 + 25%	50,000
75,000	100,000	13,750 + 34%	75,000
100,000	335,000	22,250 + 39%	100,000
335,000	10,000,000	113,900 + 34%	335,000
10,000,000	15,000,000	3,400,000 + 35%	10,000,000
15,000,000	18,333,333	5,150,000 + 38%	15,000,000
18,333,333	—	35%	0

As illustrated in the example below, a number of steps are required to determine the tax liability for Future Technology, Inc.

■ **EXAMPLE** In the third year of operation, Future Technology, Inc., had taxable income of $425,000. As a result, it must pay taxes that total $144,500.

Step 1 In the tax table (Table 8.1), locate the line for taxable income that is over $335,000, but not over $10 million.

The tax is $113,900 *plus* 34 percent of the excess over the first $335,000.

Step 2 Determine the dollar excess over $335,000.

$425,000
− 335,000
$ 90,000

Step 3 Multiply the excess amount from Step 2 ($90,000) by the tax rate in Step 1 (34 percent).

$90,000 × .34 = $30,600

Step 4 To determine the total tax amount, add the base amount from Step 1 ($113,900) to the additional tax amount from Step 3 ($30,600).

$113,900
+   30,600
$144,500 ■

Note that the tax rate used in Step 3 (34 percent) has been converted to a decimal. This step may be omitted if you use your calculator's percent (%) key. Try the sample problem above on your calculator to see if you can obtain the correct answer.

Recommendation: If you did not obtain the correct answer for the sample problem, determine if the difficulty is multiplication, addition, or subtraction. For problems with multiplication, review the material in Chapter 5. For problems with addition or subtraction, review the material in Chapter 4.

Applications
Problems

53. _____

54. _____

55. _____

56. ____$176,800____

Corporate Taxation:
Applications Problems 53 Through 68

Instructions	*Machine Setting*
1. All problems for this assignment are based on current tax rates at publication. (Use Table 8.1.) 2. Determine the dollar amount of corporate tax for the following problems.	1. Set decimal control on 2. 2. Enter all decimals in the problem with the decimal key. 3. Set round-off switch in 5/4 position (if applicable). 4. Either convert the tax rate to a decimal or use your calculator's percent key.

Group 1: Applications Problems 53 Through 56

All-American Manufacturing

Taxable Income = $520,000

Step 1 In the tax table (Table 8.1), locate the line for taxable income that is over $335,000, but not over $10 million.

53. _____

Step 2 Determine the dollar excess over $335,000.

54. _____

Step 3 Multiply the excess amount from Step 2 by the tax rate in Step 1 (34 percent).

55. _____

Step 4 To determine the total tax amount, add the base amount from Step 1 to the additional tax amount from Step 3.

56. $176,800 _____

Applications
Problems

Group 2: Applications Problems 57 Through 60

57. _____

58. _____

59. _____

60. _____

Columbia Tool & Die

Taxable Income = $1,075,000

Step 1 In the tax table (Table 8.1),
locate the line for taxable income
that is over $335,000, but not
over $10 million.   57. _____

Step 2 Determine the dollar excess
over $335,000.   58. _____

Step 3 Multiply the excess amount
from Step 2 by the tax rate in Step 1
(34 percent).   59. _____

Step 4 To determine the total tax
amount, add the base amount from
Step 1 to the additional tax amount
from Step 3.   60. _____

Group 3: Applications Problems 61 Through 64

61. _____

62. _____

63. _____

64. _____

Jackson Pest Control, Inc.

Taxable Income = $63,000

Step 1   In the tax table (Table 8.1),
locate the line for taxable income
that is over $50,000, but not over
$75,000.   61. _____

Step 2   Determine the dollar excess
over $50,000.   62. _____

Step 3   Multiply the excess amount
from Step 2 by the tax rate in
Step 1 (25 percent).   63. _____

Step 4   To determine the total tax
amount, add the base amount from
Step 1 to the additional tax amount
from Step 3.   64. _____

Applications Problems

65. _____

66. _____

67. _____

68. _____

Group 4: Applications Problems 65 Through 68

New Dimensions Furniture, Inc.

Taxable Income = $610,000

Step 1 In the tax table (Table 8.1), locate the line for taxable income that is over $335,000, but not over $10 million.

65. _____

Step 2 Determine the dollar excess over $335,000.

66. _____

Step 3 Multiply the excess amount from Step 2 by the tax rate in Step 1 (34 percent).

67. _____

Step 4 To determine the total tax amount, add the base amount from Step 1 to the additional tax amount from Step 3.

68. _____

BUSINESS APPLICATIONS: DETERMINING INSURANCE PREMIUMS

Business Situation

Since graduating from high school eighteen months ago, Jill Dorsey has worked for the Equity Life Insurance Company. Six months ago she received her first promotion and a $200-a-month salary increase. Her new job involves talking to customers and determining the premiums that they pay for different types of life insurance coverage.

An insurance *premium* is the fee that the insurance company charges for providing the coverage specified in the insurance policy. Premiums depend primarily on the age and sex of the insured and on the type of life insurance.

As illustrated in Table 8.2, the older a person is, the higher the premium is. On the average, older people are less likely to survive each year than younger people. Also, females generally pay lower premiums than males of the same age because (on the average) they live longer.

TABLE 8.2 Annual Premiums for $1,000 of Life Insurance

Age	Male	Female	Age	Male	Female
18	$4.90	$3.43	34	$ 5.60	$ 3.92
19	4.93	3.45	35	5.79	4.05
20	4.95	3.47	36	6.05	4.24
21	4.97	3.48	37	6.40	4.48
22	4.99	3.49	38	6.78	4.75
23	5.01	3.51	39	7.15	5.01
24	5.03	3.52	40	7.65	5.36
25	5.06	3.54	41	8.16	5.71
26	5.08	3.56	42	8.58	6.01
27	5.10	3.57	43	9.06	6.34
28	5.13	3.59	44	9.61	6.73
29	5.15	3.61	45	10.20	7.14
30	5.17	3.62	46	10.81	7.57
31	5.22	3.65	47	11.65	8.16
32	5.34	3.74	48	12.55	8.79
33	5.46	3.82	49	13.50	9.45
			50	14.55	10.19

The following example illustrates the steps for determining the annual premium for a life insurance policy for a 30-year-old female. Refer to Table 8.2.

■ **EXAMPLE** Determine the annual premium for an $85,000 life insurance policy. The insured is a 30-year-old female.

Step 1 The policy amount must be divided by $1,000 because the dollar amounts presented in Table 8.2 are based on what it would cost to purchase $1,000 of insurance coverage.

$85,000 ÷ $1,000 = 85

**Applications
Problems**

69. _____ **$8.58** _____

70. _____

71. _____

72. _____

73. _____

Step 2 Using Table 8.2, locate the 30 in the Age column; then go across to the Female column. The number in this column, $3.62, is the annual payment amount to purchase $1,000 of insurance coverage.

Step 3 Multiply 85, the number of $1,000 units in an $85,000 policy (Step 1), by $3.62, the annual premium amount for $1,000 of coverage (Step 2).

$85 \times \$3.62 = \$307.70$ ■

Work the example problem to review this concept. Did you obtain the correct answer?

Recommendation: If you did not obtain the correct answer for the sample problem, determine whether the difficulty is in Step 1, Step 2, or Step 3. For problems with Step 1, review the material on division presented in Chapter 6. For problems with Step 2, review the material presented in this business application. For problems with Step 3, review the material on multiplication presented in Chapter 5.

Insurance Premiums:
Applications Problems 69 Through 83

Instructions	*Machine Setting*
1. Using the life insurance premium table (Table 8.2) presented in this business application, determine the cost factor for a $1,000 policy for problems in Group 1. 2. Using Table 8.2, determine the cost factor for a $1,000 policy and the annual premium amount for each insurance policy presented in Group 2 problems.	1. Set decimal control on 2. 2. Enter all decimals in the problem with the decimal key. 3. Set round-off switch in 5/4 position (if applicable).

Group 1: Applications Problems 69 Through 73

Reminder: Find the cost factor for Group 1 problems.

Male/Female	Age	Cost Factor per $1,000
Male	42	69. _____ $8.58 _____
Female	23	70. _____
Female	39	71. _____
Male	27	72. _____
Female	33	73. _____

Group 2: Applications Problems 74 Through 83

Reminder: Find the cost factor and annual premium amount for Group 2 problems.

Coverage Amount	Male/ Female	Age	Cost Factor per $1,000		Annual Premium Amount	
$ 25,000	Female	32	74.a.	$3.74	b.	$93.50
$105,000	Male	29	75.a.		b.	
$ 45,900	Male	46	76.a.		b.	
$150,000	Female	26	77.a.		b.	
$ 20,000	Male	18	78.a.		b.	
$ 34,700	Male	41	79.a.		b.	
$175,000	Female	37	80.a.		b.	
$ 86,300	Female	48	81.a.		b.	
$160,900	Male	25	82.a.		b.	
$ 45,800	Female	34	83.a.		b.	

Applications Problems

74a. _____ $3.74 _____

74b. _____ $93.50 _____

75a. _____

75b. _____

76a. _____

76b. _____

77a. _____

77b. _____

78a. _____

78b. _____

79a. _____

79b. _____

80a. _____

80b. _____

81a. _____

81b. _____

82a. _____

82b. _____

83a. _____

83b. _____

BUSINESS APPLICATIONS: WORKING WITH INSTALLMENT LOANS

Business Situation

For the past six months, Jack and Betty Richards have been looking for a new home. They finally found a three-bedroom brick in a new subdivision that they both thought was just perfect. To finance their new home, they applied for a $92,500 home mortgage at Farm and Home Savings. The loan officer who interviewed them said that they were qualified for a thirty-year loan at 7½ percent interest. The loan officer also said that the monthly payments required to pay the principal and interest on the loan would be $642.

Purchases like homes, automobiles, furniture, and appliances cost more than most people can afford to pay at one time. As a result, most consumers use an installment loan to obtain the money required to purchase these expensive items. An *installment loan* is a loan that is repaid in a series of payments. The dollar amount of the monthly payment required to repay both principal and interest can be determined by using a monthly payment chart, like the one shown in Table 8.3. This table gives the monthly payment amount required to pay off a $1,000 loan over a 5-, 10-, 15-, 20-, 25-, or 30-year period. The interest rates presented in this table range from 7 percent to 12 percent.

TABLE 8.3 Monthly Payment Chart (*Payment Amounts for Each $1,000 of Loan Value*)

Time Period	Interest Rate										
	7%	*7½%*	*8%*	*8½%*	*9%*	*9½%*	*10%*	*10½%*	*11%*	*11½%*	*12%*
5	$19.76	$20.01	$20.26	$20.51	$20.76	$21.01	$21.25	$21.50	$21.75	$22.00	$22.25
10	11.55	11.83	12.11	12.39	12.67	12.94	13.22	13.50	13.78	14.06	14.35
15	8.91	9.22	9.53	9.84	10.15	10.45	10.75	11.06	11.37	11.69	12.01
20	7.64	7.98	8.32	8.66	9.00	9.33	9.66	9.99	10.33	10.67	11.02
25	6.96	7.32	7.68	8.04	8.40	8.74	9.09	9.45	9.81	10.17	10.54
30	6.56	6.94	7.31	7.68	8.05	8.41	8.78	9.15	9.53	9.91	10.29

The following example illustrates the procedure used to determine a monthly payment for an installment loan. Refer to Table 8.3.

■ **EXAMPLE** Determine the monthly payment for a real estate loan of $92,500. The purchaser—Jack and Betty Richards—agrees to repay the loan over a thirty-year period of time. They also agree to pay 7½ percent interest.

Step 1 The loan amount must be divided by $1,000 because the dollar amounts in Table 8.3 are based on a $1,000 loan.

$92,500 ÷ 1,000 = 92.5

Step 2 Locate the 30 in the Time Period column, then go across to the 7½% column. The number in this column, $6.94, is the table factor required to repay a $1,000 loan over a thirty-year period.

Step 3   Multiply 92.5, the number of $1,000 units in the loan (Step 1), by $6.94, the table factor from Table 8.3 (Step 2).

$92.5 \times \$6.94 = \$641.95$ ∎

Work the sample problem to review this concept. Did you obtain the correct answer?

> **Recommendation:**   If you did not obtain the correct answer for the sample problem, determine whether the difficulty is in Step 1, Step 2, or Step 3. For problems with Step 1, review the material on division presented in Chapter 6. For problems with Step 2, review the material presented in this business application. For problems with Step 3, review the material on multiplication presented in Chapter 5.

Installment Loans:
Applications Problems 84 Through 98

Instructions	Machine Setting
1. Using the monthly payment chart (Table 8.3) presented in this business application, determine the table factor for a $1,000 loan for problems in Group 1. 2. Using Table 8.3, determine the table factor and the monthly payment amount for each loan presented in Group 2 problems.	1. Set decimal control on 2. 2. Enter all decimals in the problem with the decimal key. 3. Set round-off switch in 5/4 position (if applicable).

Group 1: Applications Problems 84 Through 88

Reminder: Find the table factor for Group 1 problems.

Loan Amount	Interest Rate	Term of Loan	Table Factor
$1,000	9½%	20 years	84. ___$9.33___
$1,000	7½%	5 years	85. _____
$1,000	7%	10 years	86. _____
$1,000	10%	30 years	87. _____
$1,000	8½%	25 years	88. _____

84. ___$9.33___

85. _____

86. _____

87. _____

88. _____

Applications Problems

89a. _____
89b. _____
90a. _____
90b. _____
91a. _____
91b. _____
92a. _____
92b. _____
93a. _____
93b. _____
94a. _____
94b. _____
95a. _____
95b. _____
96a. _____
96b. _____
97a. _____
97b. _____
98a. _____
98b. _____

Group 2: Applications Problems 89 Through 98

Reminder: Find the table factor and monthly payment amount for Group 2 problems.

Loan Amount	Interest Rate	Term of Loan	Table Factor	Monthly Payment Amount
$115,875	8½%	10 years	89.a. _____	b. _____
$ 79,450	7½%	10 years	90.a. _____	b. _____
$225,000	9½%	20 years	91.a. _____	b. _____
$145,780	7%	30 years	92.a. _____	b. _____
$ 34,600	9%	15 years	93.a. _____	b. _____
$ 12,230	8%	5 years	94.a. _____	b. _____
$208,000	11%	15 years	95.a. _____	b. _____
$ 5,620	9½%	5 years	96.a. _____	b. _____
$ 15,890	12%	10 years	97.a. _____	b. _____
$178,350	9%	20 years	98.a. _____	b. _____

SELF-EVALUATION: PART I

Applications Posttest

INSTRUCTION	MACHINE SETTING
1. Complete the following problems in eight minutes or less with one or no incorrect answers.	1. Set decimal control on 2 or add-mode. 2. Set round-off switch in 5/4 position.

1. Calculate the average, median, and mode for the profit amounts listed below. Profits for 1999 were $8,890, 2000 profits were $10,349, 2001 profits were $8,890, 2002 profits were $9,430, and 2003 profits were $11,567.

   a. What is the average?

   b. What is the median?

   c. What is the mode?

2. Determine the current dividend yield for the problems below.

Dividend Amount	Current Market Value	Dividend Yield
$1.74	$29.88	a. _____
$2.10	$33.63	b. _____
$3.35	$55.25	c. _____

3. Determine the per share earnings for the problems below.

Current Market Value	P–E Ratio	Per Share Earnings
$50.13	19	a. _____
$49.75	12	b. _____
$75.13	17	c. _____

4. For the following problem, determine the total cost for each inventory method discussed in this chapter. *Assume 20 units remain at the end of an accounting period.*

Date of Purchase	Quantity	Unit Cost	Total Cost
Beginning inventory	15	$ 9.75	$146.25
January 23, 20XX	10	$10.00	$100.00
January 31, 20XX	5	$11.00	$ 55.00
February 4, 20XX	10	$12.00	$120.00
March 1, 20XX	15	$11.75	$176.25
	55		$597.50

   a. Specific identification method (5 units were purchased January 23; 5 units were purchased January 31; 10 units were purchased March 1)

   b. Average cost method

1a. _____

1b. _____

1c. _____

2a. _____

2b. _____

2c. _____

3a. _____

3b. _____

3c. _____

4a. _____

4b. _____

Self-Evaluation:
Part I

5a. _____

5b. _____

5c. _____

6a. _____

6b. _____

6c. _____

6d. _____

5. Based on the assumptions below, calculate a current ratio, a net profit margin, and an inventory turnover. Also, indicate if this firm is above average, average, or below average.

Direct Computer Sales, Inc.
Financial Data

Current assets	$110,240	Net sales	$1,264,815
Current liabilities	$76,027	Cost of goods sold	$758,889
Net income after taxes	$85,375	Average inventory	$84,321

---

a. The current ratio is _____

_____ above average
_____ average
_____ below average

b. The net profit margin is _____

_____ above average
_____ average
_____ below average

c. The inventory turnover is _____

_____ above average
_____ average
_____ below average

6. Calculate the corporate tax amount for the following corporation. *Refer to Table 8.1.*

All-Electric Company, Inc.

Taxable Income = $517,000

Step 1   In the tax table (Table 8.1), locate the line for taxable income that is over $335,000, but not over $10 million.

a. _____

Step 2   Determine the dollar excess over $335,000.

b. _____

Step 3   Multiply the excess amount from Step 2 by the tax rate in Step 1 (34 percent).

c. _____

Step 4   To determine the total tax amount, add the base amount from Step 1 to the additional tax amount from Step 3.

d. _____

7. Determine the annual premium amount for the life insurance policies listed below. *Refer to Table 8.2.*

Coverage Amount	Male/Female	Age	Annual Premium Amount
$110,000	Female	34	**a.** _____
$ 69,500	Male	42	**b.** _____
$125,600	Female	28	**c.** _____

7a. _____

7b. _____

7c. _____

8. Calculate the monthly payment amount for the installment loans presented below. *Refer to Table 8.3.*

Loan Amount	Interest Rate	Term of Loan	Monthly Payment Amount
$105,000	9½%	15 years	**a.** _____
$ 46,500	7½%	20 years	**b.** _____
$ 26,300	8%	10 years	**c.** _____

8a. _____

8b. _____

8c. _____

RECOMMENDATION: If you were able to complete Part I of the Self-Evaluation Applications Posttest in eight minutes or less with no more than one incorrect answer, proceed to Part II of the Self-Evaluation. If you did not satisfactorily complete Part I of the Self-Evaluation Applications Posttest, take it again, trying for the recommended level. If you are still not able to attain the recommended level, talk with your instructor.

Self-Evaluation:
Part II

1a. _____

1b. _____

1c. _____

1d. _____

2a. _____

2b. _____

3. _____

4a. _____

4b. _____

SELF-EVALUATION: PART II

Critical Thinking Problems

INSTRUCTION	MACHINE SETTING
1. Complete the following problems with one or no incorrect answers.	1. Set decimal control on 2 or add-mode. 2. Set round-off switch in 5/4 position (if applicable).

1. Bob's telephone expenses for the first five months of the year are as follows: January—$56.78; February—$46.70; March—$66.78; April—$56.78; and May—$72.11.

   a. What is the total telephone expense for the first five months?

   b. What is the arithmetic mean?

   c. What is the median?

   d. What is the mode?

2. Peter Morales just received his quarterly dividend check from General Electric Corporation. The check was for $36. Peter owns 50 shares of this stock. The current price quotation for General Electric is $41.13.

   a. What is the dividend amount for one share of General Electric stock?

   b. What is the current dividend yield for the General Electric Corporation?

3. Marston Manufacturing's stock is selling for $75.25 per share. You look in the newspaper and find that the company has a P–E ratio of 16. What is the amount of the per share earnings?

4. Hi-Tech Audio Electronics is an exclusive retail store that specializes in stereo equipment for the discriminating listener. One item that they carry is a compact disc (CD) player that is state of the art. Inventory data for this item are presented below.

Date of Purchase	Quantity	Unit Cost	Total Cost
Beginning inventory	10	$220	$2,200
February 15, 20XX	15	$195	$2,925
May 2, 20XX	8	$200	$1,600
September 20, 20XX	20	$170	$3,400
November 25, 20XX	15	$180	$2,700

   a. Using the specific identification method, what is the dollar value of the inventory if 18 CD players remain at the end of the year? Assume that 5 CD players were purchased on February 15, 7 CD players were purchased on May 2, and 6 CD players were purchased on November 25.

   b. Using the average cost method, what is the dollar value of the inventory if 18 CD players remain at the end of the year?

5. In a discussion with your supervisor, you learn that your company has current assets of $88,640 and current liabilities of $40,290.

   a. What is the current ratio for your firm?

   b. Is this ratio above average, average, or below average?

5a. _____

5b. _____

6. In 2002, the Digitech Corporation had profits of $456,500 on net sales of $6,340,277. In 2003, the company had profits of $629,541 on net sales of $10,854,155.

   a. What is the firm's net profit margin for 2002?

   b. What is the firm's net profit margin for 2003?

6a. _____

6b. _____

7. As the owner of the Green Thumb Nursery, you are concerned that your inventory isn't selling fast enough. Your accountant tells you that last year your cost of goods sold was $77,452. During the same accounting period, your average inventory was $15,490.

   a. What is the inventory turnover for the Green Thumb Nursery?

   b. Is this turnover above average, average, or below average?

7a. _____

7b. _____

8. Last year Atlantic Flooring and Carpet Company earned taxable income of $612,400. What is the dollar amount of corporate tax that this corporation must pay? *Refer to Table 8.1.*

8. _____

9. Jackie Jensen just sold Bart Bridges a $100,000 term life insurance policy. Bart is 33 years old. What is the dollar amount of the annual premium? *Refer to Table 8.2.*

9. _____

10. Patty and Joe Washington applied for a $62,500 loan. The money will be used to start a small manufacturing business in Detroit, Michigan. Your boss—the loan officer who approved the loan—asked you to determine the monthly payment required to repay this loan in five years. The interest rate for this loan is 11 percent. What is the monthly payment amount? *Refer to Table 8.3.*

10. _____

RECOMMENDATION: If you were able to complete Part II of the Self-Evaluation with no more than one incorrect answer, you have satisfactorily completed this chapter. You are now ready to progress to Chapter 9. If you did not satisfactorily complete Part II of the Self-Evaluation, you may want to review the material presented in the business applications sections of this chapter.

Woodside Apartments: A Simulation

INTRODUCTION

"Welcome to Woodside—a friendly, total living environment!" The above statement catches your eye as you browse through a brochure for Woodside Apartments. With the swimming pool, trees and park-like setting, ample parking, and well-maintained buildings, Woodside would be a nice place to live.

Yet you are not interested in leasing an apartment. You are applying for an accounting/clerical job. Last week you noticed the following want-ad in the newspaper.

> Wanted—reliable, energetic worker to perform clerical and accounting activities four days a week for an 80-unit apartment complex in the North Dallas area. The applicant must be neat and well-organized and possess the ability to learn a proven management system. Salary negotiable. If interested, call 972-690-3021.

You did call for an appointment and talked to Lucy Bello, the manager for Woodside. Over the phone, she explained that the apartment complex is owned by three partners who own five other apartment complexes in the Dallas–Ft. Worth area. Mr. Martin, one of the owners, is active in the management of this complex. In fact, he is responsible for interviewing and hiring all employees. She also explains that he is looking for an employee to perform general clerical and accounting tasks. The person in this position must be able to work with:

1. Checks and bank deposits
2. Rent ledger forms
3. Rent audits
4. Payroll registers
5. Invoices from suppliers
6. Bank reconciliations
7. Accounting statements and financial analyses

Of course, there are other jobs that must be completed on a day-to-day basis, but this should give you a rough idea of what is involved. Ms. Bello asks if you're interested in applying for the job. You indicate that you are interested, and she agrees to mail an application for employment. She also sets up an appointment with Mr. Martin for a job interview.

OBJECTIVE

The Woodside Apartments Simulation is designed to let you gain practical "on-the-job" experience in the classroom.

Woodside Apartments is a hypothetical business that has six employees. The people involved are

Employee	Position
Jack Martin	Owner
Lucy Bello	Manager
Jo Appleton	Maintenance Worker
Alex Farmington	Maintenance Worker
Mike Benton	Maintenance Worker

You are the sixth employee, with responsibility for day-to-day clerical and accounting activities.

Each set of job instructions is divided into two parts. First, individual transactions are described. Then detailed instructions are provided. All necessary forms are provided and may be completed with a calculator or by using the Microsoft Excel Software program. *Check with your instructor to determine which method should be used to complete the required forms.*

THE EMPLOYMENT APPLICATION

Today the employment application arrived in the mail (see Exhibit 9.1). Answer all questions to the best of your ability. Often this form is filled out while waiting to see the interviewer. The fact that Ms. Bello mailed the application form to you should enable you to do a more thorough job of completing it.

Detailed Instructions

A good application should capture the employer's attention. It should be a concise and upbeat summary of your educational background, work experience, and career goals. It should include any special skills or talents you possess. It may include personal references. If you include references, make sure you have the permission of the people you list. The most important feature of your application should be that it presents essential information about you in a clear, concise manner. Make sure all information is correct. In short, put your best foot forward. A cover letter is normally included if the application is mailed to the prospective employer. You may also want to include a resume if the application does not provide enough space to include the information that you feel is important.

Job Completed ☐

EXHIBIT 9.1 Employment Application for Woodside Apartments

WOODSIDE APARTMENTS
Application for Employment

Personal Information

	Social Security
Date	Number

Name
_____ Last _____ First _____ Middle

Present Address
_____ Street _____ City _____ State _____ Zip

Permanent Address
_____ Street _____ City _____ State _____ Zip

Phone No. _____ Own Home _____ Rent

If related to anyone in our employ, _____ Referred
state name and department _____ by

Employment Desired

	Date you	Salary
Position	can start	desired

Are you employed now? _____ If so may we inquire of your present employer

Ever applied to this company before? _____ Where _____ When

Education	Name and Location of School	Years Attended	Date Graduated	Subjects Studied
High School				
College				
Trade, Business or Correspondence School				

Subjects of special study or special skills _____

What foreign languages do you speak fluently? _____

Activities other than religious (civic, athletic, fraternal, etc.) _____

(Continued on other side)

Application for Employment

Name:_____

_____

EXHIBIT 9.1 Continued

Former Employers (List below last four employers, starting with last one first.)

Date Month and Year	Name and Address of Employer	Salary	Position	Reason for Leaving
From ___				
To ___				
From ___				
To ___				
From ___				
To ___				
From ___				
To ___				

References: Give below the names of three persons not related to you, whom you have known at least one year.

Name	Address	Business	Years Acquainted
1			
2			
3			

In case of emergency notify

Name	Address	Phone No.

I authorize investigation of all statements contained in this application. I understand that misrepresentation or omission of facts called for is cause for dismissal. Further, I understand and agree that my employment is for no definite period and may, regardless of the date of payment of my wages and salary, be terminated at any time without any previous notice.

Date _____ Signature _____

Do Not Write Below This Line

Interviewed by _____ Date _____

Remarks: _____
_____
_____

THE INTERVIEW PROCESS

With application in hand, you are now ready for the job interview. Mr. Martin, the manager and part owner of Woodside Apartments, is tied up on the phone. Ms. Bello asks you to have a seat and tells you he will be with you shortly. As you sit in the outer office, many thoughts are racing through your mind. The best application can only be an introduction. The job interview is usually the deciding factor in the hiring process. It is up to you to prepare for the interview, so keep the following hints in mind.

1. Do your homework. Research the company and be ready to ask questions. Know why you want the job and what you believe you can offer.

2. View the session as a two-way conversation, not strictly a question-and-answer situation. Be yourself and don't hesitate to volunteer information.

3. Pay attention to your appearance. This includes not only the way you dress but also how you present yourself. Interviewers notice an applicant's eye contact, hand-shake, and grooming just as they notice academic records and work experience.

4. Emphasize the positive. The interviewer may skip some points that you feel are important to the position. Not all interviewers are skilled in focusing on important areas. It is up to you to present your strengths.

A distinguished-looking man steps out of his office, walks over to your chair, and introduces himself as Mr. Martin. He asks you to come in and have a seat. Twenty-five minutes later the interview is over. He must be interested because he asks you to take a short employment test.

Detailed Instructions

Complete the ten problems on the Employment Test in six minutes or less with zero or one incorrect answer—See Exhibit 9.2. The six minute time limit includes time for recording your answers below each problem.

EXHIBIT 9.2 Employment Test for Woodside Apartments

WOODSIDE APARTMENTS

Employment Test

Start Time_____

1. 1,323.61	2. 523.90	3. 3.63	4. 1,453.83	5. 4,013.53
44.79	5.62	2,775.40	78.11	451.45
1.56	.56	71.29	600.36	1.81
352.81	2,259.00	455.92	1.58	49.98
788.34	.51	4,672.61	4.72	67.80
3,679.03	567.92	31.89	6.90	1.15
50.06	1,580.20	7.88	27.13	7,893.05
800.10	66.39	851.39	3,781.76	83.54
6,227.76	900.45	1,670.43	86.70	113.02
1.38	47.80	90.10	558.74	522.80

6. 428.75	7. 6,700.83	8. 65.70	9. 1,140.30	10. 34.85
37.89	289.11	165.20	560.02	1,356.78
3,671.69	54.30	6.50	981.39	486.30
4.80	.99	23.50	6,333.62	79.10
.31	500.32	2,997.64	200.51	6.23
1,448.20	1,530.81	602.56	411.28	2,800.47
38.60	29.75	14.02	89.98	724.52
9.71	.88	3,900.36	1,299.86	48.04
123.60	200.57	404.29	54.82	1.56
325.32	.69	638.22	6.78	265.40

Number Right_____

Finish Time_____

Number of Minutes_____

Name:_____

_____

GOOD NEWS!

Today is Friday, October 28, 20XX. The phone rings and Mr. Martin is on the other end of the line. As the tension builds, he asks if you can report to work next Monday. Without hesitation and even before the fact sinks in that he is offering you a job, you reply, "Certainly." After a short conversation, he tells you that both Ms. Bello and he are looking forward to working with you at Woodside and that they will see you next Monday. The job is yours!

DAY 1

As you walk from the parking lot to the leasing office, there are many thoughts rushing through your mind. The grounds and buildings are pleasant and well maintained, and this looks like a good place to work. Yet you never know—especially the first day. Probably the only way to find the answers to your questions is to walk through the office door and go to work. Good luck!

JOB 1

Forms 1 and 2

Transaction

Today is October 31, your first day on the job. Ms. Bello, the office manager, asks you to complete the rent ledger form for the last two days. This form helps account for all monies and checks received during a specific time period. All information needed to complete this ledger (form 2) is contained in interoffice memo 132 (form 1). When finished, proceed to the next job.

Detailed Instructions

The rent ledger form provides a number of columns to record different types of payments. Each tenant's entry should be itemized in the proper columns. Then the total received from each tenant should be recorded in column 7. Finally, it is necessary to add the individual dollar amounts in columns 1–7 and place the totals at the bottom of the rent ledger form before proceeding to the next job.

Job Completed ☐

Procedure Using Excel

Open form 02 from the Student Data Disk. Post all information from form 01 into the appropriate columns in the Excel spreadsheet on form 02. Use the right arrow key to move forward and the down arrow key to move to the next line. Dollar signs are not required when entering dollar amounts.

JOB 2

Forms 2 and 3

Transaction

It is now necessary to check the accuracy of your work by completing a rent audit (form 3).

Detailed Instructions

Woodside Apartments uses a rent audit form to ensure the accuracy of the rent ledger. Individual column totals must be transferred from the ledger to the audit form. It is now possible to add the individual totals and compare the answer with the total for column 7 on the rent ledger form. If the two answers do not agree, you have made a mistake and it must be found and corrected.

Job Completed ☐

Procedure Using Excel

Open form 03 from the Student Data Disk. Using the information from form 02, complete the Rent Audit Form. Use the down arrow key to move to the next line.

JOB 3

Forms 1 and 4

Transaction

Your next job for Woodside Apartments involves making the weekly bank deposit. For information needed to complete this job, refer to interoffice memo 132 (form 1).

Detailed Instructions

To complete a bank deposit form, it is necessary to list checks by the name of the tenant from whom the check was received. Once the checks are recorded, it is necessary to add all entries to determine the total for the bank deposit form.

Job Completed ☐

Procedure Using Excel

Open form 04 from the Student Data Disk. Complete the bank deposit by listing the checks individually. Use the right arrow key and the down arrow key to move forward to the next cell or down to the next row.

JOB 4

Forms 5, 6, and 7

Transaction

Yesterday Ms. Bello received three invoices from Woodside's suppliers. She asks you to check the extensions, series discounts, and cash discount on each invoice. If you should find a mistake, draw one line through the mistake and recalculate the total for the remainder of the invoice. Write all corrected entries in small numbers above the original amounts.

Detailed Instructions

This job seems very similar to one of the business applications you completed in your business machines class. You may want to review the material on discounts and invoices in your textbook.

     When verifying the total for each invoice, you must first multiply the quantity of each item purchased by the unit price. Second, you must work with the series discounts. Finally, you must verify the cash discount and invoice total amount.

Job Completed ☐

JOB 5

Form 8/Checks 431 and 432

Transaction

You just received interoffice memo 133 (form 8) from Jack Martin, one of the owners of Woodside Apartments. In the memo, he asks that you issue checks to two different suppliers. All needed information is contained in the memo.

Detailed Instructions

Notice that a deposit has already been recorded on the stub for check 431. This deposit must be added to the beginning balance before this check can be subtracted.

     Begin with check 431. Be sure to verify the dollar amount on each check with the amount in Mr. Martin's memo. As the accounting clerk, you are authorized to sign each check. You must also complete each check stub. Some bankers make the following suggestion:

> Complete your work on the check stub before actually writing the check. This avoids a situation where someone completes a check, forgets to record it, and can't remember the amount or to whom the check was given.

Job Completed ☐

Procedure Using Excel

Open check 431 from the Student Data Disk. Enter the amount of the check in the check stub. Complete the check using the right and down arrow keys to move to the correct cell.

Open check 432. Key in the Balance Forward on each check. Follow the same procedure for writing all checks.

JOB 6

Form 9

Transaction

Ms. Bello asks you to reconcile last month's bank statement. She gives you the following information, which you will need to complete this job.

Balance in checkbook	$12,662.50
Deposits in transit	$1,357.25
	$4,155.00
Outstanding checks	$185.90
	376.00
	49.00
	19.50
	1,149.15
	115.20
	490.35
	115.20
	176.35
	395.65
Bank statement balance	$10,222.55

Detailed Instructions

Three situations may develop that may explain a difference between the checkbook balance for Woodside Apartments and the bank statement balance: (1) time lag, (2) your mistakes, and (3) bank errors. Most banks provide a reconciliation form similar to form 9. When completing this form, you must be careful to "plug" in the correct information in the right place. Then it is a matter of adding or subtracting the right amounts. When completed, the balance on the checkbook side and the balance on the bank statement side should agree. If they do not agree, an error(s) has been made. The error(s) must be found and corrected.

Job Completed ☐

JOB 7

Forms 10 and 11

Transaction

Each week the office fund voucher must be brought up to date. Form 11 is used to account for all small payments made out of the cash box. All necessary information is contained in interoffice memo 134 (form 10).

Detailed Instructions

Most small firms use an office fund for small cash payments. Although most companies limit the amount of cash payments from the office fund, most firms maintain a cash balance of $50 to $100 in this type of fund.

Job Completed ☐

Procedure Using Excel

Open form 11 from the Student Data Disk. Enter the information from form 10 into the appropriate columns in Form 11.

DAY 2

Good morning. This is your second day at Woodside Apartments. Naturally, you felt a little uneasy yesterday, but that's to be expected after just one day.

Ms. Bello is already at work, but stops by your desk to ask you to come into her office for a little chat.

Please have a seat. Do you have any questions after your first day at Woodside?

She does seem to like your work. Then she confirms your hunch by suggesting it is time to move on to "bigger and better" jobs.

JOB 1

Forms 12 and 13

Transaction

Today is November 1, 20XX. At the end of your conversation with Ms. Bello, she asked you to complete a rent ledger form (form 13) for all rents collected since the last rent ledger was completed. All of the information needed to complete this form is contained in interoffice memo 135 (form 12). When finished with this job, proceed to the next job.

Detailed Instructions

Notice that this job is like job 1 that you completed yesterday. Be sure to record each amount from interoffice memo 135 (form 12) in the proper column on the rent ledger form. Then be sure to add the amounts in each individual column to determine the total for each column.

Job Completed ☐

Procedure Using Excel

Open form 13 from the Student Data Disk. Using the information from form 12, complete the Rent Ledger Form. Use the right arrow key to move forward and the down arrow key to move to the next line.

JOB 2

Forms 13 and 14

Transaction

Each time rent payments are posted to the multicolumn rent ledger form, it is also necessary to complete a rent audit (form 14) to verify the accuracy of your work.

Detailed Instructions

Again, this audit must be completed each time rent is received and recorded. Since rent income is the apartment's primary source of income, accuracy is extremely important. All of the tenants' checks must be accounted for.

Job Completed ☐

Procedure Using Excel

Open form 14 from the Student Data Disk. Using the information from form 13, complete the Rent Audit Form. Use the down arrow key to move to the next line.

JOB 3

Forms 12 and 15

Transaction

After the rent ledger and rent audit forms are completed, it is possible to prepare the daily bank deposit. All needed information is contained in interoffice memo 135 (form 12).

Detailed Instructions

Remember, checks are listed by the last name of the tenant.

Job Completed ☐

Procedure Using Excel

Open form 15 from the Student Data Disk. Complete the bank deposit by listing the checks individually. Use the right arrow key and the down arrow key to move forward to the next cell or down to the next row.

JOB 4

Forms 16, 17, and 18

Transaction

Ms. Bello stops by your desk and asks you to complete the weekly payroll register. She has already done some of the work, but total wages must be calculated. Also, federal withholding and FICA (Social Security) must be determined for each employee. Then total deductions can be calculated by adding the amounts for federal withholding and FICA tax. Finally, you must find each employee's amount of net wages paid or take-home pay. Once this job is completed, proceed to the next job.

Detailed Instructions

You may want to review the material on payroll calculations in your text before beginning work on the payroll register for Woodside Apartments. Ms. Bello has listed all current employees. She has also indicated the following information:

a. Marital status

b. Number of exemptions

c. Number of hours worked during this pay period

d. Hourly pay rate for each employee

First, you must determine the total wages by multiplying the number of hours by the hourly rate for each employee.

Second, you must find the amount of federal withholding for each employee. Federal withholding tables for both married and single employees are provided (forms 17 and 18). Be sure to use the right table. Also, the number of withholding allowances claimed by each employee will make a difference in the amount of federal withholding. For example, for a single employee who claims one withholding allowance and makes a weekly salary of at least $260 but less than $270, the federal withholding amount is $24.

Third, you must find the amount of FICA tax. When calculating the FICA deduction amount, marital status and number of exemptions make *no* difference. Ignore these two factors. To determine the FICA tax amount, multiply each employee's total wages before deductions by the FICA tax rate. At the time of publication, the FICA tax rate was 7.65 percent (for the two components of FICA—Social Security and Medicare). For an employee with a weekly salary of $300, the FICA tax amount is $22.95 ($300 × .0765 = $22.95).

Fourth, now that the amounts for federal withholding and FICA have been determined, it is possible to calculate total deductions for each employee. Add the federal withholding and FICA amounts together.

Fifth, to determine the amount of net wages paid, subtract the amount of total deductions from total wages for each employee.

Sixth, determine the total for the following columns:

a. Total wages

b. Federal withholding

c. FICA tax

d. Total deductions

e. Net wages paid

You should complete the formula at the bottom of the payroll register. This crossfooting procedure will help ensure the accuracy of your work.

Job Completed ☐

Procedure Using Excel

Open form 16 from the Student Data Disk. Enter the regular hours worked for each employee. Use forms 17 and 18 to determine the Federal Withholding tax. Enter that figure in column J. Net Wages will be calculated automatically. The totals will be calculated after entering all five employees' information.

JOB 5

Checks 433, 434, 435, 436, and 437

Transaction

Mr. Martin just stopped by your desk and took a look at the completed payroll register. Then he asks you to go ahead and complete the payroll process by issuing checks for all employees. Use checks 433 through 437 and today's date, November 1, 20XX.

Detailed Instructions

Be sure the amount on each employee's check is identical to the net wages paid amount on the payroll register. Don't forget that it is also necessary to complete each check stub.

Job Completed ☐

Procedure Using Excel

Open check 433; issue to Jo Appleton.
Open check 434; issue to Lucy Bello
Open check 435; issue to A. Farmington
Open check 436; issue to Jack Martin
Open check 437; issue to Mike Benton

Update all check stubs.

JOB 6

Forms 19 and 20

Transaction

Ms. Bello asks you to complete some cost comparisons for merchandise that Woodside will need to purchase next month. She has obtained the suggested retail prices and recorded all the necessary information relating to series discounts and cash discounts for each item on forms 19 and 20. It is your job to determine which supplier offers the merchandise at the lowest price.

Detailed Instructions

Before completing this job, you may want to review the material on discounts in your text. Remember, the size and number of the discounts can lower the cost for merchandise. Also, the terms of the cash discount may make a difference. For comparison purposes, assume the cash discount will be taken if one is offered.

Job Completed ☐

Procedure Using Excel

Open form 19 from the Student Data Disk. Enter the Suggested Retail Price for each item. The Net Amount will be calculated automatically. Fill in the name of the supplier with the lowest price in the space provided at the bottom of the form.

Open form 20 from the Student Data Disk. Enter the Suggested Retail Price for each item. The Net Amount will be calculated automatically. Fill in the name of the supplier with the lowest price in the space provided at the bottom of the form.

JOB 7

Forms 21 and 22

Transaction

Two invoices from different suppliers have just arrived, and you must check the accuracy of the extension work and discounts before checks can be issued. If you find an error, draw one line through the mistake and write the correct amount above the error. Then you must recalculate the total for the invoice.

Detailed Instructions

Again, you are dealing with money; therefore, all calculations must be accurate. Suppliers occasionally make mistakes, and the errors must be found before your check is written and the payment is mailed. If you need help on this job, review the material on discounts in your text.

Job Completed ☐

JOB 8

Form 23

Transaction

Last week Mr. Martin authorized a $13,000 swimming pool renovation. The repair company just sent him its statement and to his surprise, they offer their customers a 2 percent discount if the bill is paid within ten days. Naturally, Mr. Martin would like to take advantage of the discount, but the apartment is a little short on cash at this time of the month. He asks you to determine if it would be a good idea to borrow the money and pay the bill in time to save the discount. He has already checked at the bank and the money is available at 10 percent simple interest. If you decide to borrow the money, the loan will be made for a twenty-five-day period. Use form 23 to complete your analysis. Notice that there is room at the bottom of the form for you to write a short paragraph to explain your recommendation. Describe the pros and cons of your decision.

Detailed Instructions

Normally, cash discounts look like this: 2/10, N/30. Once you have determined the discount amount and the net amount after the discount, you can determine the interest amount for a bank loan. Remember that the loan is for the net amount at 10 percent for twenty-five days. Use a 360-day ordinary year for your calculations. You may want to review cash discounts and simple interest in your text before completing this job.

      Once the interest amount has been determined, you can make your recommendations in a short paragraph at the bottom of form 23.

Job Completed ☐

JOB 9

Forms 5, 6, and 7/Checks 438, 439, and 440

Transaction

Mr. Martin has looked over the three invoices you checked for accuracy yesterday. Retrieve the invoices (forms 5, 6, and 7) and issue checks 438, 439, and 440 to the three suppliers involved. Write "paid," the date 11-1-XX, and the check number on each invoice.

Detailed Instructions

Notice that these invoices are paid within the cash discount period. Make sure the amount on each check is the same as the total for each invoice. Be sure to place the proper notation on each invoice. This helps to eliminate the possibility of paying the same invoice twice.

Job Completed ☐

Procedures Using Excel

Open check 438; issue to Heritage Office Supply
Open check 439; issue to All-City Electric Supply
Open check 440; issue to Sunshine Pool Sales

Update all check stubs.

Congratulations. It is quitting time. You've made it through a second day at Woodside. As you leave, Mr. Martin calls you back and tells you he is pleased with your work.

DAY 3

You could tell when you opened the door that today was going to be a busy one. Ms. Bello was already at her desk and busy at work. Mr. Martin was on the phone and two maintenance men were looking at the repair orders written yesterday. Ms. Bello motions for you to come in and have a seat. She explains that the completed financial statements for last month have been returned by the accountant, and Mr. Martin uses the statements as a basis for a deeper look at Woodside's financial condition. Besides this additional work, there are always the *normal* activities.

JOB 1

Form 24

Transaction

Today is November 2, 20XX. The following people have deposited their rent in the night deposit box.

Tenant	Apt. No.	Amount Received
Bob Norton	139	$275 plus $20 late fee
Sally Nance	208	$310 plus $20 late fee
Bill Johnson	145	$310 plus $20 late fee
Susan Brown	110	$310.00
Rich Smith	118	$415.00

When finished recording the above information on the rent ledger form, proceed to the next job.

Detailed Instructions

Again, be sure to enter all amounts in the proper columns. Then determine the total amount for each individual column.

Job Completed ☐

Procedure Using Excel

Open form 24 from the Student Data Disk. Using the information above, complete the Rent Ledger Form. Use the right arrow key to move forward and the down arrow key to move to the next line.

JOB 2

Forms 24 and 25

Transaction

Even though only five tenants actually paid rent since yesterday, it is still necessary to complete a rent audit form.

Detailed Instructions

The only purpose in completing the rent audit is to verify the totals on the rent ledger form. As pointed out before, this audit ensures the accuracy of your work.

Job Completed ☐

Procedure Using Excel

Open form 25 from the Student Data Disk. Using the information from form 24, complete the Rent Audit Form. Use the down arrow key to move to the next line.

JOB 3

Form 26

Transaction

It is now necessary to complete the bank deposit form. In addition to the five rent checks listed in job 1, Woodside Apartments has received a check for $89.50 for returned merchandise from Spencer Office Supply.

Detailed Instructions

List the checks for the five tenants first. After the tenants' checks, list the supplier's check for unused merchandise. Be sure to total all items on the bank deposit form.

Job Completed ☐

Procedure Using Excel

Open form 26 from the Student Data Disk. Complete the bank deposit by listing the checks individually. Use the right arrow key and the down arrow key to move forward to the next cell or down to the next row.

JOB 4

Forms 27 and 28

Transaction

The accountant just delivered the completed financial statements for last month. Mr. Martin asks you to look over the statements and become familiar with the accounts and amounts listed on each statement. Then proceed to the next job.

Detailed Instructions

Before beginning your work on the next job, it may be helpful to review the following information. A statement of financial position is used to ensure that assets = liabilities + owner's equity. Assets are usually defined as something a firm owns—its cash, inventory, machinery, land, buildings, and so on. A firm's liabilities are its debts. Today most accountants use the term *owner's equity* to refer to the money, land, buildings, equipment, or other items of value an owner(s) has invested in a business.

Another statement extensively used in business today is the income statement. The information contained in the income statement reflects the firm's profits or losses for a stated accounting period. Revenue is listed at the top of the statement, while various itemized expenses are listed toward the bottom. The difference between revenue and expenses results in the firm's profit or loss or bottom-line profit.

Job Completed ☐

JOB 5

Forms 27 and 29

Transaction

Mr. Martin explains it is customary for Woodside Apartments to use the information from the statement of financial position for a more in-depth look at the company's financial status. He explains that this can be accomplished by dividing each individual asset amount by the total asset amount. For example:

Cash	Total Assets	Percent of Total Assets
$25,000	÷ $890,000	= .0281 = 2.81%

Notice that the first answer is in decimal form and must be converted to a percent. You can also divide each individual liability or owner's equity amount by the total for liabilities and owner's equity.

Detailed Instructions

When analyzing a firm's statement of financial position, it is customary to state *individual* asset amounts as a percent of total assets. Therefore, the total asset amount is considered to be 100 percent. Likewise, it is customary to state *individual* liability or owner's equity amounts as a percent of total liabilities and owner's equity. Therefore, the total liabilities and owner's equity amount is considered to be 100 percent. Your calculations will enable Woodside's management to compare the firm's financial position with those of similar businesses. It is also possible to compare its present position with calculations for previous accounting periods. *Hint:* Since each individual amount is divided by the total amount, you may want to use the constant feature on your calculator. Most electronic calculators will keep the second number in a division problem constant. To increase the accuracy of your work, use four decimal places.

Job Completed ☐

Procedure Using Excel

Open form 29 from the Student Data Disk. Enter the Dollar Amount for each item. The Percent will be calculated automatically.

JOB 6

Forms 28 and 30

Transaction

It is also possible to use the information on the income statement for a more in-depth look at the company's financial status. This can be accomplished by dividing each line item amount by total revenue. For example:

Salary Expense	Total Revenue	Percent of Total Revenue
$5,175	÷ $28,250	= .1832 = 18.32%

The first answer is in decimal form and must be converted to a percent.

Detailed Instructions

When analyzing a firm's income statement, it is customary to state *individual* expense amounts as a percent of total revenue. Therefore, the total revenue amount is considered to be 100 percent. Again, your calculations will enable Woodside's management to compare its financial position with those of similar businesses. It is also possible to compare its present position with calculations for previous accounting periods. *Hint:* Since each individual amount is divided by the total revenue amount, you may want to use the constant feature on your calculator. Most electronic calculators will keep the second number in a division problem constant. To increase the accuracy of your work, use four decimal places.

Job Completed ☐

Procedure Using Excel

Open form 30 from the Student Data Disk. Enter the Dollar Amount for each item. The Percent will be calculated automatically.

JOB 7

Forms 27, 28, and 31

Transaction

Mr. Martin asks you to complete the following financial ratios:

   a. Current ratio

   b. Acid-test ratio

   c. Return on assets

   d. Return on owner's equity

All needed information is available on the company's statement of financial position and income statement. When these calculations are completed, it is possible to compare Woodside's financial position with similar firms in the same industry. Also, it is possible to compare present calculations with Woodside's figures from previous accounting periods. For Woodside to improve its financial position, the figures for the four ratios in this job must be higher than ratio figures from previous accounting periods. For example, a current ratio of 2.10 to 1 calculated today is better than a current ratio of 1.85 to 1 calculated a year ago. Thus, improvement for all the ratios in this job should be higher.

Detailed Instructions

Ratio analysis is often a way for managers to dig a little deeper when trying to solve or anticipate a company's financial problems.

To calculate a current ratio, divide the total current asset amount by the total current liability amount. The average current ratio for all industries is 2.0 to 1. This means that for each $1 in current liabilities, a company should have $2.00 in current assets.

To calculate the acid-test ratio: (1) add the amounts for cash and receivables and (2) divide this total by the total for current liabilities. The average acid-test ratio for all industries is 1.0 to 1.0. This means that for every $1.00 in current liabilities, a company should have $1.00 in very liquid assets.

To calculate the return on assets, divide the projected yearly profit by the total asset amount. Since the profit amount needed for calculating this ratio is based on projected yearly profit, it is necessary to multiply October profit by 12. The return on assets for most companies is between 8 and 10 percent. The calculation for Woodside's return on assets indicates this business is above average.

To calculate return on owner's equity, divide the projected yearly profit amount by the total amount for owner's equity. The return on owner's equity for most companies is between 12 and 15 percent. The calculation for Woodside's return on owner's equity indicates this business is above average.

Job Completed ☐

JOB 8

Form 32

Transaction

After looking over last month's income statement, Mr. Martin seems perplexed. The bottom-line profit amount looks good, but some of the monthly expenses look like they have increased dramatically over the past twelve months. He asks if you would calculate the percent of increase or decrease for the following four monthly expenses.

Expense	October of Last Year	October of This Year
Salary	$6,150.00	$5,175.00
Utilities	1,090.40	1,383.35
Maintenance	1,134.00	1,560.00
Furniture Rental	425.00	570.00

Use form 32 to report your findings. Use four decimals for these calculations.

Detailed Instructions

Naturally, an owner or manager must be concerned with the expenses a business incurs. One way of getting a handle on expenses is by comparing the expenses of one accounting period with the same expenses for a previous accounting period. Often, it is more meaningful to compare expenses if the amount of change is stated as a percent. To complete this assignment, divide the dollar amount of change by the total amount for the earlier period. Normally, your answer is in decimal form and must be converted to a percent. Most managers want to reduce expenses whenever and wherever possible. Although it may be impossible to reduce expenses in inflationary times, it may be possible to hold the line or lower the amount and percent of increase for various expenses. Certainly an awareness of the problem is a step in the right direction. To increase the accuracy of your work, use four decimal places.

Procedure Using Excel

Open form 32 from the Student Data Disk. Enter the Expense totals for last year and this year. The Amount of Change and Percent of Change will be calculated automatically. Determine whether the Percent of Change is an increase or decrease and key that in the last column of the form.

JOB 9

Forms 21 and 22/Checks 441 and 442

Transaction

Mr. Martin has looked over the two invoices you checked for accuracy yesterday (forms 21 and 22), and he wants you to issue checks 441 and 442 to the two suppliers. Write "paid," the date 11-2-20XX, and check number on each invoice.

Detailed Instructions

Again, make sure the amount on each check is the same as the total for each invoice. Be sure to place the proper notation on each invoice. This helps to eliminate the possibility of paying the same invoice twice.

Job Completed ☐

Procedure Using Excel

Open check 441; issue to Master Sprinkler Supply
Open check 442; issue to Green Thumb Plants

Update all check stubs.

It has been a busy day, but a productive day. You have completed clerical and accounting work that is a practical necessity for an ongoing business. In reality, sometimes people forget the real reason why they keep accounting records. Records should help an owner or manager operate a business, and Woodside Apartments is no exception.

DAY 4

It doesn't seem possible, but this begins your fourth day "on the job" at Woodside Apartments. There are a number of tasks that must be performed today. Ms. Bello has already received notification that three tenants will be moving today. It sure looks like she will be busy today, and that means you will probably perform more of the day-to-day accounting and clerical work.

JOB 1

Form 33

Transaction

Today is November 3, 20XX. Although all rents were collected earlier for the month of November, Ms. Bello has received deposits from three future tenants. Record the three checks on the bank deposit slip (form 33) using the information below.

Future Tenant	Amount of Deposit
Jack Tyler	$300
Marie and Bob Newsom	$450
Mike and Peggy Barnhart	$375

Detailed Instructions

Woodside Apartments requires a deposit from all future tenants before their application can be processed. Although the deposit amount required by Woodside is substantial, it is refundable if the prospective tenant is rejected or an apartment is not available within sixty days. The required deposits are as follows:

One bedroom	$300
Two bedroom	$375
Two-bedroom with a loft	$450

Job Completed ☐

Procedure Using Excel

Open form 33 from the Student Data Disk. Complete the bank deposit by listing the checks individually.

JOB 2

Checks 443, 444, and 445

Transaction

Woodside Apartments has a policy of paying within five days after receiving individual bills. The following three bills have been received and have been approved by Mr. Martin. Date all checks November 3, 20XX.

Texas Power & Light	$485.00
Lone Star Gas	291.50
Southwestern Bell	163.49

Detailed Instructions

Be sure to complete the check stub along with the check. Also, make sure the amount of the check is correct.

Job Completed ☐

Procedure Using Excel

Open check 443; issue to Texas Power & Light
Open check 444; issue to Lone Star Gas
Open check 445; issue to Southwestern Bell.

Update all check stubs. Verify the amount of each check for accuracy.

JOB 3

Forms 34 and 35

Transaction

Ms. Bello has just received two invoices from suppliers. You must check the accuracy of the extension work and discounts before checks can be issued. Remember, you have found mistakes when checking suppliers' invoices. You certainly don't want to pay too much. Use the customary procedure for correcting an invoice if an error is found.

Detailed Instructions

If an error goes undetected and the supplier is paid too much, it can be a real problem to obtain a refund. The best advice is to catch and correct the mistake as soon as possible.

Job Completed ☐

JOB 4

Form 36

Transaction

Mr. Martin asks you to step into his office. Although Woodside is currently renting furniture for the Clubhouse, he is thinking about purchasing new furniture for the clubhouse. He has even gotten a price quotation of $2,950 from a furniture wholesaler that has sold to Woodside before. From past experience, he expects that the furniture should last five years and have a salvage value of $150. He asks you to determine the amount of depreciation expense and book value for the first two years if he decides to use the straight-line method. Then he wants you to determine the depreciation expense and book value for the first two years if he chooses the declining-balance method.

Detailed Instructions

The following formula can be used to determine the annual depreciation expense if the straight-line method is used.

$$\frac{\text{original cost} - \text{estimated salvage value}}{\text{estimated life}} = \text{annual depreciation}$$

When the straight-line method is used, first-year book value is determined by subtracting the annual depreciation amount from the original cost. The second-year book value is determined by subtracting the annual depreciation from the first-year book value.

Normally, three steps are required to calculate depreciation expense when the declining-balance method is used.

1. Divide 100 percent by the estimated life of the article.
2. Multiply the answer from Step 1 by 2. The rate found in Step 1 is multiplied by 2 because this results in a depreciation rate that is twice the straight-line amount.
3. Multiply the original cost by the depreciation rate you obtained in Step 2.

When the declining balance method is used, the first-year book value is found by subtracting the first-year depreciation amount from the original cost. The second-year depreciation expense is found by multiplying the first-year book value by the depreciation rate found in Step 2. The second-year book value is found by subtracting the second-year depreciation amount from the first-year book value. If the declining-balance method is used, the estimated salvage value is not used *except* as a dollar amount the book value cannot fall below. You may want to review depreciation in your text before beginning work on this assignment.

Job Completed ☐

JOB 5

Form 37

Transaction

Mr. Martin is concerned about the increasing cost of maintenance. He asks you to compare the total for maintenance expense to total revenue for the past five years. He has researched the needed information, which is presented below.

Year	Maintenance Expense	Total Revenue
2003	$13,099	$208,259
2004	14,513	228,856
2005	17,552	235,428
2006	21,750	288,960
2007	24,300	316,000

At the bottom of the form, there is space provided for you to write a short paragraph describing your findings. Indicate in your paragraph whether there is an increase or a decrease over the five-year period. Also, describe any future trends that seem appropriate. Use four decimal places for your answers.

Detailed Instructions

In order to complete this job, you must divide the yearly expense figure for maintenance by the total revenue for the same year. Normally, your answer is in decimal form and must be converted to a percent. Be sure to describe your findings in a short paragraph at the bottom of the analysis form. To increase the accuracy of your work, use four decimal places.

Job Completed ☐

Procedure Using Excel

Open form 37 from the Student Data Disk. Enter the Maintenance Expense and Total Revenue for each year. The Percent of Total Revenue will be calculated automatically. Key your findings in the space provided at the bottom of the form.

JOB 6

Forms 38 and 39

Transaction

Mr. Martin returns with more work, and this time he seems really upset. It seems that both the gas company and the electric company have increased their commercial rates. Although each tenant's apartment has a separate meter for both gas and electricity, the apartment complex must pay the bills for the office, clubhouse, laundry rooms, and manager's apartment. This month the electric bill is $675.00, while the natural gas bill is $483.35. He asks you to distribute each expense on the basis of square footage. The following information may be helpful as you complete this job.

Specific Area	Square Footage
Office	650
Clubhouse	1,230
Laundry rooms	515
Manager's apt.	1,080

This procedure does not reduce the expense, but it does show which areas use the largest amounts of electricity and natural gas. With this information, management may be able to reduce gas and electrical usage in certain areas.

Detailed Instructions

When there is a relationship between an expense and square footage, it is possible to distribute the expense by following the steps below.

1. Determine the total square footage involved.
2. Divide the square footage for each area by the total square footage. Round the answer for this step to six decimal places.
3. Multiply your answer from Step 2 by the expense amount. Use two decimal places for this step because your final answers represent dollars and cents. You may want to check your work. If so, add the individual answers and check to see if the total is the same as the amount you started with. If not, you may need to add or subtract the difference and *force* the balance to equal the original amount.

Job Completed ☐

JOB 7

Form 40

Transaction

It seems the apartment owners have spent $6,210 on a joint advertising campaign to improve the image of all six apartment complexes that they own in the Dallas–Ft. Worth area. Mr. Martin asks you to prorate the advertising expense based on total revenue for each apartment complex. The following information may be helpful as you work on this job.

Apartment Complex	October Monthly Revenue
Woodside Apartments	$28,250
Brockport Apartments	$18,800
Columbia Manor	$24,370
Martin's Woods	$16,930
Brookside Apartments	$30,640
Leisure Tree Manor	$21,345

Detailed Instructions

When there is a relationship between an expense and revenue, it is possible to prorate the expense by following the steps below.

1. Determine the total revenue amount for all six apartment complexes.
2. Divide the $6,210 advertising expense by the total revenue amount. Use six decimal places for this step.
3. Multiply the answer from Step 2 by each apartment complex's revenue amount. Use two decimal places for this step because your final answers represent dollars and cents.

Like the last job, you may check your work. Add the individual answers and check to see if the total is the same as the expense amount you started with. If not, you may need to add or subtract the amount of difference and *force* the balance to equal the original amount.

Job Completed ☐

Congratulations, you have just completed your first four-day workweek at Woodside Apartments. Although you were uneasy about some of your work, both Ms. Bello and Mr. Martin seem pleased. Although each job was new this week, they both promise that next week will be easier. Ms. Bello points out that many jobs are repeated and in some cases must be completed on a weekly basis. This fact alone should make your job easier next week. Other jobs are performed less often. As you get your coat and prepare to leave for the weekend, Mr. Martin makes the following statement, which is worth remembering: "Experience is often the best teacher!"

Form 1

WOODSIDE APARTMENTS

Interoffice Memo
No. 132

To: Bookkeeper
From: Lucy Bello

Date: October 31, 20XX

The following people have paid checks to Woodside Apartments. Please post the information below in the appropriate columns on the rent ledger form.

Date	Name	Apt. No.	Total Received	Comments
10-30	Echols, B	101	$375	$350 rent; $25 key deposit
10-30	Barnes, J	103	$415	$415 rent
10-30	Smith, A	111	$335	$275 rent; $25 key deposit; $35 cleaning
10-30	Meyer, S	115	$355	$310 rent; $45 furniture
10-30	James, B	118	$415	$310 rent; $45 furniture; $25 key deposit; $35 cleaning
10-31	Miller, H	130	$380	$310 rent; $25 key deposit; $45 furniture
10-31	Newbury, S	144	$450	$450 rent
10-31	Baxter, H	202	$345	$310 rent; $35 cleaning
10-31	Newman, B	243	$610	$310 rent; $300 security deposit
10-31	Hartley, B	248	$475	$475 rent

Name:_____

_____

Form 2

WOODSIDE APARTMENTS

Rent Ledger Form
Sheet No._____

Period: October 1 through October 31, 20XX

Date	Name	Apt. No.	(1) Rent	(2) Key Deposit	(3) Security Deposit	(4) Furniture Rental	(5) Late Charge	(6) Cleaning Fee	(7) Total Received	
1										1
2										2
3										3
4										4
5										5
6										6
7										7
8										8
9										9
10										10
11										11
12										12
13										13
14										14
	Totals									

Name:_____

Form 3

WOODSIDE APARTMENTS
Rent Audit Form

Part 1

Column No.	Description	Total Dollar Amount
1	Rent	$ _____
2	Key Deposit	$ _____
3	Security Deposit	$ _____
4	Furniture Rental	$ _____
5	Late Charge	$ _____
6	Cleaning Fee	$ _____
	Total	$ _____

Part 2*

Total Received—Amount from   =   Total from Part 1 Above
Column 7 Rent Ledger Form

	=	

*If these two totals do not agree, a mistake(s) has been made and it must be found and corrected before the bank deposit can be completed.

Name:_____

_____

Form 4

IF BANKING BY MAIL

1. Endorse checks as follows. Pay to the order of bank (your signature).

2. Originate in duplicate – enclose in envelope both copies with items for deposit. Duplicate will be returned by mail.

3. If currency or coin is contained in the deposit, please send by registered mail.

Record Checks for Deposit	Dollars	Cents

IMPORTANT
Include amount of above checks in total on front side

Record Checks for Deposit	Dollars	Cents
Currency Please send by registered mail		
Coins		
Use back side for listing additional checks **Total Deposit**		

If you are banking by mail please refer to instructions on reverse side.

Checks and other items are received for deposit subject to the terms and conditions of this bank's collection agreement now in effect.

Woodside Apartments
909 Woodside Drive
Dallas, TX 75248

Name:_____

_____

Form 5

Heritage Office Supply

515 North Star Road

Dallas, TX 75243

October 28   **20** XX

TO   Woodside Apartments

ADDRESS   909 Woodside Drive

CITY   Dallas, TX 75248

TERMS   2/10, N/30   ORDER NO.   AZ - 4215

Quantity	Description	Unit Cost		Total	
2	2-Drawer Files	89	50	179	00
1	Desk	229	25	229	25
1	Desk Chair	149	50	149	50
2	Side Chairs	79	95	159	90
		Subtotal		717	65
		Less 20%, 15%, 8%		268	69
		Subtotal		448	96
		Less 2/10, N/30		8	98
		Invoice Total		439	98

Name:_____

_____

Form 6

All-City Electric Supply

707 N. Beckley

Dallas, TX 75208

October 28   20   XX

TO   Woodside Apartments

ADDRESS   909 Woodside Drive

CITY   Dallas, TX 75248

TERMS   2/10, N/30   ORDER NO.   89912

Quantity	Description	Unit Cost		Total	
2	Fan Motors 1.3 H.P.	89	25	178	50
2	Transformers	44	10	88	20
2	Capacitors	39	80	59	60
		Subtotal		326	30
		Less 30%		97	89
		Subtotal		228	41
		Less 2/10, N/30		4	57
		Invoice Total		223	84

Name:_____

_____

Form 7

Sunshine Pool Sales

13410 Central Expressway

Dallas, TX 75216

October 30   **20**   XX

TO   Woodside Apartments

ADDRESS   909 Woodside Drive

CITY   Dallas, TX 75248

TERMS   3/10, N/60   ORDER NO.   10954

Quantity	Description	Unit Cost		Total	
1	Dry Chlorine	109	00	109	00
6	Muriatic Acid, Case	7	95	47	70
2	Stain Protector, Case	39	95	79	90
		Subtotal		236	60
		Less 10%, 10%		44	95
		Subtotal		191	65
		Less 3/10, N/60		5	75
		Invoice Total		185	90

Name:_____

_____

Form 8

WOODSIDE APARTMENTS

Interoffice Memo

To: Bookkeeper

No. 133

From: Jack Martin

Date: October 31, 20XX

1. Issue check no. 431 to Commerce Business Forms for $19.50 for a two-month supply of rent receipts.

2. Issue check no. 432 to Hess Carpet Cleaning Service for $49.00 for work in Apartments 112 and 203.

Name:_____

_____

Form 9

This is provided to help you balance your bank statement.

Bank balance shown on this statement $ _____

Add + (if any) deposits not shown on this statement   _____

Total   _____

Subtract − (if any) checks outstanding   _____

Balance $ _____
Should agree with your checkbook balance

Checks Outstanding	
No.	Amount
Total	

This is provided to help you balance your checkbook.

Checkbook balance at statement date $ _____

Subtract − (if any) activity charge   _____

Subtotal   _____

Subtract − (if any) other bank charges   _____

Balance $ _____
Should agree with your statement balance

If your account does not balance — please check the following carefully

☐ Have you correctly entered the amount of each check on your checkbook stubs?

☐ Are the amounts of your deposits entered on checkbook stubs the same as in your statement?

☐ Have all checks been deducted from your stubs?

☐ Have you deducted all bank charges from your stubs?

☐ Have you carried the correct balance forward from one checkbook stub to the next?

☐ Have you checked all additions and subtractions on your checkbook stubs?

Name:_____

_____

Form 10

WOODSIDE APARTMENTS

Interoffice Memo
To: Bookkeeper
No. 134
From: Jack Martin
Date: October 31, 20XX

The following cash payments were made from the office fund this week.

Date	To Whom Paid	For What	Account	Amount
10-27	U.S. Postal Service	Postage Due	515	$3.75
10-28	A-1 Delivery	Delivery Charge	519	5.60
10-28	Alex Farmington	Gas	528	5.00
10-28	Jack Martin	Office Supplies	524	2.85

Please post each entry to the office fund voucher for this week. Also, determine the total for cash payments made from the office fund.

Name:_____

_____

Form 11

WOODSIDE APARTMENTS
Office Fund Voucher

Date	To Whom Paid	For What	Account	Amount
			Grand Total	

Name:_____

_____

Form 12

WOODSIDE APARTMENTS

Interoffice Memo

To: Bookkeeper No. 135

From: Lucy Bello Date: November 1, 20XX

The following people have paid checks to Woodside Apartments. Please post the information below in the appropriate columns on the rent ledger form.

Date	Name	Apt. No.	Total Received	Comments
11-1	Masters, B	104	$350	$350 rent
11-2	Cox, R	126	$635	$310 rent; $325 security deposit
11-2	Johns, B	136	$350	$350 rent
11-3	Palmer, C	204	$400	$310 rent; $90 furniture
11-3	Martin, C	206	$390	$310 rent; $35 cleaning; $45 furniture
11-3	Aday, V	233	$610	$310 rent; $300 security deposit
11-3	Victor, N	235	$415	$310 rent; $45 furniture; $25 key deposit; $35 cleaning
11-4	Overly, B	240	$510	$275 rent; $235 security deposit
11-4	Norris, A	247	$370	$310 rent; $60 furniture

Name:_____

Form 13

WOODSIDE APARTMENTS

Period: November 1 through November 30, 20XX

Rent Ledger Form
Sheet No. _____

Date	Name	Apt. No.	(1) Rent	(2) Key Deposit	(3) Security Deposit	(4) Furniture Rental	(5) Late Charge	(6) Cleaning Fee	(7) Total Received	
1										1
2										2
3										3
4										4
5										5
6										6
7										7
8										8
9										9
10										10
11										11
12										12
13										13
14										14
	Totals									

Name: _____

Form 14

WOODSIDE APARTMENTS
Rent Audit Form

Part 1

Column No.	Description	Total Dollar Amount
1	Rent	$_____
2	Key Deposit	$_____
3	Security Deposit	$_____
4	Furniture Rental	$_____
5	Late Charge	$_____
6	Cleaning Fee	$_____
	Total	$_____

Part 2*
Total Received—Amount from   =   Total from Part 1 Above
Column 7 Rent Ledger Form

[ ]	=	[ ]

*If these two totals do not agree, a mistake(s) has been made and it must be found and corrected before the bank deposit can be completed.

Name:_____

_____

Form 15

IF BANKING BY MAIL

1. Endorse checks as follows. Pay to the order of bank (your signature).

2. Originate in duplicate – enclose in envelope both copies with items for deposit. Duplicate will be returned by mail.

3. If currency or coin is contained in the deposit, please send by registered mail.

Record Checks for Deposit	Dollars	Cents

IMPORTANT
Include amount of above checks in total on front side

Record Checks for Deposit	Dollars	Cents
Currency Please send by registered mail		
Coins		
Use back side for listing additional checks **Total Deposit**		

If you are banking by mail please refer to instructions on reverse side.

Checks and other items are received for deposit subject to the terms and conditions of this bank's collection agreement now in effect.

Woodside Apartments
909 Woodside Drive
Dallas, TX 75248

Name:_____

_____

Form 16

Payroll Register

Date_____   Sheet No._____

Employee's Name	Marital Status	Exemptions	Regular Hours	Overtime Hours	Hourly Rate of Pay	Regular Wages	Overtime Wages	Total Wages	Federal Withholding	FICA Tax	Total Deductions	Net Wages Paid
Appleton, Jo	S	1	32.5		8.00							
Bello, Lucy	M	1	40		9.50							
Farmington, A.	S	2	32.5		7.60							
Martin, Jack	M	3	40		12.75							
Benton, Mike	S	1	40		7.60							
Totals	XXXXX	XXXXX	XXXXXX	XXXXX	XXXXXX	XXXXXX	XXXXXXX					

Net Wages Paid = Total Wages − Total Deductions

$ _____ = $ _____ − $ _____

$ _____ = $ _____ − $ _____

Name: _____

Form 17

MARRIED Persons—WEEKLY Payroll Period

(For Wages Paid in July Dec 2001)

If the wages are—		And the number of withholding allowances claimed is—										
At least	But less than	0	1	2	3	4	5	6	7	8	9	10
		The amount of income tax to be withheld is—										
$0	$125	0	0	0	0	0	0	0	0	0	0	0
125	130	1	0	0	0	0	0	0	0	0	0	0
130	135	1	0	0	0	0	0	0	0	0	0	0
135	140	2	0	0	0	0	0	0	0	0	0	0
140	145	3	0	0	0	0	0	0	0	0	0	0
145	150	4	0	0	0	0	0	0	0	0	0	0
150	155	4	0	0	0	0	0	0	0	0	0	0
155	160	5	0	0	0	0	0	0	0	0	0	0
160	165	6	0	0	0	0	0	0	0	0	0	0
165	170	7	0	0	0	0	0	0	0	0	0	0
170	175	7	0	0	0	0	0	0	0	0	0	0
175	180	8	0	0	0	0	0	0	0	0	0	0
180	185	9	0	0	0	0	0	0	0	0	0	0
185	190	10	1	0	0	0	0	0	0	0	0	0
190	195	10	2	0	0	0	0	0	0	0	0	0
195	200	11	3	0	0	0	0	0	0	0	0	0
200	210	12	4	0	0	0	0	0	0	0	0	0
210	220	14	5	0	0	0	0	0	0	0	0	0
220	230	15	7	0	0	0	0	0	0	0	0	0
230	240	17	8	0	0	0	0	0	0	0	0	0
240	250	18	10	1	0	0	0	0	0	0	0	0
250	260	20	11	3	0	0	0	0	0	0	0	0
260	270	21	13	4	0	0	0	0	0	0	0	0
270	280	23	14	6	0	0	0	0	0	0	0	0
280	290	24	16	7	0	0	0	0	0	0	0	0
290	300	26	17	9	1	0	0	0	0	0	0	0
300	310	27	19	10	2	0	0	0	0	0	0	0
310	320	29	20	12	4	0	0	0	0	0	0	0
320	330	30	22	13	5	0	0	0	0	0	0	0
330	340	32	23	15	7	0	0	0	0	0	0	0
340	350	33	25	16	8	0	0	0	0	0	0	0
350	360	35	26	18	10	1	0	0	0	0	0	0
360	370	36	28	19	11	3	0	0	0	0	0	0
370	380	38	29	21	13	4	0	0	0	0	0	0
380	390	39	31	22	14	6	0	0	0	0	0	0
390	400	41	32	24	16	7	0	0	0	0	0	0
400	410	42	34	25	17	9	0	0	0	0	0	0
410	420	44	35	27	19	10	2	0	0	0	0	0
420	430	45	37	28	20	12	3	0	0	0	0	0
430	440	47	38	30	22	13	5	0	0	0	0	0
440	450	48	40	31	23	15	6	0	0	0	0	0
450	460	50	41	33	25	16	8	0	0	0	0	0
460	470	51	43	34	26	18	9	1	0	0	0	0
470	480	53	44	36	28	19	11	2	0	0	0	0
480	490	54	46	37	29	21	12	4	0	0	0	0
490	500	56	47	39	31	22	14	5	0	0	0	0
500	510	57	49	40	32	24	15	7	0	0	0	0
510	520	59	50	42	34	25	17	8	0	0	0	0
520	530	60	52	43	35	27	18	10	2	0	0	0
530	540	62	53	45	37	28	20	11	3	0	0	0
540	550	63	55	46	38	30	21	13	5	0	0	0
550	560	65	56	48	40	31	23	14	6	0	0	0
560	570	66	58	49	41	33	24	16	8	0	0	0
570	580	68	59	51	43	34	26	17	9	1	0	0
580	590	69	61	52	44	36	27	19	11	2	0	0
590	600	71	62	54	46	37	27	20	12	4	0	0
600	610	72	64	55	47	39	30	22	14	5	0	0
610	620	74	65	57	49	40	32	23	15	7	0	0
620	630	75	67	58	50	42	33	25	17	8	0	0
630	640	77	68	60	52	43	35	26	18	10	1	0
640	650	78	70	61	53	45	36	28	20	11	3	0
650	660	80	71	63	55	46	38	29	21	13	4	0
660	670	81	73	64	56	48	39	31	23	14	6	0
670	680	83	74	66	58	49	41	32	24	16	7	0
680	690	84	76	67	59	51	42	34	26	17	9	0
690	700	86	77	69	61	52	44	35	27	19	10	2
700	710	87	79	70	62	54	45	37	29	20	12	3
710	720	89	80	72	64	55	47	38	30	22	13	5
720	730	90	82	73	65	57	48	40	32	23	15	6
730	740	92	83	75	67	58	50	41	33	25	16	8

Form 18

SINGLE Persons—WEEKLY Payroll Period

(For Wages Paid in July Dec 2001)

At least	But less than	0	1	2	3	4	5	6	7	8	9	10
$0	$55	0	0	0	0	0	0	0	0	0	0	0
55	60	1	0	0	0	0	0	0	0	0	0	0
60	65	2	0	0	0	0	0	0	0	0	0	0
65	70	2	0	0	0	0	0	0	0	0	0	0
70	75	3	0	0	0	0	0	0	0	0	0	0
75	80	4	0	0	0	0	0	0	0	0	0	0
80	85	5	0	0	0	0	0	0	0	0	0	0
85	90	5	0	0	0	0	0	0	0	0	0	0
90	95	6	0	0	0	0	0	0	0	0	0	0
95	100	7	0	0	0	0	0	0	0	0	0	0
100	105	8	0	0	0	0	0	0	0	0	0	0
105	110	8	0	0	0	0	0	0	0	0	0	0
110	115	9	1	0	0	0	0	0	0	0	0	0
115	120	10	2	0	0	0	0	0	0	0	0	0
120	125	11	2	0	0	0	0	0	0	0	0	0
125	130	11	3	0	0	0	0	0	0	0	0	0
130	135	12	4	0	0	0	0	0	0	0	0	0
135	140	13	5	0	0	0	0	0	0	0	0	0
140	145	14	5	0	0	0	0	0	0	0	0	0
145	150	14	6	0	0	0	0	0	0	0	0	0
150	155	15	7	0	0	0	0	0	0	0	0	0
155	160	16	8	0	0	0	0	0	0	0	0	0
160	165	17	8	0	0	0	0	0	0	0	0	0
165	170	17	9	1	0	0	0	0	0	0	0	0
170	175	18	10	2	0	0	0	0	0	0	0	0
175	180	19	11	2	0	0	0	0	0	0	0	0
180	185	20	11	3	0	0	0	0	0	0	0	0
185	190	20	12	4	0	0	0	0	0	0	0	0
190	195	21	13	5	0	0	0	0	0	0	0	0
195	200	22	14	5	0	0	0	0	0	0	0	0
200	210	23	15	6	0	0	0	0	0	0	0	0
210	220	25	16	8	0	0	0	0	0	0	0	0
220	230	26	18	9	1	0	0	0	0	0	0	0
230	240	28	19	11	3	0	0	0	0	0	0	0
240	250	29	21	12	4	0	0	0	0	0	0	0
250	260	31	22	14	6	0	0	0	0	0	0	0
260	270	32	24	15	7	0	0	0	0	0	0	0
270	280	34	25	17	9	0	0	0	0	0	0	0
280	290	35	27	18	10	2	0	0	0	0	0	0
290	300	37	28	20	12	3	0	0	0	0	0	0
300	310	38	30	21	13	5	0	0	0	0	0	0
310	320	40	31	23	15	6	0	0	0	0	0	0
320	330	41	33	24	16	8	0	0	0	0	0	0
330	340	43	34	26	18	9	1	0	0	0	0	0
340	350	44	36	27	19	11	2	0	0	0	0	0
350	360	46	37	29	21	12	4	0	0	0	0	0
360	370	47	39	30	22	14	5	0	0	0	0	0
370	380	49	40	32	24	15	7	0	0	0	0	0
380	390	50	42	33	25	17	8	0	0	0	0	0
390	400	52	43	35	27	18	10	1	0	0	0	0
400	410	53	45	36	28	20	11	3	0	0	0	0
410	420	55	46	38	30	21	13	4	0	0	0	0
420	430	56	48	39	31	23	14	6	0	0	0	0
430	440	58	49	41	33	24	16	7	0	0	0	0
440	450	59	51	42	34	26	17	9	1	0	0	0
450	460	61	52	44	36	27	19	10	2	0	0	0
460	470	62	54	45	37	29	20	12	4	0	0	0
470	480	64	55	47	39	30	22	13	5	0	0	0
480	490	65	57	48	40	32	23	15	7	0	0	0
490	500	67	58	50	42	33	25	16	8	0	0	0
500	510	68	60	51	43	35	26	18	10	1	0	0
510	520	70	61	53	45	36	28	19	11	3	0	0
520	530	71	63	54	46	38	29	21	13	4	0	0
530	540	73	64	56	48	39	31	22	14	6	0	0
540	550	74	66	57	49	41	32	24	16	7	0	0
550	560	76	67	59	51	42	34	25	17	9	0	0
560	570	79	69	60	52	44	35	27	19	10	2	0
570	580	81	70	62	54	45	37	28	20	12	3	0
580	590	84	72	63	55	47	38	30	22	13	5	0
590	600	87	73	65	57	48	40	31	23	15	6	0

Form 19

WOODSIDE APARTMENTS

Merchandise: Gas Clothes Dryers   Cost Comparisons

Supplier	Model No.	Suggested Retail Price	Discounts	Wholesale Price	Cash Discount Terms	Cash Discount Amount	Net Amount
Ford & Co	GS–800	$425.95	10%, 10%, 10%	$ _____	2/10, N/30	$ _____	$ _____
Young	GS–800	$439.50	15%, 10%, 10%	$ _____	3/10, N/30	$ _____	$ _____
AAA	X–102D	$405.00	10%, 10%, 5%	$ _____	None	$ _____	$ _____
Midway	HD–380D	$415.00	20%, 5%	$ _____	1/10, N/30	$ _____	$ _____

Name: _____

Form 20

WOODSIDE APARTMENTS

Merchandise: Washing Machines   Cost Comparisons

Supplier	Model No.	Suggested Retail Price	Discounts	Wholesale Price	Cash Discount Terms	Cash Discount Amount	Net Amount
Ford & Co.	GD–505	$498.50	10%, 10%, 10%	$_____	2/10, N/30	$_____	$_____
Marston	X–102A	$529.95	25%, 10%	$_____	2/10, N/30	$_____	$_____
Newsome	HD–380	$509.00	20%, 5%, 5%	$_____	None	$_____	$_____
Taylor	GD–510	$500.00	15%, 10%, 10%	$_____	1/10, N/30	$_____	$_____

Name: _____

Form 21

Master Sprinkler Supply

8102 N. Jefferson

Dallas, TX 75222

October 28   20   XX

TO   Woodside Apartments

ADDRESS   909 Woodside Drive

CITY   Dallas, TX 75248

TERMS   2/10, N/30   ORDER NO.   AB - 4092

Quantity	Description	Unit Cost		Total	
3	24-Hour Timers	69	70	209	10
18	3-inch Pop-up Heads	4	35	78	30
5	3/4-in. Pipe Sections	3	29	16	45
		Subtotal		303	85
		Less 15%, 10%, 5%		83	03
		Subtotal		220	82
		Less 2/10, N/30		4	42
		Invoice Total		216	40

Name:_____

Form 22

Green Thumb Plants

10236 Forest Lane

Garland, TX 75042

October 31   20   XX

TO   Woodside Apartments

ADDRESS   909 Woodside Drive

CITY   Dallas, TX 75248

TERMS   3/10, N/30   ORDER NO.   678932

Quantity	Description	Unit Cost		Total	
4	6-inch mums	3	99	15	96
12	6-inch copper plants	4	95	59	40
3	8-inch ferns	5	89	17	67
20	3-inch English ivy	2	90	58	00
36	1-gallon boxwood	1	99	71	64
42	1-gallon wax leaf	2	29	96	18
		Subtotal		318	85
		Less 20%, 10%		89	28
		Subtotal		229	57
		Less 3/10, N/30		6	89
		Invoice Total		222	68

Name:_____

Form 23

WOODSIDE APARTMENTS

Cash Discount/Simple Interest—An Analysis

1. Total Statement Amount Before the Cash Discount $ _____

2. Less 2/10, N/30 $ _____

3. Required Loan Amount If Cash Discount Is Taken
   (Subtract Line 2 from Line 1) $ _____

4. Dollar Amount of Interest for the Loan Amount
   (Line 3) at 10% for 25 days $ _____

Summary

5. Cash Discount Amount from Line 2 $ _____

6. *Minus* Dollar Amount of Interest from Line 4 $ _____

7. Dollar Amount of Savings $ _____

Your Findings

Name:_____

_____

Form 24

WOODSIDE APARTMENTS

Period: November 1 through November 30, 20XX

Rent Ledger Form
Sheet No. _____

Date	Name	Apt. No.	(1) Rent	(2) Key Deposit	(3) Security Deposit	(4) Furniture Rental	(5) Late Charge	(6) Cleaning Fee	(7) Total Received	
1										1
2										2
3										3
4										4
5										5
6										6
7										7
8										8
9										9
10										10
11										11
12										12
13										13
14										14
		Totals								

Name: _____

Form 25

WOODSIDE APARTMENTS

Rent Audit Form

Part 1

Column No.	Description	Total Dollar Amount
1	Rent	$ _____
2	Key Deposit	$ _____
3	Security Deposit	$ _____
4	Furniture Rental	$ _____
5	Late Charge	$ _____
6	Cleaning Fee	$ _____
	Total	$ _____

Part 2*

Total Received—Amount from   =   Total from Part 1 Above
Column 7 Rent Ledger Form

| _____ | = | _____ |

*If these two totals do not agree, a mistake(s) has been made and it must be found and corrected before the bank deposit can be completed.

Name: _____

_____

Form 26

IF BANKING BY MAIL

1. Endorse checks as follows. Pay to the order of bank (your signature).

2. Originate in duplicate – enclose in envelope both copies with items for deposit. Duplicate will be returned by mail.

3. If currency or coin is contained in the deposit, please send by registered mail.

Record Checks for Deposit	Dollars	Cents

IMPORTANT
Include amount of above checks in total on front side

Record Checks for Deposit — Dollars — Cents

Currency Please send by registered mail
Coins
Use back side for listing additional checks   **Total Deposit**
If you are banking by mail please refer to instructions on reverse side.

Checks and other items are received for deposit subject to the terms and conditions of this bank's collection agreement now in effect.

Woodside Apartments
909 Woodside Drive
Dallas, TX 75248

Name:_____
_____

Form 27

WOODSIDE APARTMENTS

Statement of Financial Position
for Month Ended October 31, 20XX

Assets

Current Assets

Cash	$ 25,000.00
Accounts Receivable	2,130.65
Office Supplies	310.35
Repair Supplies	175.92
Pool Supplies	285.30
Prepaid Insurance	1,835.20
Total Current Assets	$ 29,737.42

Fixed Assets

Land	$124,500.00
Buildings Less Depreciation	609,420.88
Office Equip. Less Depreciation	1,841.70
Total Fixed Assets	$735,762.58

Other Assets

Land for Future Development	$124,500.00
Total Assets	$890,000.00

Liabilities

Current Liabilities

Accounts Payable		$ 7,035.00
Mortgage Note Payable (Current)		7,155.00
Total Current Liabilities		$ 14,190.00

Long-Term Liabilities

Mortgage Note Payable (20XX)		$478,600.00
Total Liabilities		$492,790.00

Owner's Equity

Common Stock		$255,000.00
Retained Earnings		142,210.00
Total Owner's Equity		$397,210.00
Total Liabilities and Owner's Equity		$890,000.00

Name: _____

Form 28

WOODSIDE APARTMENTS

Income Statement
For Month Ended October 31, 20XX

Revenue	Amount
Apartmental Rental and Other Monies	$28,250.00
Operating Expenses	
Salary Expense	$ 5,175.00
Depreciation Expense—Apartment Buildings	3,361.95
Maintenance Expense	1,560.00
Utilities	1,383.35
Advertising	714.30
Property Taxes	583.33
Furniture Rental—Clubhouse	570.00
Apartment Selector Commission Expense	410.20
Repair Supplies	385.45
Pool Supplies	382.30
Insurance Expense	344.90
Office Supplies	179.85
Delivery Expense	92.50
Gasoline and Oil	74.80
Depreciation Expense—Office Equipment	70.83
Postage	66.75
Miscellaneous Expense	61.48
Total Operating Expenses	$15,416.99
Net Profit Before Taxes	$12,833.01

Name:_____

_____

Form 29 (Reminder: Use four decimal places.)

WOODSIDE APARTMENTS

Analysis of Statement of Financial Position
For Month Ended_____

Account Name	Dollar Amount	÷	Total Assets	=	Amount Stated as a Percent of Total Assets
Cash	$ 25,000.00	÷	$890,000	=	_____ %
Accounts Receivable	2,130.65	÷	(Constant)	=	_____ %
Office Supplies	310.65	÷		=	_____ %
Repair Supplies	175.92	÷		=	_____ %
Pool Supplies	285.30	÷		=	_____ %
Prepaid Insurance	1,835.20	÷		=	_____ %
Total Current Assets	29,737.42	÷		=	_____ %
Land	124,500.00	÷		=	_____ %
Bldg. Less Deprec.	609,420.88	÷		=	_____ %
Office Equip. Less Deprec.	1,841.70	÷		=	_____ %
Total Fixed Assets	735,762.58	÷		=	_____ %
Land for Future Dev.	124,500.00	÷		=	_____ %

Analysis of Statement of Financial Position   Continued, p. 2
for Month Ended_____

Account Name	Dollar Amount	÷	Total Liabilities & Owner's Equity	=	Amount Stated as a Percent of Total Liab. & O. Equity
Accounts Payable	$ 7,035.00	÷	$890,000	=	_____ %
Mort. Pay (Curr.)	7,155.00	÷	(Constant)	=	_____ %
Total Cur. Liab.	14,190.00	÷		=	_____ %
Mort. Pay. (20XX)	478,600.00	÷		=	_____ %
Total Liabilities	492,790.00	÷		=	_____ %
Common Stock	255,000.00	÷		=	_____ %
Retained Earnings	142,210.00	÷		=	_____ %
Total Owner's Equity	397,210.00	÷		=	_____ %

Name:_____

_____

Form 30 (Reminder: Use four decimal places.)

WOODSIDE APARTMENTS

Analysis of Income Statement
for Month Ended_____

Expense Account	Dollar Amount	÷	Total Revenue	=	Expense Stated as a Percent of Revenue
Salary	$ 5,175.00	÷	$28,250.00	=	_____ %
Depreciation—Apt.	3,361.95	÷	(Constant)	=	_____ %
Maintenance	1,560.00	÷		=	_____ %
Utilities	1,383.35	÷		=	_____ %
Advertising	714.30	÷		=	_____ %
Property Taxes	583.33	÷		=	_____ %
Furniture Rental	570.00	÷		=	_____ %
Apt. Selector	410.20	÷		=	_____ %
Repair Supplies	385.45	÷		=	_____ %
Pool Supplies	382.30	÷		=	_____ %
Insurance Expense	344.90	÷		=	_____ %
Office Supplies	179.85	÷		=	_____ %
Delivery Expense	92.50	÷		=	_____ %
Gasoline and Oil	74.80	÷		=	_____ %
Depreciation—Equip.	70.83	÷		=	_____ %
Postage	66.75	÷		=	_____ %
Miscellaneous Expense	61.48	÷		=	_____ %
Total Expenses	$ 15,416.99	÷		=	_____ %
Net Profit Before Taxes	$ 12,833.01	÷		=	_____ %

Name:_____

_____

Form 31

WOODSIDE APARTMENTS

Financial Ratios—An Analysis

I. Current Ratio

$$\frac{\text{Current Assets}}{\text{Current Liabilities}} \quad \frac{\$_____}{\$_____} = _____ \text{ to 1.0} \quad \text{Reference: 2.0 to 1.0}$$

II. Acid Test Ratio

$$\frac{\text{Cash + Receivables}}{\text{Current Liabilities}} \quad \frac{\$_____}{\$_____} = _____ \text{ to 1.0} \quad \text{Reference: 1.0 to 1.0}$$

III. Return on Assets

Step 1: October Profit

$\$_____ \times 12 = \$_____$ Projected Yearly Profit

Step 2:

$$\frac{\text{Projected Yearly Profit}}{\text{Total Assets}} \quad \frac{\$_____}{\$_____} = _____ \% \quad \text{Reference: 8\%–10\%}$$

IV. Return on Owner's Equity

Step 1: October Profit

$\$_____ \times 12 = \$_____$ Projected Yearly Profit

Step 2:

$$\frac{\text{Projected Yearly Profit}}{\text{Total Owner's Equity}} \quad \frac{\$_____}{\$_____} = _____ \% \quad \text{Reference: 12\%–15\%}$$

Name:___
___

Form 32 (Reminder: Use four decimal places.)

WOODSIDE APARTMENTS
Percent of Increase and Decrease

Expense	October Last Year	October This Year	Amount of Change	Percent of Change	Increase or Decrease
Salary	$6,150.00	$5,175.00	$_____	_____	_____
Utilities	1,090.40	1,383.35	$_____	_____	_____
Maintenance	1,134.00	1,560.00	$_____	_____	_____
Furniture Rental	425.00	570.00	$_____	_____	_____

Name:_____

_____

Form 33

IF BANKING BY MAIL

1. Endorse checks as follows. Pay to the order of bank (your signature).

2. Originate in duplicate – enclose in envelope both copies with items for deposit. Duplicate will be returned by mail.

3. If currency or coin is contained in the deposit, please send by registered mail.

Record Checks for Deposit	Dollars	Cents

IMPORTANT
Include amount of above checks in total on front side

Record Checks for Deposit	Dollars	Cents
Currency Please send by registered mail		
Coins		
Use back side for listing additional checks **Total Deposit**		

If you are banking by mail please refer to instructions on reverse side.

Checks and other items are received for deposit subject to the terms and conditions of this bank's collection agreement now in effect.

Woodside Apartments
909 Woodside Drive
Dallas, TX 75248

Name:_____

_____

Form 34

Newton Maintenance Supply
1512 Ervay Street
Dallas, TX 75201

November 3   20   XX

TO   Woodside Apartments

ADDRESS   909 Woodside Drive

CITY   Dallas, TX 75248

TERMS   3/15, N/45   ORDER NO.   10234

Quantity	Description	Unit Cost		Total	
6	Industrial Cleaner	3	99	23	94
2	Floor Wax–per gallon	9	98	19	96
3	Light Bulbs–per case	17	49	52	47
			Subtotal	96	37
			Less 20%	19	27
			Subtotal	77	10
			Less 3/15, N/45	2	31
			Invoice Total	74	79

Name:_____

Form 35

Heritage Office Supply
515 North Star Road
Dallas, TX 75243

November 3   20 XX

TO   Woodside Apartments
ADDRESS   909 Woodside Drive
CITY   Dallas, TX 75248
TERMS   2/10, N/30   ORDER NO.   AZ - 5316

Quantity	Description	Unit Cost		Total	
24	Ball Point Pens	1	19	28	56
6	Liquid Paper	1	75	22	50
4	Typewriter Ribbons	4	75	19	00
2	Boxes Legal File Folders	7	95	15	90
1	Word Division Book	3	98	3	98
1	Dictionary	12	50	12	50
		Subtotal		102	44
		Less 20%, 15%, 8%		38	35
		Subtotal		64	09
		Less 2/10, N/30		1	28
		Invoice Total		62	81

Name:_____

_____

Form 36

WOODSIDE APARTMENTS

Comparison of Depreciation Methods

Factors: $2,950 Original Cost
5-Year Estimated Life
$150 Estimated Salvage Value

Straight-Line Method		Declining-Balance Method	
First-Year Depreciation	$____	First-Year Depreciation	$____
First-Year Book Value	$____	First-Year Book Value	$____
Second-Year Depreciation	$____	Second-Year Depreciation	$____
Second-Year Book Value	$____	Second-Year Book Value	$____

Name:_____

Form 37 (Reminder: Use four decimal places.)

WOODSIDE APARTMENTS

Maintenance Expense—An Analysis

Year	Maintenance Expense	Total Revenue	Percent of Total Revenue
2003	$13,099	$208,259	_____ %
2004	14,513	228,856	_____ %
2005	17,552	235,428	_____ %
2006	21,750	288,960	_____ %
2007	24,300	316,000	_____ %

Your Findings

Name:_____

Form 38

WOODSIDE APARTMENTS

Natural Gas—An Analysis

Specific Area	Square Footage	Dollar Distribution of Expense
Office	650	$_____
Clubhouse	1,230	$_____
Laundry Rooms	515	$_____
Manager's Apt.	1,080	$_____
Total		$483.35 Natural Gas Expense

Name:_____

_____

Form 39

WOODSIDE APARTMENTS

Electric Expense—An Analysis

Specific Area	Square Footage	Dollar Distribution of Expense
Office	650	$_____
Clubhouse	1,230	$_____
Laundry Rooms	515	$_____
Manager's Apt.	1,080	$_____
Total		$675 Electric Expense

Name:_____

_____

Form 40

WOODSIDE APARTMENTS

Advertising Expense—An Analysis

Apartment Complex	Monthly Revenue	Prorated Expense
Woodside Apts.	$28,250	$ _____
Brockport Apts.	18,800	$ _____
Columbia Manor	24,370	$ _____
Martin's Woods	16,930	$ _____
Brookside Apts.	30,640	$ _____
Leisure Tree Manor	21,345	$ _____
Total		$6,210 Advertising Expense

Name:_____

_____

Date			Bal. For'd		
			Deposits	4,155	00
10/31/20XX					
			Total		
To the Order of			Amt. this Check		
			Balance		

Woodside Apartments
909 Woodside Dr.
Dallas, TX 75248

431

20____   75-148/919

PAY TO THE
ORDER OF _____

$ _____

_____ DOLLARS

Woodside Apartments

For _____

⑉ı:091901480ı:85300021ı83ı4ıı' 0366

····

Date			Bal. For'd		
			Deposits		
			Total		
To the Order of			Amt. this Check		
			Balance		

Woodside Apartments
909 Woodside Dr.
Dallas, TX 75248

432

20____   75-148/919

PAY TO THE
ORDER OF _____

$ _____

_____ DOLLARS

Woodside Apartments

For _____

⑉ı:091901480ı:85300021ı83ı4ıı' 0366

····

Date		Bal. For'd		
		Deposits	4,030	00
11/1/20XX				
To the Order of		Total		
		Amt. this Check		
		Balance		

Woodside Apartments
909 Woodside Dr.
Dallas, TX 75248

433

_____ 20 ____   75-148/919

PAY TO THE
ORDER OF _____ $ _____

_____ DOLLARS

Woodside Apartments

For _____

⑈¦⁚091901480⁚85300021⑈83141⑈" 0366

Date		Bal. For'd		
		Deposits		
To the Order of		Total		
		Amt. this Check		
		Balance		

Woodside Apartments
909 Woodside Dr.
Dallas, TX 75248

434

_____ 20 ____   75-148/919

PAY TO THE
ORDER OF _____ $ _____

_____ DOLLARS

Woodside Apartments

For _____

⑈¦⁚091901480⁚85300021⑈83141⑈" 0366

Woodside Apartments
909 Woodside Dr.
Dallas, TX 75248

435

20____

75-148/919

PAY TO THE
ORDER OF _____

$ _____

_____ DOLLARS

Woodside Apartments

For _____

⑆091901480⑆853000211831411⑈ 0366

Date

Bal. For'd

Deposits

Total

To the Order of

Amt. this Check

Balance

Woodside Apartments
909 Woodside Dr.
Dallas, TX 75248

436

20____

75-148/919

PAY TO THE
ORDER OF _____

$ _____

_____ DOLLARS

Woodside Apartments

For _____

⑆091901480⑆853000211831411⑈ 0366

Date

Bal. For'd

Deposits

Total

To the Order of

Amt. this Check

Balance

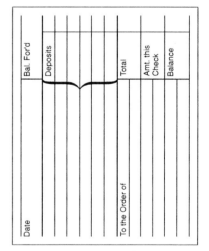

Date
Bal. For'd

Deposits

Total

To the Order of

Amt. this
Check

Balance

437

20

75-148/919

Woodside Apartments
909 Woodside Dr.
Dallas, TX 75248

PAY TO THE
ORDER OF

$

DOLLARS

Woodside Apartments

For

⑆ ⑈091901480⑈ 8530002118314⑈ 0366

Date
Bal. For'd

Deposits

Total

To the Order of

Amt. this
Check

Balance

438

20

75-148/919

Woodside Apartments
909 Woodside Dr.
Dallas, TX 75248

PAY TO THE
ORDER OF

$

DOLLARS

Woodside Apartments

For

⑆ ⑈091901480⑈ 8530002118314⑈ 0366

Woodside Apartments
909 Woodside Dr.
Dallas, TX 75248

439

75-148/919

20____

PAY TO THE
ORDER OF ____

$____

____ DOLLARS

Woodside Apartments

For ____

⑆091901480⑆ 8530002118314⑈ 0366

Date

Bal. For'd		
Deposits		
Total		
Amt. this Check		
Balance		

To the Order of

Woodside Apartments
909 Woodside Dr.
Dallas, TX 75248

440

75-148/919

20____

PAY TO THE
ORDER OF ____

$____

____ DOLLARS

Woodside Apartments

For ____

⑆091901480⑆ 8530002118314⑈ 0366

Date

Bal. For'd		
Deposits		
Total		
Amt. this Check		
Balance		

To the Order of

Woodside Apartments
909 Woodside Dr.
Dallas, TX 75248

441

75-148/919

20____

PAY TO THE
ORDER OF _____ $ _____

_____ DOLLARS

Woodside Apartments

For _____

⑈⑆091901480⑆8530002118314⑈ 0366

Date	Bal. For'd		
	Deposits		
11/2/20XX		$1,769	50
To the Order of	Total		
	Amt. this Check		
	Balance		

Woodside Apartments
909 Woodside Dr.
Dallas, TX 75248

442

75-148/919

20____

PAY TO THE
ORDER OF _____ $ _____

_____ DOLLARS

Woodside Apartments

For _____

⑈⑆091901480⑆8530002118314⑈ 0366

Date	Bal. For'd		
	Deposits		
To the Order of	Total		
	Amt. this Check		
	Balance		

Woodside Apartments
909 Woodside Dr.
Dallas, TX 75248

443

_____ 20 ___ 75-148/919

PAY TO THE
ORDER OF _____

$ _____

_____ DOLLARS

Woodside Apartments

For _____

⑆091901480⑈85300021183114⑆ 0366

Date	Bal. For'd	
	Deposits	
11/3/20XX	$1,125	00
To the Order of	Total	
	Amt. this Check	
	Balance	

Woodside Apartments
909 Woodside Dr.
Dallas, TX 75248

444

_____ 20 ___ 75-148/919

PAY TO THE
ORDER OF _____

$ _____

_____ DOLLARS

Woodside Apartments

For _____

⑆091901480⑈85300021183114⑆ 0366

Date	Bal. For'd	
	Deposits	
To the Order of	Total	
	Amt. this Check	
	Balance	

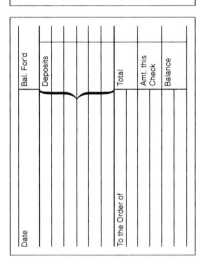

Woodside Apartments
909 Woodside Dr.
Dallas, TX 75248

445

20 _____

75-148/919

PAY TO THE
ORDER OF _____

$ _____

_____ DOLLARS

Woodside Apartments

For _____

⊕ ⑆091901480⑆853000211831⑈4⑈ 0366

Date		Bal. For'd	
		Deposits	
		Total	
To the Order of		Amt. this Check	
		Balance	

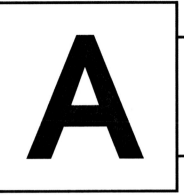

Using the Computer Numeric Keypad

Use of the computer will become more and more a necessity as you progress through your professional career in business. The computer keyboard contains two separate keypads. One is the standard typewriter keyboard containing letter keys, number keys, punctuation keys, and space bar. The other, located at the right of the typing keyboard, is the standard ten-key numeric keyboard. This keyboard is a quick, easy way to type numbers in manuscript material or on a spread sheet. By using the calculator option contained in most software packages, the numeric keyboard becomes the major input source for a calculator.

Most software offers options ranging from the standard calculator to the scientific calculator and the financial calculator. These calculators have most of the same options and operations as your electronic calculator, but a few of the symbols and locations of the action keys will vary. Table A.1 lists the standard symbols and operations contained in most calculator software programs.

The numeric keypad is the same as the ten-key keyboard on the electronic calculator. Continue to use proper posture at the computer keypad and operate the keypad using the same skills developed on the electronic calculator. Note the demonstrated posture, placement of working papers, and placement of hands on the keypad in Figure A.1.

Methods used to perform basic calculations on computers using the keypad are presented in the following illustrations.

Addition

$23 + 4.5 + 0.077 + 7 =$

Set 23	Depress +
Set 4.5	Depress +
Set 0.077	Depress +
Set 7	Depress Enter or =
Read the answer:	34.577

TABLE A.1 Standard Symbols and Locations

Button	Key	Function
+	+	Adds
−	−	Subtracts
*	*	Multiplies
/	/	Divides
sqrt	@	Calculates square root
%	%	Calculates percentage
1/x	r	Calculates reciprocal
=	= or Enter	Performs any operation between the previous two numbers
+/−	F9	Changes sign of displayed number
Back	Backspace or Left Arrow	Deletes last digit displayed on right
CE	DEL	Clears the displayed number
C	ESC	Clears the current calculation
MC	CTRL + L	Clears memory
MR	CTRL + R	Recalls number stored in memory
MS	CTRL + M	Stores displayed number in memory
M+	CTRL + P	Adds number displayed to value stored in memory

FIGURE A.1 Correct Posture

Subtraction

$27.55 - 3.45 =$

Set 27.55   Depress $-$
Set 3.45   Depress Enter or $=$
Read the answer: 24.10

Multiplication

$70.14 \times 3.2 =$

Set 70.14   Depress *
Set 3.2   Depress Enter or $=$
Read the answer: 224.448

Division

$419/26.8 =$

Set 419   Depress /
Set 26.8   Depress Enter or $=$
Read the answer: 15.634

B

Answers to Selected Problems and Self-Evaluations

CHAPTER 1   BUSINESS MATHEMATICS REVIEW

Addition

1. 72.82	**7.** 80.386	**13.** 12.16
3. 9.29	**9.** 3,430.6048	**15.** 799.0058
5. 201.733	**11.** 19.762	

Subtraction

1. 32.77	**7.** 37.520	**13.** 0.9395
3. 236.26	**9.** 4,005.541	**15.** 26.4472
5. 35.48	**11.** 2.815	

Multiplication

1. 21.252	**7.** 0.47544	**11.** 3.2805
3. 308.18247	**9.** 2.64825	**13.** 9.23019
5. 0.00027125		

Division

1. 227	**3.** 81.5

Rounding Numbers with Decimals

1. 46.35	**5.** 406.01	**9.** 4.0076
3. 76.67	**7.** 129.6675	**11.** 77.2001

Self-Check

1. 58.63	**5.** 94.13	**7.** 78.8
3. 9.29		

Converting Decimals and Fractions

1. 0.625	**9.** 0.75	**15.** 3/4
3. 0.8	**11.** 1/5	**17.** 1/2
5. 0.167	**13.** 5/8	**19.** 7/8
7. 0.1		

Self-Check

1. 0.4	**3.** 0.9	**5.** 2/5

Proofreading Numbers

1. x	**7.** 15.91	**13.** 78,963
3. .11	**9.** 14¢	**15.** $17.10
5. x	**11.** x	

Self-Check

1. 9.63, 4.59, 4.68, 8.43	**3.** 6.45, 4.60, 3.53

Base, Rate, and Portion

1. 70.80	**5.** 145	**9.** 10%
3. 187.50	**7.** 20	**11.** 40%

Self-Check

1. 80.85	**7.** 11.17%	**11.** 226.38
3. 56.45	**9.** 78.34%	**13.** 48.47%
5. 282.5		

Solving Narative Problems

1. $73.00	**3.** $13.57

Estimations

1. 2,467	**5.** OK	**7.** $0.01
3. OK		

CHAPTER 2   OPERATING THE TEN-KEY KEYBOARD BY THE TOUCH METHOD

1. 3,360	**19.** 47.44	**37.** 457.79
3. 2,694	**21.** 35.16	**39.** 5,133.95
5. 3,966	**23.** 45.00	**41.** 4,140.04
7. 3,120	**25.** 59.26	**43.** 52,677.75
9. 3,339	**27.** 44.54	**45.** 423,810.02
11. 3,119	**29.** 308.65	**47.** 107,464.82
13. 35.52	**31.** 132.34	**49.** 126,661.00
15. 53.28	**33.** 106.46	**51.** 119, 494.01
17. 38.31	**35.** 1,135.01	

Self-Check

1. 3,016.73	**3.** 143,401.79	**5.** 5,300.35

CHAPTER 3   PRACTICE AND SPEED DEVELOPMENT

Speed Development 1

1. 6,378	**5.** 4,854	**9.** 2,615
3. 4,166	**7.** 5,551	

Speed Development 2

1. 474.30	**5.** 547.42	**9.** 382.90
3. 321.14	**7.** 676.01	

Speed Development 3

1. 21,283.80	**5.** 15,649.57	**9.** 5,451.44
3. 10,397.57	**7.** 3,076.42	

Self-Evaluation Skills Posttest

1. 684.43	**5.** 1,203.13	**8.** 2,407.49
2. 1,467.78	**6.** 1,170.97	**9.** 5,693.16
3. 1,145.40	**7.** 1,681.12	**10.** 5,947.57
4. 2,746.84		

CHAPTER 4 ADDITION AND SUBTRACTION ON THE ELECTRONIC CALCULATOR

11. 12,968.68	**47.** 282.16 cr.	**83.** 531.85
13. 14,988.18	**49.** 3,857.68 cr.	**85.** 386.01
15. 19,576.71	**51.** 1.70	**87.** 108.71
17. 16,986.98	**53.** 22.54	**89.** 7.35
19. 30,225.03	**55.** 116.26	**91.** 1.48
21. 10.89	**57.** 3.72 cr.	**93.** 118.68 cr.
23. 132.23	**59.** 5.30	**95.** 7.87 cr.
25. 22.42	**61.** 105.52 cr.	**97.** 224.04
27. 103.74	**63.** 609.29	**99.** 299.24
29. 446.34	**65.** 68.03	**101.** 236.03
31. 1,417.54	**67.** 767.14 cr.	**103.** 68.58
33. 1,126.82	**69.** 147.26	**105.** 7.87
35. 3.28	**71.** 354.90	**107.** 116.58
37. 3,125.82	**73.** 272.60	**109.** 278.82
39. 115.63	**75.** 1,486.94	**111.** 363.78
41. 325.35 cr.	**77.** 1,941.86	**113.** 32.10 cr.
43. 238.52 cr.	**79.** 2,030.51	**115.** 68.10
45. 11.47 cr.	**81.** 74.97	

Self-Evaluation

1. 4,527	**5.** 242.01	**9.** 48.92 cr.
2. 42.66	**6.** 197.11	**10.** 33.5
3. 564.92	**7.** 31	**11.** 5.44
4. 81.08	**8.** 5.19	**12d.** 1,120.31

Business Applications: Maintaining Check Registers

1g. $1,419.19   **3i.** $647.81

Business Applications: Completing Bank Statement Reconciliation

5j. $1,126.53

Business Applications: Processing Consumer Payment Cards

7h. $73.80   **9h.** $414.64

Business Applications: Working with Accounting Forms

11e. $388.97   **13e.** $5,878.09

Business Applications: Completing a Payroll Journal

15h. $665.97   **17h.** $1,107.86

Self-Evaluation: Part I

1d. $388.01	**4a.** $3,772.70	**5a.** $1,307.25
2. $541.05	**4b.** $41.01	**5b.** $183.01
3. $435.63	**4c.** $3,731.69	**5c.** $1,124.24

Self-Evaluation: Part II

1. $4,352.33	**4.** $63.39	**6b.** $15,001.54
2. $858.07	**5.** $515.83	**6c.** yes
3j. $40,424.08	**6a.** $15,001.54	**7.** $234.58

CHAPTER 5   MULTIPLICATION ON THE ELECTRONIC CALCULATOR

1. 8,970	**31.** 41.54	**61.** 6,233.76
3. 46,134	**33.** 45.83	**63.** 3,306.80
5. 80,352	**35.** 2,236.50	**65.** 2,883.74
7. 3,358,664	**37.** 10,386.94	**67.** 267.30
9. 7,008,603	**39.** 57.63	**69.** 2,916.72
11. 15,257,452	**41.** 10.20	**71.** 63
13. 75.88	**43.** 145.16	**73.** 44,365
15. 99.54	**45.** 136.23	**75.** 2,724.03
17. 892.62	**47.** 682.28	**77.** 1,139.04
19. 45,674.06	**49.** 554.83	**79.** 417.44
21. 5.25	**51.** 352	**81.** 50
23. 29.77	**53.** 55.00	**83.** 523.69
25. 1,215.64	**55.** 90.75	**85.** 1,595.47
27. 0.78	**57.** 248.49	
29. 1.86	**59.** 222.29	

Self-Evaluation

1. 333.31	**6.** 372.33	**11.** 37.89
2. 24.14	**7.** 260.04	**12.** 109.20
3. 29.08 cr.	**8.** 272.27	**13.** 1,832.40
4. 18,088	**9.** 31.53	**14.** 2,054.73
5. 430.56	**10.** 2,781	**15.** 690.73

Business Applications: Working Markdown Problems

1. 85%	**13.** $1.13	**25.** $31.46
3. 60%	**15.** $2.75	**27.** $28.75
5. 72%	**17.** $18.89	**29.** $25.46
7. $5.95	**19.** $10.85	**31.** $15.96
9. $8.00	**21.** $15.96	**33.** $12.76
11. $0.45	**23.** $21.75	**35.** $9.06

Business Applications: Calculating Cash Discounts

37. $235.50	**45.** 98%	**51b.** $1,494.04
39. $35.99	**47.** $2,619.00	**53b.** $2,584.30
41. 97%	**49.** $6,618.54	**55b.** $1,831.22
43. 96%		

Business Applications: Determining Compound Interest Amounts

57. 1.0609	**65.** $1,461.24	**71.** $2,973.93
59. 1.1255	**67.** $4,535.66	**73.** $34,695.57
61. 1.2682	**69.** $2,706.00	**75.** $11,153.85
63. $2,720.36		

Business Applications: Calculating Commissions

77. $272.30	**85.** $1,486.70	**91.** $428.89
79. $281.60	**87.** $334.40	**93.** $350.79
81. $350.31	**89.** $435.60	**95.** $3,451.69
83. $374.21		

Business Applications: Working with Markup—Cost Method

97. $45.00	**103.** $444.50	**109b.** $249.25
99. $124.00	**105.** $565.80	
101. $384.40	**107b.** $154.44	

Self-Evaluation: Part I

1b. $12.71	**2f.** $3,455.59	**4b.** $379.58
1d. $23.60	**3a.** $3,416.84	**4c.** $534.68
1f. $14.96	**3b.** $4,371.57	**5b.** $2.98
2b. $1,503.91	**3c.** $7,255.56	**5d.** $12.98
2d. $849.09	**4a.** $280.80	**5f.** $29.95

Self-Evaluation: Part II

1a. $21.99	**2b.** $3,146.78	**5.** $260.30
1b. $87.96	**3.** $14,060.40	**6a.** $1.44
2a. $64.22	**4.** $4,810	**6b.** $5.04

CHAPTER 6   DIVISION ON THE ELECTRONIC CALCULATOR

1. 2.89	**15.** 7.76	**29.** 80.88
3. 6.74	**17.** 1.29	**31.** 12.29
5. 15.37	**19.** 0.05	**33.** 8.81
7. 35.82	**21.** 17.22	**35.** 6.09
9. 263.14	**23.** 8.78	**37.** 614.86
11. 1.19	**25.** 24.49	**39.** 450.68
13. 1.45	**27.** 33.79	

Self-Evaluation Skills Posttest

1. 3,517.50	**6.** 23.68	**11.** 2.30
2. 119.45	**7.** 49.88	**12.** 1.35
3. 150,892	**8.** 0.68	**13.** 0.14
4. 0.02	**9.** 4,702	**14.** 409.59
5. 1,571.20	**10.** 3.73	**15.** 32.49

Business Applications: Working with Markup—Retail Method

1. 75%	**9b.** $29.99	**15b.** $12.00
3. 65%	**11b.** $31.99	**17b.** $20.00
5. 61%	**13b.** $10.00	**19b.** $30.77
7. 57%		

Business Applications: Calculating Percent of Increase/Decrease

22a. $2,000	**28b.** 47.44%	**34b.** 3.01%
24a. $5,280	**30b.** 20.14%	
26b. 10.20%	**32b.** 6.88%	

Business Applications:
Analyzing Statements of Financial Position

37. 9.6%	**47.** 56.9%	**57.** 5.7%
39. 56.2%	**49.** 4.2%	**59.** 76.5%
41. 6.9%	**51.** 9.2%	**61.** 6.7%
43. 16.2%	**53.** 8.1%	**63.** 68.0%
45. 20.2%	**55.** 23.5%	**65.** 84.3%

Business Applications: Analyzing Income Statements

67. 12.2%	**77.** 1%	**87.** 1.6%
69. 2.4%	**79.** 16.3%	**89.** 1.5%
71. 3.4%	**81.** 67.4%	**91.** 2.0%
73. 0.9%	**83.** 57.3%	**93.** 0.6%
75. 9.6%	**85.** 19.6%	**95.** 9.8%

Business Applications:
Calculating Depreciation—Straight Line

97. $2,300	**103.** $1,013.13	**109c.** $5,571.42
99. $442.78	**105.** $880.40	**111c.** $4,132.50
101. $678.57	**107c.** $2,225	**113c.** $6,903.74

Self-Evaluation: Part I

1b. $59.95	**2h.** −13%	**4b.** 24.3%
1d. $15.99	**3a.** 15.5%	**4c.** 4.4%
1f. $9.99	**3b.** 8.1%	**5a.** $125.73
2b. 5%	**3c.** 41.5%	**5b.** $193.75
2e. 19%	**4a.** 40.4%	**5c.** $98.69

Self-Evaluation: Part II

1. $83.25	**3a.** $3,544	**5.** 1.8%
2a. $249	**3b.** 11.4%	**6a.** $3,160
2b. $62.25	**4.** 37%	**6b.** $7,320

CHAPTER 7   MULTIPLE OPERATIONS ON THE ELECTRONIC CALCULATOR

1. 120	**7.** 16.53	**13.** 217.51
3. 56.73	**9.** 55.82	**15.** 17.89
5. 37.55	**11.** 27.28	

Self-Evaluation Skills Posttest

1. 56.73	**6.** 1.96	**11.** 34.67
2. 1.47 cr.	**7.** 5,600	**12.** 7.23 cr.
3. 25.95	**8.** 9,563.19	**13.** 55.22
4. 23.93	**9.** 1.82	**14.** 24.74
5. 188.27	**10.** 61.73	**15.** 31,957.94 cr.

Business Applications: Calculating Depreciation—Declining Balance

1c. $1,980.00	**9c.** $3,675.00	**15c.** $450.00
3c. $1,445.00	**11c.** $360.00	**17c.** $1,111.11
5c. $1,096.00	**13c.** $1,426.67	**19c.** $466.67
7c. $1,103.40		

Business Applications: Working with Series (Chain) Discounts

22. $562.95	**28b.** $163.68	**34b.** $161.79
24. $336.15	**30b.** $168.46	
26b. $131.24	**32b.** $220.02	

Business Applications: Completing Invoices

36h. $251.99	**38h.** $1,478.55

Business Applications: Calculating Simple Interest

40b. $1,590.00	**46b.** $3,471.58
42b. $3,104.88	**48b.** $1,010.36
44b. $2,280.18	

Business Applications: Calculating Distribution of Expense

50. 1,625	**56b.** $912.00	**62b.** $1,372.16
52b. $1,125.97	**58.** 880	
54. 750	**60b.** $2,103.98 (−.01)	

Self-Evaluation: Part I

1c. $1,956	**2c.** $4,319.69	**5b.** $549.71
1f. $487.50	**3f.** $602.71	**5d.** $613.14
1i. $1,720	**4b.** $1,609.61	**5f.** $687.14 (+.01)
2a. $508.73	**4d.** $4,851.38	
2b. $2,120.79	**4f.** $13,837.48	

Self-Evaluation: Part II

1a. $7,400	**2.** $1,074.73	**5a.** $238.87
1b. $11,100	**3a.** $2,461.39	**5b.** $4,113.87
1c. $4,400	**3b.** $1,828.61	**6.** 5,210
1d. $6,600	**4a.** $6.21	**7.** $1,800
1e. $2,664	**4b.** $304.19	

CHAPTER 8 DEVELOPING KEYBOARDING AND CRITICAL THINKING SKILLS

1. 1,732.45	**9.** 43.02	**17.** 145.29
3. 1,979.40	**11.** 35,118.16	**19.** 37.37
5. 13,125.52	**13.** 934.74	**21.** 22.75
7. 6,436.71	**15.** 752.94	

Self-Evaluation Skills Posttest

1. 115.82	**6.** 2.27	**11.** 21.85
2. 18.12 cr.	**7.** 3,315	**12.** 0.03
3. 51.92	**8.** 2,514.04	**13.** 64.24
4. 8.91	**9.** 0.13	**14.** 17.92
5. 151.65	**10.** 17.18	**15.** 33.36

Business Applications: Finding Statistical Averages

1. $30,571.17	**5.** $260,144.14	**9.** $24,205.29
3. $6,089.72	**7.** $34,000	**11.** $3,540.30

Business Applications: Calculating Dividend Yield and Stock Earnings

13. 2.8%	**19.** 3.4%	**25.** $0.39
15. 1.7%	**21.** $2.29	**27.** $1.19
17. 5.8%	**23.** $3.28	

Business Applications: Working with Inventory Valuation

29. 905	**35.** $338.75
31. $1,717.50	**37.** 50
33. 105	**39.** $12,567.50

Business Applications: Calculating Financial Ratios

41.	1.48 below	**47.**	3.08
43.	13	**49.**	10.50
45.	3%	**51.**	3%

Business Applications: Examining Corporate Taxation

56.	$176,800	**64.**	$10,750

Business Applications: Determining Insurance Premiums

70.	$3.51	**76b.**	$496.18	**80b.**	$784.00
72.	$5.10	**78b.**	$98.00	**82b.**	$814.15
74b.	$93.50				

Business Applications: Working with Installment Loans

84.	$9.33	**92b.**	$956.32
86.	$11.55	**94b.**	$247.78
88.	$8.04	**96b.**	$118.08
90b.	$939.83	**98b.**	$1,605.15

Self-Evaluation: Part I

1a.	$9,825.20	**3b.**	$4.15	**6d.**	$175,780
1b.	$9,430	**3c.**	$4.42	**7a.**	$431.20
1c.	$8,890	**4a.**	$222.50	**7b.**	$596.31
2a.	6%	**4b.**	$217.20	**7c.**	$450.90
2b.	6%	**5a.**	1.45	**8a.**	$1,097.25
2c.	6%	**5b.**	7%	**8b.**	$371.07
3a.	$2.64	**5c.**	9	**8c.**	$318.49

Self-Evaluation: Part II

1a.	$299.15	**3.**	$4.70	**6b.**	6%
1b.	$59.83	**4a.**	$3,455	**7a.**	5
1c.	$56.78	**4b.**	$3,394.80	**7b.**	Below average
1d.	$56.78	**5a.**	2.20	**8.**	$208,216
2a.	$0.72	**5b.**	Above average	**9.**	$546
2b.	1.8%	**6a.**	7%	**10.**	$1,359.38

CHAPTER 9   WOODSIDE APARTMENTS:
A SIMULATION

See Instructor for Check Figures.

SINGLE PC LICENSE AGREEMENT AND LIMITED WARRANTY

READ THIS LICENSE CAREFULLY BEFORE OPENING THIS PACKAGE. BY OPENING THIS PACKAGE, YOU ARE AGREEING TO THE TERMS AND CONDITIONS OF THIS LICENSE. IF YOU DO NOT AGREE, DO NOT OPEN THE PACKAGE. PROMPTLY RETURN THE UNOPENED PACKAGE AND ALL ACCOMPANYING ITEMS TO THE PLACE YOU OBTAINED THEM FOR A FULL REFUND OF ANY SUMS YOU HAVE PAID FOR THE SOFTWARE. THESE TERMS APPLY TO ALL LICENSED SOFTWARE ON THE CD-ROM EXCEPT THAT THE TERMS FOR USE OF ANY SHAREWARE OR FREEWARE ON THE CD-ROM ARE AS SET FORTH IN THE ELECTRONIC LICENSE LOCATED ON THE CD:

1. GRANT OF LICENSE and OWNERSHIP: The enclosed computer programs and data ("Software") are licensed, not sold, to you by Prentice-Hall, Inc. ("We" or the "Company") and in consideration of your payment of the license fee, which is part of the price you paid and your agreement to these terms. We reserve any rights not granted to you. You own only the disk(s) but we and/or our licensors own the Software itself. This license allows you to use and display your copy of the Software on a single computer (i.e., with a single CPU) at a single location for academic use only, so long as you comply with the terms of this Agreement. You may make one copy for back up, or transfer your copy to another CPU, provided that the Software is usable on only one computer.

2. RESTRICTIONS: You may not transfer or distribute the Software or documentation to anyone else. Except for backup, you may not copy the documentation or the Software. You may not network the Software or otherwise use it on more than one computer or computer terminal at the same time. You may not reverse engineer, disassemble, decompile, modify, adapt, translate, or create derivative works based on the Software or the Documentation. You may be held legally responsible for any copying or copyright infringement which is caused by your failure to abide by the terms of these restrictions.

3. TERMINATION: This license is effective until terminated. This license will terminate automatically without notice from the Company if you fail to comply with any provisions or limitations of this license. Upon termination, you shall destroy the Documentation and all copies of the Software. All provisions of this Agreement as to limitation and disclaimer of warranties, limitation of liability, remedies or damages, and our ownership rights shall survive termination.

4. LIMITED WARRANTY AND DISCLAIMER OF WARRANTY: Company warrants that for a period of 60 days from the date you purchase this SOFTWARE (or purchase or adopt the accompanying textbook), the Software, when properly installed and used in accordance with the Documentation, will operate in substantial conformity with the description of the Software set forth in the Documentation, and that for a period of 30 days the disk(s) on which the Software is delivered shall be free from defects in materials and workmanship under normal use. The Company does not warrant that the Software will meet your requirements or that the operation of the Software will be uninterrupted or error-free. Your only remedy and the Company's only obligation under these limited warranties is, at the Company's option, return of the disk for a refund of any amounts paid for it by you or replacement of the disk. THIS LIMITED WARRANTY IS THE ONLY WARRANTY PROVIDED BY THE COMPANY AND ITS LICENSORS, AND THE COMPANY AND ITS LICENSORS DISCLAIM ALL OTHER WARRANTIES, EXPRESS OR IMPLIED, INCLUDING WITHOUT LIMITATION, THE IMPLIED WARRANTIES OF MERCHANTABILITY AND FITNESS FOR A PARTICULAR PURPOSE. THE COMPANY DOES NOT WARRANT, GUARANTEE OR MAKE ANY REPRESENTATION REGARDING THE ACCURACY, RELIABILITY, CURRENTNESS, USE, OR RESULTS OF USE, OF THE SOFTWARE.

5. LIMITATION OF REMEDIES AND DAMAGES: IN NO EVENT, SHALL THE COMPANY OR ITS EMPLOYEES, AGENTS, LICENSORS, OR CONTRACTORS BE LIABLE FOR ANY INCIDENTAL, INDIRECT, SPECIAL, OR CONSEQUENTIAL DAMAGES ARISING OUT OF OR IN CONNECTION WITH THIS LICENSE OR THE SOFTWARE, INCLUDING FOR LOSS OF USE, LOSS OF DATA, LOSS OF INCOME OR PROFIT, OR OTHER LOSSES, SUSTAINED AS A RESULT OF INJURY TO ANY PERSON, OR LOSS OF OR DAMAGE TO PROPERTY, OR CLAIMS OF THIRD PARTIES, EVEN IF THE COMPANY OR AN AUTHORIZED REPRESENTATIVE OF THE COMPANY HAS BEEN ADVISED OF THE POSSIBILITY OF SUCH DAMAGES. IN NO EVENT SHALL THE LIABILITY OF THE COMPANY FOR DAMAGES WITH RESPECT TO THE SOFTWARE EXCEED THE AMOUNTS ACTUALLY PAID BY YOU, IF ANY, FOR THE SOFTWARE OR THE ACCOMPANYING TEXTBOOK. BECAUSE SOME JURISDICTIONS DO NOT ALLOW THE LIMITATION OF LIABILITY IN CERTAIN CIRCUMSTANCES, THE ABOVE LIMITATIONS MAY NOT ALWAYS APPLY TO YOU.

6. GENERAL: THIS AGREEMENT SHALL BE CONSTRUED IN ACCORDANCE WITH THE LAWS OF THE UNITED STATES OF AMERICA AND THE STATE OF NEW YORK, APPLICABLE TO CONTRACTS MADE IN NEW YORK, AND SHALL BENEFIT THE COMPANY, ITS AFFILIATES AND ASSIGNEES. HIS AGREEMENT IS THE COMPLETE AND EXCLUSIVE STATEMENT OF THE AGREEMENT BETWEEN YOU AND THE COMPANY AND SUPERSEDES ALL PROPOSALS OR PRIOR AGREEMENTS, ORAL, OR WRITTEN, AND ANY OTHER COMMUNICATIONS BETWEEN YOU AND THE COMPANY OR ANY REPRESENTATIVE OF THE COMPANY RELATING TO THE SUBJECT MATTER OF THIS AGREEMENT.

If you are a U.S. Government user, this Software is licensed with "restricted rights" as set forth in subparagraphs (a)–(d) of the Commercial Computer-Restricted Rights clause at FAR 52.227-19 or in subparagraphs (c)(1)(ii) of the Rights in Technical Data and Computer Software clause at DFARS 252.227-7013, and similar clauses, as applicable.